Praise for *Marathon Woman*

"Kathrine Switzer's memoir is a testimony to her unwavering determination, her unflagging energy, and her unfailing, and often unwarranted, optimism."
—*Running Times*

"When I think of running, I think of Kathrine Switzer."
—Billie Jean King

"Kathrine Switzer's work for the women's marathon is a gold medal triumph for women everywhere."
—Grete Waitz, nine-time winner of the
New York City Marathon and
Olympic silver medalist

"Without the efforts of Kathrine Switzer, there probably would not have been a women's marathon in the 1984 Olympic Games."
—Peter V. Ueberroth, former president of
the Los Angeles Olympic Organizing
Committee and author of *Made in America*

"Kathrine Switzer is the Susan B. Anthony of women's marathoning. Her gutsy and historic run through Boston opened the roads to women marathoners around the world."
—Joan Benoit Samuelson, first Olympic
gold medalist in the women's marathon

"Switzer's past is a page-turner."   —*Detroit Free Press*

"[Switzer] chronicles her battles for equality."   —*Her Sports*

"The perfect gift for your favorite female runner. . . . The best running book I've read this year." —Diane Sherrer, *Star-Gazette*

"Switzer's hard-fought journey is an engaging, compelling read, and one of long distance running's greatest pioneers uses all the skill and daring at her command to become a grand bellwether of an epic dream come true." —*Running Stats*

"Interesting and enlightening." —*This Week*, Durham

"Chronicles a career of creating opportunities and equal sport status for women." —*Rapid City Journal*

MARATHON WOMAN

Running the Race
to Revolutionize Women's Sports

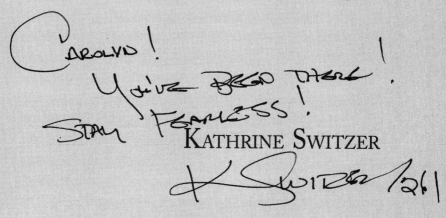

CAROLYN !
YOU'VE BEEN THERE !
STAY FEARLESS !

KATHRINE SWITZER

DA CAPO PRESS
A MEMBER OF THE PERSEUS BOOKS GROUP

To Roger Robinson
"Rejoice, we conquer!"

Copyright © 2007 by Katherine Switzer

Interior design by Ivelisse Robles Marerro

Cataloging-in-Publication data for this book is available
from the Library of Congress.
HC ISBN: 978-0-7867-1967-9
PB ISBN: 978-0-7382-1329-3

First Da Capo Press paperback edition 2009
Published by Da Capo Press
A Member of the Perseus Books Group
www.dacapopress.com

Da Capo Press books are available at special discounts for
bulk purchases in the U.S. by corporations, institutions, and other
organizations. For more information, please contact the Special Markets
Department at the Perseus Books Group, 2300 Chestnut Street,
Suite 200, Philadelphia, PA 19103, or call (800) 810-4145,
ext. 5000, or e-mail special.markets@perseusbooks.com.

10 9

ACKNOWLEDGMENTS

It is with great joy that I thank John Radziewicz and Da Capo Press for publishing *Marathon Woman* in paperback. I'm delighted to be associated with Da Capo and the Perseus Books Group and also must thank Wendie Carr and Ashley St. Thomas for their tireless support of the book.

While of course I'm thrilled we sold out of the hardcover edition, the fact is, runners don't like to carry heavy books or have them fall on their noses when they drop quickly asleep, so I'm happy we can accommodate them.

The responses from you, the readers, to *Marathon Woman* have been phenomenal, and I'm deeply touched. Some of you laughed, some cried, some claimed your lives were changed forever and hundreds of you wrote to say so. Especially interesting were the surprised men who wrote when they found it was not a "girlie" book, or the couch potatoes who realized that running was only the metaphor for overcoming the impossible. Thank you all.

Huge thanks also to the many race directors and promoters around the world who have invited me to speak at their events and sign my book. It is gratifying to meet so many wonderful people and share our enthusiasms.

Marathon Woman originally was published by my friend Will Balliett at Carroll & Graf. I will always be indebted to Will for his belief in women and in this book. Thanks also to my agent, Jennifer Lyons, for her help with this and my previous books.

My appreciation continues to my original editors, Tom Dyja—who is also a wonderfully calming coach!—and Roger Robinson, my husband, who lovingly, loyally, and expertly took on the Herculean task of slashing and burning. With his always balanced eye, he made order out of chaos. He got to cut out old boyfriends, too; there must be great satisfaction in that. In any case, I cannot thank Roger enough for this, as well as his unflagging help in the ensuing promotion and travel, and for so much more in our wonderful life together.

If your name appears in the book, that's an automatic thank-you for your help!

But some people must be thanked again for their direct contribution to the ongoing success of this project. They are as follows:

Valerie Andrews; Eva Auchincloss; Gordon Bakoulis; Joan Barker; I. W. Barkis, PhD; Joan Benoit Samuelson; Richard Benyo; Sara Mae and Larry Berman; Amy, Susan, and Matt at the Brearley Collection, Inc.; Arnie Briggs; Ian Brooks; Amby Burfoot; David Carson-Parker; Tim Chamberlain; Paul Christman; Peter Ciaccia; John H. G. Clark Jr.; Jeannine Shao Collins; Jeremy Commons; John Cowell, PhD; Harry Dees; Tom Derderian; Shaun Dillon; Loraine Day; Elaine Doll Dunn; Mary Engel; Tony Fisk; Jack Fleming; Mike Frankfurt; Hamish French; Janet Guthrie; Roger W. H. Gynn; Scotty Hart; Anni and Heinz Hemmo; Joe Henderson; Hal and Rose Higdon; Nancy and Pat Higgs; Ron Hill; Jeff Johnson; Mike Keohane; Billie Jean King; Arthur Klonsky; Ilana Kloss; Linda Kosarin; Zan Knudson; Marty Krakower, MD; Nina

Kuscsik; Ryan Lamppa; Deborah Slaner Larkin; John Leonard; John Linscott; Frank Litsky; Jean Marmoreo, MD; David Martin, PhD; Joan McCullough; Jamie McNeely; Lorraine Moller; Lin and Kevin Molloy; Jane and Dave Monti; Guy Morse; Robert Moss; Jane and Gary Muhrcke; Walt Murphy; Martina Navratilova; Cristina Negron; Sandra Noakes; Peggy Northrop; Ruth Orkin; Carol and Dick Parker; Elizabeth Phillips; Rhonda Provost; Stephanie Quesada; Marilyn Rader; Bob Ramsay; Gloria Ratti; Nikki and Jim Robinson; Ivy Robles; Bill and Charlie Rodgers; Allison Roe; Running USA; Richard Rybinski; Beth Salisch; Scott Samuelson; Millie Sampson; Dick Sargent; Sir Ron Scott; Jan Colarusso Seeley; Michele Slung; Joyce and Brian Smith; Jane Sobel; Julia Santos Solomon; Kaye Durland Spilker; Allan Steinfeld; Jennifer Street; Anne Switzer; Warren Switzer, PhD; Wayne Switzer; Youngsun Choi Switzer; Debbie Tawse; Fred Thompson; Jack Toms; Joan and Harry Trask; Cathy Troisi; Lennie Tucker; Sue and Bruce Tulloh; Peter Ueberroth; Greg Vitiello; Jane Kagan Vitiello; Grete and Jack Waitz; Kimberly Waldman; Nancy and Jon Whitney; David Willey; Mary Wittenberg; Bart Yasso; and Stephanie Young.

My thanks to all of you.
Kathrine Switzer
March 2009

CONTENTS

MARATHON
WOMAN

PART I | BASE

In distance running, "base training" or just "base," is the foundation on which you build the rest of your running. It's the core strength that allows you to build the ability to go longer and go faster. With luck, it also will help prevent injury.

CHAPTER | 1

A LONG LINE OF PIONEERS

"Here's a set of papers. Put these away and show them to your doctor when you arrive. Here's another set, show *these* to the authorities when you are processed to get on the boat. Good luck."

My mother, Virginia, took the papers and thanked her doctor.

She was nearly eight months pregnant with me and heading over on the first ship carrying military family members to war-torn Europe to join my father, whom she hadn't seen in seven months. It was November of the terrible winter of 1946 and if she didn't go then, it might be never, because traveling with a tiny infant and my two-year-old brother Warren was much more difficult than traveling pregnant with one child. The papers the sympathetic doctor gave Mother for the processing authorities said she was only six months pregnant and therefore allowed to sail. Just.

Midway across the North Atlantic, the old refitted steamer broke down and tossed back and forth for nine days while it waited for a tow. Undetected mines, unmitigated seasickness, or the thought of my being born at sea did not concern my mother; being towed back to New York did. Instead, they were towed to Bremerhaven, where a train waited to take the boatload of women and children into Germany.

It is a mighty thing to travel to one you love. I can imagine my parents' reunion, my huge father, Homer, picking up my tiny mother and laughing at how she'd changed since they last saw each other. It is a good thing to have such a love when you go to a difficult place, for my mother was horrified at what she saw in Germany. City after city in ruins, piles of rubble everywhere, huge groups of homeless and war-displaced people huddling on the streets; it seemed everyone was hungry and seeking shelter from the bitter cold.

My father was a major in the army then, and one of his jobs was to organize DP (displaced persons) camps to shelter these people until they could find their own family members, or a way home or to a new life. Family unity was important to both my parents; they had it, they wanted to help others have it, and they wanted to pass it on to their own kids. Mother had begun by hiring a nanny from out of the lines of desperate people around our house for the yet-to-be-born me. Nanny Anni asked if she could bring a friend to become our cook, and then Anni's brother showed up to act as houseboy, and soon we had a piano teacher (there was a grand piano in the house), and a tailor to make our clothes, most of these people living in our house. My mother, the one-woman Marshall Plan, shared everything she had, even the heat, which was frighteningly scarce.

In fact, there was so little heat in the army hospital where I was born that I was put in an incubator, to the amusement of the staff, since I was well over nine pounds and twenty-three inches long. My father filled out the birth certificate and in his excited state misspelled my name, leaving the "e" out of the middle of it, and resulting in Kathrine. My long legs pleased my father, who was six feet five inches tall. He thought it would be great if I grew up to be tall, too, and then he made a slightly wicked reference to the fact that since I was conceived after a riotous The War Is Over party at the Kentucky Derby, I might turn out to be a racehorse. Funny, that.

Actually, I didn't even walk until I was eighteen months old, and my parents were quite concerned. I had no inclination to walk; why should I when I had *meine Anni* to carry me everywhere? Anni adored me; I was the child she was sure she'd never have, because there were few young men left alive in Germany and she was already twenty-eight. She was a second mother to me, and a wonderful sister to my mother, who was very busy helping my father.

One day, my father told Anni there was a dance in the next town and she should go. Anni demurred; she had no way of getting there and nothing to wear. My mother loaned her a party dress and my dad drove her in his Jeep. Inside the dance hall, a young accordian player named Heinz saw Anni walk in wearing the nicest dress he'd ever seen. They met and began seeing each other.

This was a very good thing, because three years later, when it came time for us to leave Germany, my parents wanted to bring Anni back with us to America, but American immigration only allowed for family members. The parting for all of us, and me especially, was devastating. I wailed and tried to claw my way back to her, until finally my dad, crying like everyone else, had to drive away, leaving Anni in the road with the supportive Heinz by her side.

Anni and Heinz eventually married and settled in what became an isolated Communist East Germany. Fearful of reprisals, my parents and Anni and Heinz stopped writing to each other. For fifty years, a holiday did not pass without one of us wondering where Anni was, and raising a glass to her. It was my first experience of a great loss, and despite close family love, it left me feeling vulnerable. I didn't like being left alone. Two years later, though, when my father left to fight in the Korean War, I could see I had to get used to it because it might be a permanent condition. Few Americans think about the Korean War today, but it was nasty, like all wars, and my father saw action. He was away eighteen months, and every day before I went off to school my mother would read aloud at the breakfast table the list of those killed or missing in action from the *Washington Post*. At the age of five, I didn't understand the process of family notification and thought this was how you were told if your father was dead. I didn't know what would happen to me, but I knew I should be very strong for the day it did.

My mother was sensitive, kind, feminine, and utterly fearless— of war, of spiders, and of things that go bump in the night. Her aplomb and resourcefulness did not inspire me so much as set such a strong example that I was simply ashamed to be afraid. By the time my father got home from Korea, I was becoming self-reliant, and primed to soak up the many stories he told me and my brother about our ancestors' strength and determination.

Again and again I heard about how our Protestant forebears came to the New World in 1727 to escape religious persecution, onerous taxation, military drafts and to seek a decent, pacifist, God-fearing life as "Pennsylvania Dutch" farmers. The stories followed them westward, as they hacked out farms in the Northwest Territories (now Illinois), and always included the tale of W. H. (Washington Harrison) Switzer, who walked (not ran) away from home to join the Union Army. After the Civil War, he packed up his wife and three children to homestead his "soldier's service grant" of land in South Dakota in the 1870s. The dream of a farm, even a ranch, was worth the certainty of a lifetime of backbreaking work and huge personal risk. I was told it was important always to make a better place for the next generation.

Nobody in our family and none of my ancestors are cavalier; quite the contrary. We err on the side of prudence—even overpreparation. Despite that, W. H. was surprised by a diabolical South Dakota winter that was black with blizzards and froze the family inside a semisubterranean sod hut. How they survived by salting down and eating the last cow and root vegetables and melting ice for drinking water became the stuff of legend when they returned to their Illinois farm two years later, not in failure but in the triumph of having tried. Eventually, W. H. and his wife had eleven children; ten surviving to maturity—an unimaginable accomplishment then and even now, 130 years later!—and W. H. died in his bed at eighty-eight. So it never occurred to me as a child to ask why someone would leave somewhere sure to pursue a dream of something better, or to think anything too difficult to try. Determination was part of the Switzer genetic code.

The stories were picked up in the Great Depression by my parents, two penniless farm and small-town kids so set on a college education that they wrangled scholarships and worked enough jobs to make each of them the first in their families to do so. They were engaged for seven years before they felt financially secure enough to marry, and then my mother took herself down to the university health service to be fitted for a diaphragm so they could plan their family. Nothing was left to chance. My brother and I were raised with equal expectation and not a jot of favoritism, an amazing thing for that era. It was a family requirement for us both to get a college education; I was allowed to think of nothing less, and heaven help you if you screwed up this opportunity. Perseverance, patience, and delayed gratification were the other part of the code.

The men in my family were always big. No, huge. (My father was so big that when I was little I confused him with God, because they said God was a big man in the sky looking down on you.) None of these men were less than six foot two, with sizeable girth and tremendous power. They would have been great athletes, but with a lack of time and money, such a thought was not only inconceivable, it was extravagant. They prided themselves on their strength and used it well: really, they could do anything. The women they chose as wives were their equals—feminine, yet capable and resolute. As I grew up in the 1950s and early '60s in suburban Chicago and Washington, D.C., the mothers of my friends mostly stayed at home, played bridge, and met their husbands at the door with a cold drink. My mother often made a martini for my father and met him at the door, too, but only after she'd come home from a busy day as an important guidance counselor and teacher and changed into a clingy dress. My mother could do it all, and my father respected her enormously; besides, her paycheck was an important resource.

I grew up climbing ropes and trees, playing "war" with the neighborhood boys (and outrunning almost all of them), and jumping off our roof to show that I, too, could be a paratrooper. I was the first girl picked when the guys had to choose up sides. When my older brother outdid me at sports (which was always), I never thought it was because he was a boy but because he was older. At the same time, I loved wearing frilly dresses, played dolls very seriously with my girlfriends, and had a terrible crush on the boy next door with whom I loved to slow-dance when our elementary school had a kids' dance.

I was my parents' daughter. I had no other role models but them and my brother, and perhaps that was a lucky thing for me. I thought it was an exciting world, where I could be both feminine and strong, determined and dreaming, methodical and daring, and at the same time live up to my family's expectation of my improving a situation for the next generation. I came from a long line of pioneers. Not famous, but indefatigable. I didn't want to let them down.

CHAPTER | 2

"LIFE IS FOR PARTICIPATING, NOT SPECTATING."

"Oh Gawwwwd, honey, you don't want to be a *cheerleader!* They are so, well, *silly*," my dad said at dinner. Yeah, silly is right; I thought they were pretty brainless, too. I mean, they didn't even know the game of football, chanting cheers like "First and ten, do it again" when we had just lost the ball. But still, I was going to try out for the junior varsity cheerleading squad at Madison High School. Being a cheerleader was like having a passport to being considered pretty and popular, and going out with the captain of the football team. I was skinny, had frizzy hair, wore glasses, and worst of all had no breasts. I was hoping for some kind of miraculous transformation and I thought maybe being a cheerleader would do it.

"I'm not having you hanging around outside locker rooms waiting for boys," Mother said, looking at me over her reading glasses.

"They don't hang around waiting for boys!" I said.

"They do, too," said my brother.

Oh, thanks a lot, I thought. "Do not."

"Do too."

Dad interrupted with, "You know, honey, you shouldn't be on the sidelines cheering for other people. People should cheer for *you*. You are a real good little athlete. You love to run and score goals and strategize." Dad was great at flattery when he wanted to convince you to do things his way. I pouted. "The real game is on the field. Life is for participating, not spectating. Now you know, your school even has a girls' field hockey team. You should go out there, play hard, be a leader." It was true I loved to play hard, but the only girls I saw on the teams were such tomboys; nobody would ask them out in a million years. I didn't want to say that, though, as that would make my mother right.

"I don't know how to play field hockey. I would never make the team," I said. This was true, too. I'd never even held a hockey stick.

"Well, now that's easy, kid! All you have to do is get in shape! Just run a mile a day and you'll be in shape by hockey season."

"A *mile?* Run a *mile* a day?!!" Really, I was incredulous. He might as well have said to go climb Mount Kilimanjaro. A mile was *far*.

"Look, I'll show you how you can do this." He pulled out a pencil and paper. "Our yard is somewhat less than an acre—hmmm, about forty-five yards by eighty-five yards, so how many yards is that around?"

I calculated. "About two hundred and sixty yards."

"Okay, that's seven hundred and eighty feet. How many feet in a mile?"

"Five thousand two hundred eighty!"

"Right, just testing you. So let's see . . ." The pencil flew. "I make it seven laps."

I groaned. "That's far."

"You could do it right now, just going out the door. Anyway, you start slowly at first, and over time you'll get better. Heck, I trained a whole battalion and then marched the entire group twenty-five miles a day many a time. And I had to jog up and back and carry plenty of laggards' packs for them, too, to keep the group together!"

Dad always managed to show how difficult things could be accomplished bit by bit, and he'd always give some extreme and motivating example that would demonstrate that it was not all that hard anyway. It was a great formula. And then the best part: he'd set a challenge. "I guarantee you, run a mile a day all summer long and you'll make that team by autumn." It was a great diversionary tactic; cheerleading was never brought up again.

I set out the next day to run the seven laps. I jogged very slowly, as I was sure I'd never finish. It was a shuffle, actually. The grass in our yard was lumpy and uneven, with plenty of rocks and stumps in the woodsy back section. I felt awkward and breathless and knew I probably looked pretty stupid. And it was so hot! I was red all over. But I hung on and did it. I did it the first time out like Dad said I could, and I felt, well, I felt like the King of the Hill.

There were several pivotal moments in my life, and that dinner-table conversation with my father was the first. He knew that I was lurching awkwardly into high school and, like so many prepubescent kids struggling with questions of identity, self-esteem, and sexuality, I was facing challenges. One of my biggest had begun when my parents put me in a special accelerated program when I was five. The problem with starting school when you're five is that when you're in the eighth grade you're only twelve, and while everyone else is reaching puberty, you are still a child. Compounding this, my eighth grade was the first year of high school—there were no middle schools then—and being in this accelerated program meant that I was taking courses like algebra, and with seventeen- and eighteen-year-olds. In one class, I sat next to the gorgeous hero-hunk captain of the football team, and I don't know who felt more idiotic, he or I, but the point is that many of these kids were young adults preparing for jobs, college, or marriage, and I was still playing with dolls.

As only a child among adults can feel, I felt worse than unable to keep up; I didn't even know what the hell was going on, socially or academically. Puberty was a long way away. Having no clue about sex, I determined that the secret to social acceptance had to do with wearing a bra and lipstick, so I begged my disapproving mother for a training bra (which I padded) and a Tangee natural lipstick so I could play the part. As an adult myself now, I can see how insidious these pressures can be on a young girl, and I can see why my parents were happy for me to stay a child as long as possible.

Academically, it was the same story. Sometimes a twelve-year-old mind is just not ready for some concepts, like the "unknown" of algebra (The unknown what? The great unknown of outer space? The Unknown Soldier?) or the structure of language. I panicked after my first French class because I had no idea what "conjugate" meant. But what can you do? Being held back a year was not even considered—it was a kind of disgrace in those days, and even though she could see me struggling, my mom the educator was pleased that I was in advanced classes. I couldn't say "It's too hard" because that was just not acceptable in a home where nothing was "too hard." If you had an opportunity, your job was to rise to the challenge and muscle through, which I did, often resorting to sheer memorization.

Fortunately, ours was an incredibly supportive family, and every night there were lively conversations at dinner. Weekends involved everyone working on the house or in the yard together, vacations were long camping trips, and for all of our lives, happy occasions were always celebrated together. So it was natural that when I started running my mile a day I heard "atta girl" a lot of from them. This was really helpful, too, because people—like the milkman or mailman—would see me out running laps around our yard and ask me, "Is everything all right at home?" and then they would knock on the door and ask my mother if I was okay. My girlfriends told me I shouldn't do it because their parents said I'd get big legs and grow a moustache. We all got used to the fact that I looked strange to everyone else, but at home I was just fine.

The miles built up. Every day. For no explicable reason, one day my one mile would be easy and on other days I thought it would never end. Most of the time I found myself so lost in thought that I carried a piece of chalk so I could mark a tree to remember the laps. No matter how hard it was or how much I didn't want to run that day, I always felt better afterward. Some days, that is what got me out the door. The best part was at the end of every day, when I had a sharp sense of having accomplished something measurable and definable. I won a little victory every day that nobody could take away from me. I didn't have that sense when I didn't run, so I tried not to miss a day. As the summer drifted on, I looked forward to the coming school term with a new confidence. Not about some remote hockey team possibility, but about myself.

Then it was autumn, school began, and I tried out for the hockey team. Sure, I was nervous; I listened to everything Coach Margaret Birch said and followed it to the letter. An amazing thing happened: because I didn't get tired, winded, or sore, I learned the skills faster than the other beginners. When we took to the field, I could already run with the best. Wow, how did *that* happen? When I made the junior varsity team, there were whoops of joy at home, and I was the proudest girl who ever wore a hockey tunic.

I was also exceedingly grateful. Not quite understanding how physical conditioning worked, I thought I had discovered magic. Forty-five years later, I still think it's magic—but I'm getting ahead of myself.

I began to believe that as long as I ran, I'd keep the magic, but if I stopped, I'd lose it. Which is actually true. I called running my Secret Weapon; I was afraid if I told others about it, they would think I was nuts about all this magic stuff, so I did it quietly on my own. Having a secret weapon gave me the confidence to try other sports; I made the basketball team, too. Then I found that the Secret Weapon somehow worked when I wanted to participate in other activities, such as join dance committees or write for the school newspaper.

The school newspaper work began because there was so little coverage of the girls' sports (some things never change) and I wanted to give our team some hype. I loved my team! These were girls just like me—some were tomboys, some were prom queens—and I felt bad about my earlier prejudging of the tomboys. We all played our hearts out, and despite our different social and economic backgrounds, we came to enjoy each other off the field at dances, football games, and slumber parties, beyond the reach of all the catty cliques in the high school.

Friends called me Kathy, but my closest pals called me Switz. I thought Kathy sounded a bit lightweight for a sports byline, but the faculty adviser wouldn't let me use just Switz, which I thought was very cool. Thanks to Dad, Kathrine was always changed by the typesetter (yes, they had to set type in those days) into "Katherine" and I got annoyed at seeing a misspelled name corrected into an incorrect one, so I often wrote simply using my initials, K. V. Switzer. At this time I was reading—and salivating over—*The Catcher in the Rye*; J. D. Salinger was a god to me, and hard on his heels came T. S. Eliot and e. e. cummings; all of whom made me feel very good about being K. V. Switzer, Sports Writer.

By the end of my freshman year, I was tired of being a skinny kid. For ten months, I'd done my "breast enhancing" exercises to no avail. I'd purchased Kotex, thinking that might make my period start. Then, in an article in one of the dozens of my mother's magazines stacked up around the house, I found a fascinating article about caloric values for food, and caloric expenditure. The two highest-calorie foods were peanut butter and chocolate, and the article advised eating earlier in the day to expend calories to help with weight loss. This made perfect sense to me, so I had a peanut butter and jelly sandwich and a big glass of chocolate milk every night before bedtime. I gained fifteen pounds the next year and grew nearly four inches. Whether the peanut butter helped puberty or womanhood was thundering on anyway, I'll never know, but suddenly I was a woman. I'll never forget the expression on my father's face one day when he looked at me and then went in the other room to talk to my mother. I overheard only part of the conversation which was, "Holy cow, when did *that* happen?"

Because I was running every day, I adjusted to my new body without a stumble. I loved having a menstrual period; its cyclic regularity made me feel a part of nature as much as the seasons. My new body weight seemed to give me more strength, and I added push-ups and leg lifts to my routine. My brother said the real pros did one-legged full squats so I started doing ten of those on each leg, and shimmied up a thick climbing rope my dad had hung for us in the backyard.

Though I was devoted to keeping fit, I was not passionate then about someday becoming a professional athlete. First, such an opportunity didn't exist, and I didn't pine for it the way I understand Billie Jean King did when she was a kid and wanted to play men's professional baseball. It might have been very different, of course, if there had been professional running like there is today. Anyway, the second reason was because I wanted a career that also utilized my education. It's an awful thing to say now, but when I was growing up there was a feeling that people who earned their living in physical labor—and that often included pro athletes—were to be pitied because they either didn't have an education or sufficient intellect for an executive kind of job. I wanted to keep it in balance; the Roman writer Juvenal's concept of *mens sana in corpore sano* (a healthy mind in a healthy body) resonated strongly with me.

Another Roman captivated me. I ogled pictures of the statue of Diana the Huntress, and loving how my new body looked and felt, I would compare my naked self in the mirror to her statue, marveling at the similarities of body and—oh yes—spirit! Diana was athletic *and* feminine *and* self-possessed *and* she had small breasts, too, so she was my new role model. I felt as in control of my body as she did, and since guys were beginning to hit on me in school, I was not an easy mark. I didn't need the boys' attentions for self-esteem; despite having no sex education, running gave me enough physical confidence to thwart those needy little nerds. There was no doubt in my mind it was running that did it and that it was truly magic.

It probably seems strange that I'd choose an ancient goddess for a role model, but the fact is that I hadn't any modern ones in sports until the Rome Olympics in 1960. But even alongside the graceful images of Wilma Rudolph winning the sprints, I'll never forget the compelling photo of Tamara Press, the Soviet shot-putter in full grunt, with arms like hams, a jelly roll on her midriff, and grimy bra straps showing. It was scary; was that what it meant to be a female athlete? A lot of people said yes, and I'm sure if it upset me, I can imagine how it discouraged thousands of other readers of *Life* magazine, including plenty of young girls who would swear off sports forever.

I didn't know it then, but the Rome Olympics offered another contrast in the perception of women's capability; it was the first time in thirty-two years that the women's 800-meter (half-mile) run was held. Women were barred under penalty of death from even watching the ancient Olympic Games, and were excluded from participation in the first modern Olympics in 1896. After a great deal of protesting, women had been admitted to the Olympics in 1900 in golf, tennis, and croquet. In 1928, women's track and field was also added. The longest event was 800 meters (two laps around the track, about a half mile), and when the first three women ran a hotly contested race and Lina Radke set a new world record, they tumbled breathlessly into the infield—as you do when you run an all-out 800. This "display of exhaustion" horrified spectators, officials, and worse, the media. Harold Abrahams, the redoubtable Olympic runner turned journalist whose feats were depicted in the movie *Chariots of Fire*, wrote that this spectacle of exhaustion was a disgrace to womanhood and a danger to all females. He recommended that the event be struck from future Olympics. It was.

These women runners were even more horrifying to people in 1928 than Tamara Press was to me. For the next thirty-two years, women who ran more than the sprints had to prove again and again that they were not weak or fragile, endangering themselves, or disgracing womanhood. While the men had the additional Olympic events of 1,500 meters (about a mile), the 3,000-meter steeplechase, 5,000 meters (3.1 miles), 10,000 meters (6.2 miles), and the marathon (26 miles, 385 yards, or 26.2 miles), any long race for women portended danger. It was a hard-fought battle to get the 800 back in the Olympics for women in 1960, and any consideration of a still longer race was the subject of great controversy and medical debate.

At the same time, many other sports were modified for girls so they would be protected from harming themselves. Interestingly, rigorous field hockey was not, but basketball was a perfect example: in the '60s, girls played a version of basketball that limited their running, by having six players who were only allowed three dribbles and were not allowed across the center line. When I interviewed our girls' basketball coach for the school newspaper and asked if we would ever play the same version as the men, she said, "Never." The excessive number of jump balls could displace the uterus. I almost laughed out loud. Ten years later, women were getting full-ride scholarships to Big Ten universities to play the "men's" version of basketball.

By my junior year, I had a boyfriend, Dave, and a new school, George C. Marshall High School in Falls Church, Virginia. Dave was fun; he played center on the football team, and since his dad was the same rank in the navy as my dad was in the army, we had a lot in common. Every Friday night after the football game, Dave and his friend Larry the linebacker would come over to the house tired, happy, bruised, and nicked, and we'd make homemade pizza and talk through the game. Often I shared my experiences about a hockey or basketball game, and the boys always took my sports seriously. We bragged about who could do more push-ups (no contest) but they were always amazed that I could do more sit-ups and leg lifts. I lived for the annual President's Council on Physical Fitness and Sports fitness day when, among other things, we were tested on how many sit-ups we could do in a minute (I beat both the guys with sixty-three) and the 600-yard run. I was the fastest girl, but I wasn't as fast as they were, which annoyed me. One evening, I pushed Dave and Larry a bit, asking what they thought was the acceptable limit for women's exertion. It was hard for them to define, but finally they agreed that they did not like it when women played so hard they sweated through the backs of their shirts. I had no judgmental feeling about this, I simply noted it as an interesting observation. I was not a heavy sweater myself. Yet.

Dave and I were a steady item by our senior year, in love, with class rings exchanged, and promises and plans for marriage after college. It is incredible now for me to imagine this reasoning, since, at sixteen the plan was already unfolding. Dave was going to be a naval officer, and his singular high school ambition was to follow in his father's footsteps by first getting an appointment to the U.S. Naval Academy at Annapolis. When Dave was accepted in the spring, there was great rejoicing. He left for training the week after graduation, and I was oddly happy to be on my own for a while.

My parents were University of Illinois grads and my ambition was also to go to a big university. Given that my mother was a nationally respected, progressive, and much-beloved director of guidance at one of the biggest high schools in our county, you'd expect that I would have gotten a real inside scoop on college choices, but there was a different agenda at work. Dad was adamant that for financial reasons I go to school in our home state of Virginia and that I attend a coed college, saying that women's schools were effete and unrealistic, something I'm embarrassed to say I agreed with at the time. Incredibly, there were only two coed schools in the whole state then—William and Mary, which I knew would not accept me with my mediocre SATs, and Lynchburg College, which was smaller than my high school! I wanted the Big Time, like the University of Michigan! I secretly applied to Michigan, and got turned down. Not that I could have gone anyway, but the process was humbling me. Dad knew I was very disappointed, so as usual he made a deal with me: since he was paying, the first two years would be his choice and that was Lynchburg, and then the next two years I could choose if I wanted to transfer elsewhere. I said yes to Lynchburg, and I could see that Dad was confident that once I was there, I'd love it and stay.

One of the compensations about going to Lynchburg was that they had a women's field hockey team. It seemed a bit perverse that the big-time universities didn't have women's sports but the small colleges often did. I thought I should prepare myself for this new team by increasing my running distance. If a mile a day would get me on the high school team, I'd need more to make a college team. I heard that the boys on the high school cross-country team ran three miles; I'd never heard of anybody running farther than that, so I set three miles a day as my ultimate goal. If I could do that, the Secret Weapon would kick into overdrive!

Every evening after my summer job, I'd go to my high school track and run laps, adding a lap each week to the total. I was astonished at how easy it was, and it's funny that, being quite fit, I certainly could have run three miles right away. I didn't know that, though, and I felt I should increase the mileage carefully to avoid injury. Instinctively, I was right: moving up by increments is a key training principle and builds a strong base. I also had good thinking time, and in one of those Eureka! moments that occur only while running or in the shower, I saw what I really wanted to do as my career. The thing I loved most next to running was to write for the student newspaper. It had never occurred to me that I could study journalism and combine my two loves. By the end of July I was running three miles a day. I was coated in sweat. I felt like the King of the Hill again.

CHAPTER 3

"CAN YOU RUN A MILE?"

I arrived at Lynchburg College with a small chip on my shoulder but extremely happy to be away from home. I was surprised to find the college a very pretty and friendly place and, as much as I hated to admit it, I mostly loved being there from the first week. I had been dreading what I thought would be some overbearing religiosity throughout the campus, but it turned out that only the ministerial students were pushing religion and the rest of the school was amazingly balanced, considering it was stuck smack in the middle of the fundamentalist South.

Some of these supposedly angelic guys studying to be ministers were little devils, though! They'd ask you to the movies, only to pull off into a country lane instead and try to park for the evening. The first time this happened, I found myself standing outside the car and refusing to get back in until he promised to drive me straight back to my dorm. After all this, I was stunned when he asked if he could accompany me to church the next day, as if he were some kind of young innocent!

Academically, I found the atmosphere to my liking. It was challenging without being intimidating, and classes were small enough to make you feel that you had an identity. It allowed the teachers to reveal their own personalities, too. Since I was convinced I wanted to be a journalist—even though my military father hated them with a passion since they were mostly "wheedling pinko guys who had never looked down a gun barrel in their lives"—I was psyched for the first time about studying.

So naturally I was gung ho for my first college English class. It was a day I will never forget. The professor was Charles Barrett, a quietly droll and engaging man. He assigned the class an essay on an Orwell short story. Then he chortled, saying that giving an essay a title is always difficult because it needs to grab the reader. A great title is either "Snakes" or "Sex," either of which grabs readers when they see those two words. I'd never heard a teacher use the word "sex" in the classroom before and I thought it was deliciously wicked. I worked hard on my essay, signed it K. V. Switzer, and in a moment of breathless nerve, titled it "SEX." The next week, Dr. Barrett said he wanted to read one of the essays to the class and he began, "SEX." There was a collective gasp, and I slunk down in my seat. Then he read the whole piece and said why it was good and why he had given it an A. I was scared witless. As we left the room, one of my classmates said, "Can you imagine someone using that title!?" I answered, "I know, I know." I eventually took all of Barrett's classes in English and creative writing, as well as some in journalism, and soon I was writing for the college newspaper, the *Critograph*.

The only thing that really disappointed me at LC was the level of play on the women's field hockey team; well, that and the Southern accents and panty girdles. Once you get a regional inflection, it's hard to shake it, and it seemed to me then that women who spoke with a slow Southern accent did not sound as serious as those with neutral ones. Worried that I might start using syrupytalk, I worked on affecting a crisper accent. I must have sounded like such an ass, but I really believe many years later that this benefited me when I got into broadcasting.

As for the panty girdles, it seemed all the girls wore these horrid, hot rubbery things that sealed them from the waist to just above the knees. Ostensibly, they were for holding up stockings and slimming the hips, but even slender girls wore them. Why anyone would wear a garment that ruined your muscle tone and turned a simple pee into a ten-minute ordeal was beyond me until I figured out The Code. At a certain point I noticed that my standard-issue cotton garter belt was eliciting raised eyebrows and some shakes of the head from my dorm-mates. However, if you wore a long-line triple-zip panty girdle, it signaled that you were Not Easy. As it turned out, by the end of my freshman year, several of those latex maidens were knocked up, and for the life of me I cannot imagine how they got those things off in the backseat of a car and then got them back on in time for the midnight curfew.

I had hoped to be among stronger field hockey players to raise my game; it turned out that I was already one of the better players. This was not an ego boost; it was frustrating. When some players got winded and had to walk after one sprint down the field, I knew we were doomed as an effective team. When one of the defensive players insisted on wearing her Playtex long-line bra and panty girdle, I knew it was hopeless.

The field was a joke; it was so littered with rocks and crabgrass clumps and bare patches that the ball caromed everywhere regardless of the direction you hit it. Very occasionally, however, we could win on this home field, because nobody else could play on it. The teams who came, especially from the fancy schools like Hollins, were used to playing on gorgeous fields that resembled golf greens and were totally flummoxed here.

One day, Constance Appleby, the legendary Englishwoman who introduced the sport of field hockey to America in 1901, came to give us a small clinic and training session. I just adored her. I thought then she was about eighty, so you can imagine how dumbfounded I was when I found out she was ninety-three! She was not frail in the slightest, quite sturdy in the midsection, and kitted out in a chocolate brown tunic with matching sash and shin guards.

After a brief talk, Miss Applebee shocked us all by hustling us out onto the field with her. We were charging toward the goal and she was not far from my side when she tripped over one of those big dirt clods and did a body slam. I ran to her crying, "Oh, Miss Appleby, are you all right? Oh oh oh!" I thought, oh God, we've killed Miss Appleby, but when I got to her she jumped to her feet, extended her arm down the field like a general, and shouted in an incredible English accent, "Play on!"

From that moment, I knew I wanted to play sports and stay in shape for the rest of my life. Miss Appleby was one fit, feisty old bird, and that's how I wanted to be when I was old. The problem was, there were no sports teams for women to play on once you got out of college unless you were a coach, in which case you could kind of play along. I didn't want to be a coach, and I didn't want to play along. I wanted to be an athlete, but I didn't want to be *just* an athlete, either; I also wanted a career, a journalism career. I wanted to be like the Greek philosopher-athletes—strong mind, strong body; balanced, challenged, rising to the challenge.

I had this conversation many times with myself, mostly when I was out running, which I still did almost every day after hockey practice. Running was incredibly satisfying, even going around the field, or occasionally out around the campus in a big loop. It was measurable, made me feel accomplished, and was a good way to work out the frustrations of team scrimmages where I hardly broke a sweat and never got breathless. I was worried that maybe I'd get out of shape being on the team—now that would be ironic!—and I knew that running would keep me strong and confident until I found the answer.

One beautiful autumn afternoon we had a game at nearby Sweet Briar College. I'd never seen a field that smooth, and consequently the game was fast. Our girls were not in shape, and Sweet Briar ran circles around us. Our particularly inept panty-girdle-wearing defensive player kept letting an opponent by her, and when it happened, she would laugh. Then I went off in hot pursuit to cover her position, trying to prevent a goal. Riled at having to do her job as well as mine, the next time I screamed, "It's not funny! Go *after* her!" and I swear to you she stopped, put her hands on her hips and said, "It's only a *game*, Kathy." (She pronounced "game" "gay-yum.")

Afterward, nobody on our team seemed to mind losing; they were all enthralled with taking tea with the Sweet Briar girls. I was so upset that I slipped away and looked out at the soft line of the Blue Ridge Mountains and wondered why it wasn't just a gay-yum to me, why it was more important. The coach came out and said, "You don't like losing, do you?" It was more complicated than that, but I was too inarticulate to explain how I felt. All I could say was, "No, I don't like losing," but I was beginning to wonder if maybe I wasn't cut out to be a team player. Maybe I needed an individual sport. That way I'd only have myself to blame. In just three years, there weren't going to be any more teams to play on anyway, since there were no team sports for women.

Sometimes now, forty years later, I occasionally have dreams in which I'm playing field hockey. In the dream, I have all the speed and endurance I had then, but I have all the smarts I have now. My teammates and I are working together, devising brilliant plays and shots that I never could have intellectualized at eighteen. I awaken laughing, and then I wonder how my life might have been different if women's field hockey had been an Olympic sport then, as it is now.

• • •

Dave and I always had the understanding that we'd date other people when we went to college but that we were the main item for each other. Being a plebe at the naval academy at Annapolis meant that there were only about six times a year to see each other anyway, so it was pointless not to have good time with other friends. The be-all, end-all party was at the end of the year, June Week, when there were dances at the academy every night. My mom was particularly enthralled with her daughter's going. It was one of the few times she succumbed to feminine fantasy, and the gifts I got from her that Christmas were evening dresses, purses, and the general accoutrements of June Week preparation.

That first Christmas home from college was a revelation to me because of how much Dave had changed, or, perhaps, how much the academy had changed him. Not only had the drill instructors run the puppy fat off him, but Dave himself had become quite regimented in his attitude. Instead of being the easygoing guy I knew, he'd become bossy, telling me I should transfer from Lynchburg to

Goucher College so I'd be closer to him and the academy as it didn't matter where I got my education since I wasn't going to work anyway. At this, I laughed out loud, since we'd talked about career paths in high school.

"When I am a naval officer, *my* wife is not going to work," he pronounced.

"Right," I said, "and what do I do for the six months a year you are out at sea?"

"My mother didn't work, and she was perfectly happy making a very nice home for us."

"Well, my mother works and she is perfectly happy, too, making money and a name for herself, and I plan to work, so brace yourself."

The luster of that relationship was starting to get cloudy. I still wanted to go to June Week—heck, I had all these ball gowns!—but I was increasingly less enthralled with Dave for two other reasons. The first was that he suddenly hated my running and said he thought it made me a freak. He told me this at a party, and I was so mad that I left alone and began to walk the several miles home. It was late at night and I knew it was a stupid thing to do, so when a friend came along in a car and offered to drive me home, I gratefully accepted. But when I got in the car, I was mistaken; it was not my friend but a total stranger. As we drove along, I thought, *Oh God, this is very dangerous.* When the driver slowed for a stop sign, I jumped out and took off running through dark suburban yards and did a fast barrel roll under a hedge. I lay there hidden for what seemed like ages as the guy searched for me. When I heard his car drive away and knew I was safe, I slipped back to the party and asked a friend to drive me home. Dave came later to my house; we had a tearful argument and I shouted that it was a very damn good thing I was a runner or I'd never have outrun the predator in the car.

The other reason was that in the late autumn at Lynchburg I'd begun dating a classmate named Robert Moss, who was different from any boy I'd met. He had an English mother and an American father and therefore was not quite American. He was tall and thin, had a quiet reserve, a dry wit, and carried an umbrella; all very un-American characteristics and quite fascinating to me. He was also on the cross-country team, and to me that was the epitome of romantic heroism. He was the first person with whom I shared the secrets of my soul and my desire to excel in sports, a big risk in an era of sexual stereotyping. Robert never denigrated my enthusiasm just because I was a girl, and unfortunately, I took this astonishing sense of equality for granted.

By spring, we were both smitten and spent a good deal of our library study time snuggled up instead under a sweet-smelling honeysuckle vine necking until the midnight curfew. Since I was another guy's girlfriend, these sessions created plenty of romantic steam, as forbidden fruit always does. I was in love but tied to Dave; it was oh, so hopeless until Robert suggested that I dump Dave. What, and not go to June Week? Impossible! It was the wrong answer. I stubbornly went to June Week and Robert, who felt he'd been marginalized for a few prom dresses, stubbornly refused to continue our relationship when I returned. We stayed friends, but it took me years, really, to get over him.

Eighteen months later, on a dreary, rainy afternoon between my basketball and lacrosse seasons, the hard-packed dirt and grass fields that I ran on were muddy, so I decided to do my run on the track. Normally, I hated the track, since it was so boring going around and around and also because it was flanked on one side by the men's dorms and the last time I ran there some dorky guys leaned out the windows and chanted in unison, "Bounce! Bounce!" It was raining pretty hard that day, though, and nobody was there.

Lately I'd been doing some of my running with a speedy freshman named Martha Newell. Marty and I played hockey together, and then we started running together, and even decided to join an organization called the Amateur Athletic Union (AAU), which we were told put on track meets. The longest race for women was the 880; Marty ran a very respectable 2:23 and was quick at the shorter stuff, too. My best 880 was 2:34 and I was frustrated, since I felt I couldn't even get rolling in that time. We went to a couple of meets in Baltimore. Even though I felt it was hardly worth traveling anywhere just to run two laps around a track, I was gung ho about training with Marty and so interested in running that I was prepared to give up hockey, lacrosse, and basketball. Running was something I could do with a friend, or alone, and all my life. I didn't need a coach or a team. I'd found the solution to my dilemma.

I was almost done with my three miles when I noticed that the men's track coach, Aubrey Moon, had come out and was standing trackside somewhat forlornly, dripping in his hooded slicker. He was holding a few stopwatches in each hand with the lanyards dangling between his fingers. Only there were no runners out for him to time. He called me over after my last lap.

"Can you run a mile?" he asked.

I was a bit indignant, and answered, "I can run *three* miles."

"Well, good. Because I have only sixteen guys out for track this season, and I only have two milers, Mike Lannon and Jim Tiffany. If you run the mile for us, we could pick up some points. All you have to do is finish."

It was kind of like if he could have kept his pet cocker spaniel in the inside lane for four laps, he'd have done that, too, to get the points, but I was still pleased to be able to help him and the team out. It was no big deal; nobody paid any attention to track at Lynchburg anyway.

"Sure, coach, put me in!" I laughed. I'd always wanted to use that old movie line.

Lynchburg College was in two athletic conferences, the Mason-Dixon Conference, which prohibited the participation of females on men's teams, and the Dixie Conference, which did not. The next three meets, with Frederick College, St. Andrew's, and the Baptist College of Charleston, were all in the Dixie Conference, so those would be the only ones I'd run in.

That evening I called on my friend Mike Lannon to ask for advice, since it was my first competitive mile. I guess Mike was the closest thing Lynchburg had to a scholarship runner. He was very good and he lived in the top of the old gym, which must have been the equivalent of a housing subsidy. Mike got out a piece of paper and said he thought I could probably run a six-minute mile, which would be ninety-second laps. The important thing was not to do the first one faster than ninety seconds or I would run out of gas. Mike was lively, encouraging, and not at all patronizing. As it turned out, at track practice over the next few days, not a single guy on the team gave me so much as a smirk or a wink, only encouragement. Clearly, these weren't the guys who had hooted out the dorm windows at me, and I felt great being around them.

A few days later, Coach Moon asked Marty to run in the meet, too. She was going to do the 880; thank God I didn't have to do that!

Since they had no shirts for us, we went out and bought matching red-and-white tops from a sporting goods store to match as close as we could the red of the Lynchburg College Hornets.

I am embarrassed to admit it, but around this time I was also an entrant in the Miss Lynchburg Beauty Pageant. I thought these pageants were mostly very silly and said so one evening at dinner to a few of my friends, including my roommate, hockey teammate, and best friend, Ronette Taylor, who shared my strong views on women's rights. My friends howled me down, saying pageants had changed, they included interviews and talent evaluations and they were an opportunity to win scholarships, trips, nice clothes, and have the use of a new car for a few weeks. Back in our room, Ronnie said I was nuts not to enter, that I had as good a shot as anyone. I respected Ronnie's judgment and I certainly had the evening dresses! So I entered the contest.

The pageant and the mile run for the men's track team were to take place on the same day; after the run in the afternoon, I'd shower, change, and be ready for the pageant. A zillion times throughout high school and college, I'd played a game of hockey or basketball, then changed and "gone glam" for a dance, so I saw nothing particularly unusual about this. The media, my classmates, and the public saw it differently.

It started innocently enough, when a nice guy in the LC community relations office came out to track practice and took a couple of photos of me to give to the Lynchburg papers to publicize the upcoming meet. Suddenly, it was big local news! A *girl* was going to run on the men's team, and she's going to run a *mile*! As if a mile were like climbing Mount Everest; I was even quoted in the paper as wishing girls could be allowed to run the three miles. Everyone on campus began buzzing about it. Some loved the idea and admired my gusto, others whispered darkly that running a mile was dangerous and might change me into a man (or worse, a lesbian!). The guys who were the slimy catcallers intimated that I must be having sex with the men on the team or why else would I be out there with them in shorts? I caught most of the flak since the story about my running broke first, but Marty got her share, too. My closest peers, including the five other women in my dorm apartment and Dr. Barrett, teacher Wilma Washburn, and Robert, all trumpeted support, so I listened to them and shut out the rest.

When the papers also heard from pageant officials that I was a finalist for Miss Lynchburg, the story and photos got sent on to the *Richmond Dispatch* and the wire services; within a day it was in papers everywhere. My father was reading the *Washington Post* at breakfast when my photo jumped out at him. I hadn't called my parents because I didn't want to bother them; it all seemed so insignificant at first.

The first meet was Thursday, and the next Saturday, and on both occasions when Marty and I went out to the track, we were quite unprepared for the mob scene. It seemed that the entire student body was there, more than even came out for soccer! The meager stands were packed, and people lined the wall all along the top of the hill. There were a lot of cameras on tripods—at the start/finish line, and along the first curve of the track. Somewhere my parents were there, too, having decided they'd better drive down from Washington to see firsthand what the hell was going on.

I'd made a commitment to the coach and now we had reporters here from everywhere, even the *New York Times* and the *Herald-Tribune,* and various TV stations. And I'd never even been timed in a mile before. Really, all I was supposed to do was finish, and here were all these people expecting . . . what? That I was going to win? That I was going to collapse?

Mike Lannon was uncannily accurate. I ran as he said I should and I finished in five minutes and fifty-eight seconds. As expected, I finished last, but I got the points. Then Marty ran the 880, and by golly, she pipped a guy from Frederick College at the finish! This was fantastic, as people suddenly saw us not just as girls who jogged along, but girls who could run. We were thrilled to help the team, and had no idea we were making history. The *Lynchburg News* reported that LC was "possibly the only college in Virginia with two female run-ners on its track team . . . and one of the few schools in the country which has girls competing as regulars with the men on the varsity level." It wasn't the first time that a girl had competed in the Dixie Conference, though; in 1964, Charleston College had entered a girl sprinter along with the few boys who were starting up the col-lege team.

At the pageant that Saturday night after the meet, I had to cram my swollen feet into high heels and stand around in them for hours. It was the death knell to my toenails, which had gotten badly jammed into the end of the spikes I'd worn for the last two races that were two sizes too small. Later, they turned black and fell off; it was the first time I'd seen anything like this on my own body—I thought I had gangrene or something!—and it marked the beginning of a decade of ongoing foot problems.

My "talent" at the pageant was to play my accordion. If you are not laughing now, you would have at the news reports that said, "After Kathy Switzer pumps her legs in the track meet, she will pump her accordion in the beauty pageant." I duly pumped out "Lady of Spain" or something suitably accordionlike, which as you can imagine did not impress anyone, particularly as I had a pained expression on my face due to my throbbing feet. I did not win the Miss Lynchburg Contest. I put the instrument away and never played it again.

The hubbub continued—mail began pouring in from all over. There were fan letters from old school chums and relatives, marines from Quantico asking for dates, GIs from Vietnam wanting to be pen pals, and a flat-out marriage proposal from a butcher in Alabama. I parceled these out to my apartment-mates and we regaled each other with them. Then there was the hate mail, usually from people purporting to be religiously correct and informing me that I was going to fry in hell. These I threw in the trash. The whole experience was quite a lesson in human polarization and perception, whether it was the mixed opinions on campus or the letters. No one seemed neutral about it.

It was also an interesting lesson in journalism, and it reinforced my desire to become a reporter. I was now the sports editor of the *Critograph*, and, among other things, I had to write about Marty's and my participation in the meets. That was the only objective report I read about what we'd done. At the same time, I had other events to cover, not the least of which were Robert and his friend Jim Tiffany . running a big race called the Boston Marathon. Nobody knew they were training for it, not even me, so when they got back I interviewed Robert and found out that the marathon was 26 miles, 385 yards long and that he and Jim had run it in 3:45. Ohhhhh, after all the complaints I made about all my races being too short, now here was something called the marathon that sounded like the most exciting event in the whole world. I was fascinated, and I had a sudden desire to try it myself. I asked whether any girls ran, and Robert said one did and she ran around 3:20. I couldn't help it. I said, "You let a *girl* beat you?"

I also applied to Syracuse University as a transfer student, declaring a desire for a joint major in English at the College of Arts and Sciences and journalism at the famous Newhouse School. I was happy enough at Lynchburg, but I was anxious to specialize. Was I excited when SU accepted me! On my last day of classes at LC that spring of 1966, there was an end-of-term awards presentation and I was so lost in thought about studying at Syracuse that I almost missed hearing my name called. Coach Moon was awarding the letters to the track team, and Marty and I each got one for our participation on the men's team, a real first in sports. We'd only run in three races so I didn't think we really deserved them, but it was one of the nicest awards I've ever received.

Chapter | 4

"I guess I got rid of her."

My dorm at Syracuse University was a decrepit old firetrap of a house on Comstock Avenue called Huey Cottage. I'd selected the cheapest possible accommodations to try to reduce the financial sting for my parents, which was considerable. Even in those days, Syracuse was expensive, and I felt very guilty about it.

My room was on the top floor, up three flights, and I was apparently sharing it with two other women, since there were three beds in a giant attic loft. We had our own keys and were allowed to keep our own hours, and when the "house matron" (actually a graduate student working to cover her own room and board) handed me my key, my knees went weak with excitement at having such freedom.

A few days after settling in, I came back from a daylong orientation to find that my roommates had finally arrived. They were sitting on the sides of their beds, smoking and talking. Clearly they knew each other; in fact, everyone on the floor had lived together for the last two years and I was the newcomer. I bounced in with a confident "Hi, I'm Kathy!" and they all just stared at me, and continued to smoke. Eventually, one of them exhaled and said, "Jesus H. Christ."

It didn't take me two seconds to realize that I looked a total nerd to them. Here I thought I was very "in," decked out in a round-collared flowered Villager dress, with matching shoes and purse. They were all dressed in jeans, black turtlenecks, and hoop earrings. The code here was "cool," so I hustled over to Marshall Street and got myself a pair of jeans and a turtleneck. Not that it made any difference; I was the third wheel and that was that. Of course it didn't help that one of the first questions I asked them was if they knew where the local AAU office was.

As soon as the term began officially, I beat it down to the athletics department office in Manley Field House. To be specific, *men's* athletics. There was a women's athletics department, but it was just intramural. What that told me was sports at Big Time universities meant powerful, scholarship-enriched football, basketball, and lacrosse programs, and even running, swimming, and gymnastics—for men. But scholarships for women were not to be considered. Women got "play days." I knew all this before I came to Syracuse, and frankly it didn't matter. I assumed women at Syracuse and other institutions didn't want intercollegiate sports or somehow they'd make it happen. By then I'd made the decision to run, and I had never heard of a women's college track team anyway. So, I'd run with a team if possible, or alone if not. With nothing to lose, I felt full of confidence when I walked into Coach Bob Grieve's office to ask if I could run on the men's cross-country team. "You know, I've read about you. Yep, it was in *Sports Illustrated*'s Faces in the Crowd," he said after I told him about running for the men's team at Lynchburg. He seemed nice enough. There were two other guys in the office who pretended they weren't listening. One was about fifty, skinny and totally innocuous. The other was twenty-five, very big and very attractive and every time he looked up I glared at him with my toughest "Don't mess with me, smartass" look until he got the message and left the office. Then Coach Grieve said, kindly, "Look, Syracuse is in the NCAA conference, which is all men, and so it's against the rules for women to play on a men's team. But I have no objection if you want to come out and train with the team." That was good enough for me—maybe better, as I felt sure if I couldn't outrun anybody at Lynchburg I sure as hell wasn't going to outrun anybody in the Big Time.

He explained that the team worked out at Drumlins Golf Course, about a mile from the field house. "How do they get there?" I asked. He hesitated for a moment; I could see there was doubt in his face. "They run there," he answered.

I walked the mile back to Huey calculating that it would be a two-mile run to Drumlins and a two-mile run back, and that was already more than my daily mileage. God knows how much I'd have to run during practice. I felt like an idiot thinking I was such a hot ticket running three miles a day, but I'd said I'd show up and show up I would. Back in Coach Grieve's office, after I left, he turned to the older guy in the office and said, "I guess I got rid of *her*."

The next day I took a taxi to the golf course. As I paid the driver, I made a joke to myself that this was not such a cheap sport after all, and that I'd better improve pretty fast or I was going to go broke. I had to have a pocket for the money so I wore a pair of slacks and a long-sleeved blouse. I'd never been to a cross-country workout before so I had no idea what to wear anyway. Now I was nervous, since I had to walk out there in the middle of the fairway where all these skinny guys in orange and white shorts were running around. They were going to hate me for sure. Cool girls at Syracuse joined sororities and looked great all the time; they did not run.

As I walked toward them, the innocuous older guy in Coach Grieve's office ran to meet me, jumping around like a jackrabbit. "Hey! We've never had a girl before! I'm Arnie and I've been here twenty years and we've never had a girl before! You're Kathy, right? Hey guys, this is Kathy and she's going to run with us!" All the guys called out greetings and welcomes. *Gosh*, I thought, *so far, so good*. Then suddenly they swarmed, were still, and Coach Grieve blew a whistle. Like a pack of greyhounds, they were off over the rolling lawns. The swiftness and beauty took my breath away. They sparkled over the green expanse and seemed to float up a long hill, disappearing into the trees. The attractive assistant coach clicked a stopwatch and wrote something down on a clipboard. His name was Tom, and with his size, he certainly was not a runner. He was the one I had shot dirty looks at in the coach's office, and he didn't look up at me this time.

Coach Grieve was on a motorized golf cart and Arnie got in beside him. "Okay, let's see what you can do," Coach said to me. He pointed out the whole visible perimeter of the golf course and asked if I could run that far. "Sure," I said, guessing it to be about two miles at most, then laughed. "Just not very fast!" So off I went, deciding to keep it steady since I didn't know what else he might have in store for me. When I got back, some of the freshmen runners had finished their workouts, so coach asked one of the runners to jog me over the freshman course. I apologized for how slowly I was going but the young man didn't mind, he said he was doing his cooldown anyway, whatever that was. And so ended my first day, with my covering five miles in slacks and a blouse, feeling perfectly all right, and happy that I didn't make a total fool of myself.

Arnie offered me a ride home, having no idea how grateful I was to take it, and talked nonstop in a totally stream-of-consciousness way about how he was once a good runner and even finished tenth in the Boston Marathon and still held the upstate New York record for the marathon after all these years can you imagine but now he was injured, bad knee, bad Achilles, well, that happened, he was too old to run anymore anyway it was tough enough just walking his mail route, he was really the mailman along Comstock Avenue and that is why he was driving his car out here and not running to the golf course and he'd been married for twenty-five years and ever since he was married his wife hated running, just doesn't know why he loves it so much, well, we don't know either do we? Anyway he'd been working out and helping with the boys since the year he got back from World War II where he broke his back parachuting into France where the doc told him to run to prevent arthritis so he might as well keep helping out, Coach Grieve needed him he wasn't getting any younger either, so that's me, I'm kind of the "Unofficial Team Manager." He grinned. We shook hands and I thanked him. "See you tomorrow!" he shouted when I got out of the car.

I came out to practice every day. Sometimes I ran to the course, but mostly Arnie started picking me up at Huey Cottage as he finished his mail route, drove to the field house to change, and then drove out to the country club. I decided just to try to keep running the whole time I was on the cross-country course, but I was so slow, not only couldn't I keep up with the slowest guy, I couldn't even keep him in sight and never did know the right way the course went. Pretty soon Arnie began jogging a bit with me, probably feeling sorry for me, but also thinking that, even injured, he could keep up with me. So we became a fixture, the old man limping and lurching alongside the young woman who ran smoothly but slowly.

Arnie chattered like a bird the whole time. He was full of stories, and I was so new to this much running that I didn't have the lungs yet to run and talk at the same time, so I hung on puffing like a train and very occasionally gasping out a monosyllabic reply. It was remarkable how little cardiovascular capability Arnie had lost over the years, and he looked in great shape. Well, he looked *old*—gray and balding, with a deeply lined face—but he was still lean, and like all runners he had fabulous legs. He always wore gray shorts and T-shirt, and with his gray hair and slightly ashen coloring I used to call him The Monochrome. I could tease him and he liked that. But to tell you the truth, if he hadn't had that gimpy knee, he could've kicked ass among these young guys, and I admired him a lot right off the bat. I mean, he was fifty years old! That was *ancient*.

Every day Arnie had a new story about the Boston Marathon. He'd run it fifteen times. So while occasionally I'd hear about the hot day at Yonkers that ruined Buddy Edelen, or Arnie's triumphs at Around the Bay, mostly it was another tale about Boston. Stories about how Arnie finished tenth in the heat of 1952, or legendary Johnny Kelley the Elder, who had run Boston dozens of times, and Johnny Kelley the Younger, who was no relation but won in 1957, or Tarzan Brown who jumped into a lake midrace just because he was hot. Arnie was beginning to run pain free; the soft grass and easy pace was healing him. The days and miles would fly by, and pretty soon Arnie would have told his fifteen Boston stories and begin them again. It was like a film on a two-week loop. He might as well have been telling me about Achilles and Hector and Ajax and Apollo, as Arnie's heroes all became gods to me, and Boston the most sacred of the Olympian fields.

· · ·

Three months later, in December 1966, I sat on the bleachers in the field house waiting for Tom, the young, attractive graduate assistant, to finish his coaching for the day. I felt pretty good; Arnie and I had done ten miles out on the roads and it was dark and cold. Running in the elements always made me feel purified, and running ten miles all at once was a banner day. Tom and I now had a cordial relationship. He had pointed out that my canvas sneakers were inferior but when it was clear I didn't know about other shoes, he kindly offered to take me to a special store where I could order quality ones from Germany. Tonight was shopping night.

The rest of the cross-country team had been indoors for a month now, running on an indoor board track eleven laps to the mile in Manley Field House. I hated the track, of course. Not only was it the same hamsterlike drill of running around in circles, but the purpose of indoor track was to go fast, not to go long, which did not interest me. When I did my first speed sessions indoors, the back of my throat always tasted like blood and my legs were like jelly.

I also detested it inside the field house; the surface area in those days was all dirt and it was full of dust from the lacrosse players. To keep the dust down, a truck came in every other day and sprayed oil over the dirt. So now you and your clothes were not only dirty but greasy, your hair smelled like an engine, and your nose and lungs filled with what I felt sure was dangerous particulate matter. One of the most important reasons to run was to flush out my lungs with clean air every day! I'd come to believe, and still do, that an hour's worth of hard breathing in the outdoors will cure more ills than just about anything. So Arnie and I decided to brave the winter and stay running outdoors. "Nobody ever ran through the winter with me before!" exulted Arnie. It was a bigger decision than I'd realized.

Tom was in his element as he worked with the throwers instead of the cross-country runners. I never got tired of watching him demonstrate how to get more drive from the turns in the discus or the thrust up out of the hips into the shot. It was fascinating; Tom was fluid as a dancer, an odd thing in a man so big and bulky-looking. He was only five feet ten and a half inches (the half inch was very important to him, hence he liked the nickname Big Tom) but weighed 235 pounds. He had big quads and a big back, shoulders, and neck, but not particularly popping arm or calf muscles. And tiny feet—size 7, maybe. This was Tom's particular point of pride, saying it was a real asset in his potentially being a world-class hammer thrower, as he could execute his turns faster. It was true that when he was showing the throwers how to move, his feet just kind of spun around; they were never in the way. When I watched him throw the hammer, it was phenomenal—he pirouetted, his feet just a blur. I was in awe of his ability in this strange event; as inexperienced as I was I could see genuine talent. He couldn't actually throw the hammer much because it was too dangerous, and he almost never did it indoors unless the whole arena was empty, which was next to never, and until the weather changed he couldn't throw outside. So he worked out with the undergraduate throwers, lifted, and substituted throwing a 35- or 56-pound weight, which he could safely do indoors since it didn't go very far.

His chest and belly varied from kind of pudgy out-of-season to just solidly thick when in shape, but neither ever had strong definition. He was the kind of man who looked quietly capable more than powerful; in fact, his body looked a lot like the old photos I saw of my very strong grandfather and great-grandfather—built squarely and with a low center of gravity. Hard to knock over, he made a girl feel confident to be around rather than being an overtly sexy kind of guy.

If he'd had a warmer personality or welcoming face, he'd have been a teddy bear. But he rarely had either, and was he impatient! As he worked with the throwers there was never an "Okay, that's better." It was always, "Come *on*. Hips! Hips! *Hips,* forchrissake!!!"

All of which combined to make me wildly attracted to him. He had a lot of the things I was used to and valued—strength, and capability—and he also possessed characteristics that were totally outside my experience and that intrigued me: he was often moody and imperious but most of all, he was a natural athlete. I'd never met anyone who possessed God-given talent. I only knew people who worked hard. No matter what I did, I knew I never had real talent—not just in running but in looks and brains, too. I was just better than average and thus felt I was not quite Tom's equal, which of course perversely made him more attractive, since somehow he was therefore a superior person. Really, there is no accounting for adolescent logic, although I'm not sure age nineteen is an adolescent excuse anymore.

So, that night after buying running shoes, I was surprised and flattered when Big Tom asked if I'd like to have dinner with him, where he turned out to be almost sweet, certainly less remote, and very interesting. He was still slightly intimidating as he was a Big Deal athlete and four years older than I, and knew more about sports than I could ever imagine. He told me about his plans to be in the Olympic Games; that was his ambition, but he felt very hamstrung by the AAU, the national governing body of the sport. It was the AAU who organized the trials that chose the Olympians and who was our only voice to the International Amateur Athletic Federation (IAAF), the world-governing body of track and field, and the IAAF in turn was our only voice to the International Olympic Committee (IOC). The AAU was all-powerful therefore, and their regulations prevented Tom from earning any more from the sport than his graduate assistantship at Syracuse. He told me horror stories how the AAU banned athletes for the slightest infraction and how you had to follow rules very carefully or you could be declared a professional and never compete again. It was really pretty bad as nobody even had money to travel to meets, or buy decent equipment, or worst of all to have the time to train decently. He said his fantasy was just to have a couple of years where he could do nothing but train and he knew he'd be an Olympian. Wow, I was impressed. Within a few weeks, we were a "steady" item.

• • •

On one of these last preholiday afternoons, I came out of Newhouse at 4:05 after my last class of the day, so tired that I just wanted to fall in bed for a nap before dinner. It was practically dark and just beginning to snow; it was really coming down fast. There was Arnie, parked in front of the building, in the Strictly No Parking or Standing area, looking anxiously out the car window for me, hoping to find me in the crowd of students before the campus police made him move on.

I hated his persistence. I even hated him. We hadn't had an agreement to meet today; he just showed up, knowing this was my last class of the day and that I had no escape. I got in the car, sullen, and he was as chipper as could be. "Got your gear, ready to go?" He was *always* there, like a dog with a stick, just wouldn't leave me alone. I was immediately ashamed to be thinking like this, but I wasn't going to relent. "I'm not running tonight, I'm just too tired," I snipped. "I don't have my gear; it's back at the dorm." Arnie started to drive in the direction of Huey. "Awww, gee," he whined. It was as if this was some big personal disappointment! I hated it when Arnie whined, and he whined all the time. It was his choice to wait out in the car for me for God knows how long, not mine. "How about an easy six, you'll be done in no time," he suggested.

I bickered with him until I realized how childish I was being and how much time I was wasting. I might as well run, there was no getting any sleep now anyway, kids were already heading out to the dining hall, so I got my gear and we went to the field house to change. With all my procrastination and carping, we'd lost nearly an hour, and I was now both ashamed and mad at myself since time was the one thing I needed most and it was my fault that we'd lost it. We'd have to hurry, too, or the dining hall would close before we finished our run and as it was, now all I'd get was the last crust of whatever no-name casserole was stuck to the bottom of the pan. It made me madder at Arnie than ever.

As we went out the back door of Manley Field house and up Colvin Street, the snow was already four inches deep and even in rush-hour traffic the car tracks were getting covered almost as soon as they were made. At first we fumbled along single file, finding our way along the roadside, working into a rhythm between the swishing cars and headlights and a pavement and curbing we couldn't see but were long familiar with. The snow was driving in behind us, and it truly billowed, flying overhead and rolling down in front of us like some giant sail flapping silently from the overhead rigging of street lamps. The cars were driving into the storm and I knew they could barely see where they were going, much less see us. "It's stupid night to be running anyway, we'll probably get killed, and I don't care!" I remember thinking.

Once we got out past the golf course, the road became countrified, and as there was little traffic, we moved into our usual mode of running side by side, practically in lockstep. We could see ahead for some distance, so we had time to move well off the road if a car came by. I felt safer but was still plenty irritable and was running tight. The best part of running was when that irritation suddenly disappeared, when it quietly flowed away in the stream of disconnected memories and anxieties, and you were running free and relaxed. It always happened if you let it, or if you just ran long enough. But tonight I was cranky, and for whatever spiteful and self-destructive reason, I wished to stay cranky and was running and punching the air like a boxer. Arnie sensed it and tried to start a conversation, but all he got out of me were monosyllables or grunts. In all this wide, white, open expanse, I felt like I'd been locked up in prison with this cellmate for longer than I could stand. Instead of just shutting up and running quietly, though, Arnie did the one thing guaranteed to set me off: he began another story about one of his fifteen Boston Marathons. It was his way of saying it was a foul night to be running, he knew I was tired, but look—here we are; let's make the most of it.

As we turned the corner into the top of Peck Hill Road, just past halfway, we were in the teeth of the storm. The snow was deep, over six inches now, and slick, not grippy like some good running snow can be. Worse, the road was narrow again, without a real shoulder, and when cars came we had to jump to the side, usually sliding into a ditch. The flakes were so thick and heavy that they got sucked up our noses and stuck in our eyelashes. It made the whole dark world a gauzy fluff and oncoming headlights just smeary streaks. Single file again, we were falling onto each other on the downhills and bumping on the uphills, and when cars came, Arnie was still so into his Boston story he didn't jump away; I did. It was if I'd come awake and didn't want to die after all. Then I had to slide along to catch up to him; my new shoes had not arrived yet and my black canvas tennis shoes were like hydroplanes, and the motorists who came upon us were frantic. Well, I don't blame you, you poor suckers, I thought. Anyone out tonight for *any* reason is stupid, but running in this is too stupid to be believed. And here was Arnie, blithely yammering on as if this were not a crisis. Finally I shouted, "Oh Arnie, let's quit *talking* about the Boston Marathon and run the damn thing!"

He acted so surprised that he turned and said with perfect sincerity, "Oh, a *woman* can't run the Boston Marathon!"

"Why ever not?" I asked.

"The marathon is twenty-six miles, three hundred eighty-five—"

"I KNOW how far it is, Arnie. So why can't a woman run it?"

"With women it is the Law of Diminishing Returns."

"Now what exactly does THAT mean?" Really, Arnie was so exasperating. He often used things like the Theory of Osmosis or Law of Thermodynamics or whatever "Holy Writ" popped into his head to explain things; usually it was pretty funny, since one bore no relation to the other, but tonight I was, as I said, cranky.

"Because with the marathon, it gets harder as it gets longer." He was treating me like a simpleton now.

"So?"

"Women can't do that kind of distance; they can't run that long," he said. He didn't sound sorry, condescending, or hectoring. It was simple fact.

"But I run six or even ten miles with you every night! You've been telling me all this time how good you think I am, what capability I have! Are you now telling me I am physically incapable of running a marathon?!"

"Yes, I am, because ten is a long way from twenty-six."

"Well, Arnie, you are wrong. A woman ran the Boston Marathon last April, her name was Roberta Bingay, and she was pretty good, too. She ran in something like three hours and twenty minutes." My snippiness was complete; I dealt the trump card, but I was unprepared for the reaction. Arnie exploded, and it scared me a little, as I'd never seen him angry. He stopped running (something he never did) and shouted, "No *dame* ever ran the Boston Marathon! That girl jumped in at Wellesley!"

"She did too run it, I know because I read it in *Sports Illustrated*." I emphasized the *Sports Illustrated*; if something was in *Sports Illustrated*, it was as good as being in the *Encyclopedia Britannica*, as far as I was concerned.

"I say this again, no woman ever ran no marathon." We had a moment of silence. The snow was inundating us, and some cars, seeing us at the last moment, nearly skidded into us. "Okay, let's get moving," he said grumpily.

"I'm not running with you until you believe that a woman can run a marathon," I said quietly.

"C'mon, let's just keep moving."

"Arnie, no. You have to admit that a woman is physically capable of it. Maybe you don't believe in Bingay; then, okay, but SOME woman. I can't run with you anymore if you don't believe a woman can do it. This is important."

Arnie answered quickly and articulately. I was surprised. I guessed later he'd thought about this before, maybe for months.

"If any woman can run a marathon, I believe you could. But even you would have to prove it to me. If you showed me in practice that you could run the distance, why, I'd be the first person to take you to the Boston Marathon!"

"Okay," I said, grinning. "You're on!" and we started running home. My fatigue and sullen crankiness were gone. All the way back Arnie was all business, outlining how we'd train for it, how we only had three months but maybe we could just do it. I just kept grinning. "Hot damn," I thought. "I have a coach, a partner, a plan, and a goal—the biggest race in the world. Boston! *Boston!*"

CHAPTER 5

"YOU'LL RUIN THAT GIRL, ARNIE!"

The following Saturday, just before I left the campus for Christmas, Arnie and I did our first "long run" in the Boston training program, an eleven-miler. I was ecstatic, I'd gone further than ten for the first time, and it seemed a huge leap to me, as if I were in the next league or something. It's funny how running does that; just one more mile often makes you feel like very hot stuff.

The Boston Plan was simple: continue doing what we did every day—six to ten miles, and on Saturday or Sunday, do a "long run." The plan was to try to move up the long run by about two miles every Sunday. Once I got back from the holiday break, we'd have about twelve weeks, and that would even allow for some missed days. In actuality, when I look back, I never thought about the Plan, never thought about the number of weeks or what we had to do, never thought of the possibility of injury or that there might be setbacks. It was just an exciting discovery, and I had someone leading the way. The biggest concern I had was if I had my period the day of the marathon, but I figured I could just keep taking my birth control pills and forestall it if that looked to happen. Which reminded me, I'd better punch out those tiny pills from the foil disk and put them in an aspirin bottle so my mother won't discover them when I am home for Christmas. Tom and I had started sleeping together; it was daring and romantic but I sure wasn't taking any chances, either with my mother or Mother Nature. I'd tell my parents about Tom obliquely and gradually.

But my new romance with Tom wasn't the first thing I gushed about to my parents; it was the eleven-miler that I was still so high on. When they picked me up at the airport in Washington. I said, "Hi, Mommy and Daddy! Ohhh, it's so good to see you and you'll never guess!! I ran *eleven* miles a couple of days ago!!" Well, that's pretty far, said my dad, trying to maneuver out of the traffic. I could tell running wasn't high on their priorities list then, and that was fine as from that moment on I decided to keep the Boston attempt a secret between Arnie and me. I didn't want to announce anything that I wasn't sure of actually doing. I always thought it was embarrassing or certainly nervy of people who in the first weeks of a big undertaking, said things like, "I'm writing a book!" "I'm working on a PhD!" or the worst, "I'm pregnant!" when all these things had a very high failure rate and made the person having the failure feel even worse when you had to go around and tell everyone it hadn't happened. And then you can't remember all the people you made this grand announcement to, so months later, when your failure wounds were just about healed, someone would say, "Hey, when are you getting your PhD?!" That was it; I was keeping very quiet about Boston.

. . .

By early January, I was no longer impatient with Arnie. As we ran though canyons of snowbanks, I listened with new interest to the endless repeats of his stories, hearing about his mistakes and triumphs, and my respect and admiration for him grew tremendously. I could never conceive of running a marathon fast, however, as he had done; or with the aim to RACE it. That was unimaginable to me; I never believed I could do anything but finish a marathon and so that became the simple goal. Outside of a vague feeling that I wanted to run strong and healthily for the rest of my life, I had no athletic goals beyond covering 26 miles, 385 yards.

We never timed anything; we never even wore watches when we ran. Arnie had measured three-, five-, six-, and ten-mile circuits by car, and midweek we just ran variations of those. Increasingly, John Leonard, one of the guys on the cross-country team, would come with us on the weekdays. But what Arnie and I lived for was the weekend run; midweek was just maintenance. I looked forward to these long runs with a mixture of excited discovery and stomach-sinking dread. All week I balanced the intoxicating and inevitable sense of accomplishment and the thrilling feeling of charting undiscovered territory against the other odds: would I be able to do the new distance? What if it really hurt? Did I have what it took? Was there a physical point beyond which I might not be able to go? And if I got there, did I have the guts to mentally push past it?

I always answered myself by saying that if I could do it and it felt good it could not be bad and the only way to find out was to try. I didn't look or feel worse for running; on the contrary, the longer I ran the better I felt, and indeed was, in every way. It was logical to me that hard work done progressively makes you stronger no matter what kind of animal you are. I had always reveled in the duality of being a feminine athlete, and now I felt more aware and confident than ever of my attractiveness and sexuality, both of which seemed to grow with the sense of strength and power that the long run gave me.

Arnie had his own reasons: he just loved to run, and by going a long way slowly he seemed to heal old injuries and keep them at bay. He was delighted after so many years to rekindle his athleticism, have company, feel needed, and—although unspoken—to get out of the house and away from his critical wife for a while. But at the same time and totally unbeknownst to me, Arnie had his own sinking dreads: we were in uncharted territory and he was the captain. What if the earth really was flat and I fell off the other side? Who knew how far a woman could safely run? What if I got seriously injured or ill from this; oh, how he would blame himself and be blamed! Already, the guys back at the post office were giving him serious grief, saying things like, "You'll ruin that girl, Arnie. She'll get big legs, turn into a man." "Pretty girl, Arnie, too bad what's going to happen." "Hey, what do you think you're *doing*?" Arnie felt responsible, but to whom or what? He didn't have any real answers, either.

Word of Arnie's being out running for miles alone with a girl got back to Arnie's wife pretty fast, too. Running, the longtime mistress she could not compete with, suddenly had a face and a name. She hated his running, *period*—alone, with men, on a team—and now, with a young woman it was just too much. There was no way she, or many people for that matter, could understand that our relationship was totally platonic, that my being a girl was only incidental to our friendship and to my being his pupil and training buddy. I later suspected that she just gave him hell, but at the time I never knew all these things. I did not, in fact, know these things for many years. Arnie was the most docile guy in the world; actually the word *pushover* comes to mind, but his running and especially his running with me was sacrosanct. Ultimately, he felt as I did—as long as I was improving and felt good, it had to be okay.

Arnie's wife wasn't the only woman who hated me; there seemed a whole flotilla of them who tried to drive us off the road. They were never courageous enough to actually stand near us or say something personally; no, they had to have the protection and anonymity of their cars. In all the times Arnie and I had to leap for our lives, it was because of a woman, not a man. We'd usually see them coming. There was a kind of dangerous, bearing-down look the car had as it headed toward us, and then we'd catch a glimpse of a vitriolic face behind the wheel just as we jumped.

"Shit!" I'd shout. "Dammit, Arnie, why is it always a woman?"

"Aw, she's just jealous."

"Jealous, my ass! She could have killed us. What's she jealous of?"

"I dunno. Maybe because you're doing it and she's not."

"Well, hell, Arnie, all she has to do is put on her sneakers!"

"I know that. You know that. She don't know that."

It happened more times than you would ever believe. So much so that I felt angry and betrayed and began to fear that maybe these drivers represented how most women felt about women like me who were so blatantly strong and free. They just didn't get it—and I didn't feel sorry for them, either. And then, out of the blue, the opposite would happen. Occasionally a plump lady out in her yard would shout, "Hey, honey! You keep at it or you're gonna look like me!" Other women would just stop and clap and say, "Hooray for you!" And then I'd feel happy and hopeful for women all over again.

• • •

I loved the long run because we ran on Saturday or Sunday in daylight. It sounds like such a simple thing, but just to have an occasional day full of sunshine and dripping snowbanks, after weeks and weeks of endless darkness was heartening to the point of inspiration. Anything was possible! We could run forever! I know it's corny, but on those sunny days I felt so full of hope and promise that my heart seemed to jump out of my chest.

In fact, as soon as I began running the distances, I found I no longer had any interest whatsoever in church or organized religion. I became quite critical of what I suddenly felt were unnatural rules and rituals. When I ran, I felt like I was touching God, or God was touching me, every day. So the idea of only finding God one day a week inside a building seemed absurd, when for miles around in open country and wild landscapes I felt God everywhere. I was free, protected, and approved of. The rhythm of running and my own heartbeat tapped out a universal connectedness to the environment that I had never before felt, and I was both exhilarated and humbled by this infusion of my newfound religion.

I'm sure this was brought on also by the rush of endorphins, a sensation I had not experienced at quite this level. It also creates spontaneous talk about anything and everything, without judgment. Indeed, people tell you the secrets of their souls when they run; so at just the moment in training when I was feeling close to God in an expansive way, Arnie was, too, in his way, which was as a Roman Catholic convert. Arnie always had to run early on Sundays so he could get to Mass on time; this hammered me as weekends were the only time I—like all college students—could catch up on sleep. Arnie knew the early start annoyed me, so as he coached me through the miles, he felt also compelled to convert me too what he called The One True Faith. I do believe he thought if I felt kindly to the church, I'd not mind running early, as it was some kind of passport to heaven, or at least that was his way of explaining it. I also think he was in cahoots with Tom, who was a Catholic, too, and had I not been so infused with the endorphin bonhomie, I would have sniffed a conspiracy. In any case, this collision of religions caused heated and often hilarious debates on the run as Arnie tried his evangelical mightiest to woo me to his faith, and the miles just whizzed by.

• • •

For a while, we cooked. Bam, bam, bam: twelve miles, fourteen, sixteen. It was fantastic. One Saturday in March was our eighteen-miler and I felt the way I did every other weekend, except that at about the thirteenth mile, when we were out in the country, Arnie said, "Why are you slowing down?"

"Am I?" I asked, very surprised.

"Yes, are you okay?"

"Sure, I'm fine," I said. I felt perfectly fine and tried to pick up the pace a little. In all our workouts, we never sped up and we never slowed down. We stayed at the same plodding pace the whole time, so trying to speed up felt hard for me. Another mile or so passed and Arnie spoke sharply to me: "Hey! Why are you walking?"

I looked down at my legs. "Gosh, I didn't know I was." But sure enough, they were walking. I felt both very surprised and very drowsy. I started jogging again and it became a walk. Arnie said, "Okay, we'll just jog to that telephone pole, then walk to the next, then jog to the next and so forth for a while until you feel better."

I stated to jog, looking down at my legs. They were only shuffling, and then definitely walking. I slapped my thighs.

"C'mon! Run," I scolded them as if they were disobeying me on purpose. I realized with alarm I was actually talking to my legs. I tried to walk briskly. Arnie was kind of jogging around in circles, up and back, then backward.

"Look, Arnie. I am so sleepy I just cannot move. I'm just going to sit down here for a minute and take a nap." My voice sounded weird, like a drunk. "I'll be fine with jus'a lil' nap." I sat down on the grass on the side of the road and was instantly asleep.

Arnie began shouting, "Hey, you can't do that! You can't just stop out here in the middle of nowhere!"

"Arnie, I'll be fine in just ten minutes, just a ten-minute nap, okay okay . . ." Then I was gone, fast asleep.

The next thing I knew, Arnie and someone else were helping me into a car. I didn't care about anything except sleep and was aware only that I was stretched out in the back of a nice warm car and of Arnie's apologetic yammering to the driver. It felt very comforting, like an electric fan buzzing. Whoever he was took us all the way back to the field house, where Arnie had parked his car. When we arrived, I woke up and felt right as rain but quite embarrassed, and was brief with my thanks to the driver. To Arnie, I was a bit huffy. "See, I only needed a little nap," I said. Over the years I've often wondered who it was who rescued us and how grateful I am to him.

We went back the next week to sixteen miles, and then attempted the eighteen again with no problems. We did an eighteen-miler three weekends in a row, the last one on a tougher course, with incredible hills, just to be sure. This last course was out in countryside around Syracuse and Manlius that I'd never seen, taking us to all these Italian-sounding villages like Pompey and Fabius, remote and pretty places where the snow had not all melted. In shady places, this snow still overhung the road by ten or twelve feet, like the crest of a dirty white wave. Even I could not imagine what that section of the road must have been like in January.

Now it was late March, the sun was wan and the landscape bleak, just brown and black, the ground in places getting squishy like sodden peat. We were wearing shorts, even though it was still too chilly, and in any case we still had to wear sweatshirts and gloves. I felt as if the gray sweatshirt with TRACK stamped on the front in blue had just become a part of my body. It never seemed to get wet or heavy, because I never sweated. Neither of us did. It was too cold, we were going too slowly, and so the only thing that needed a daily wash was the T-shirt closest to my skin.

Since we never sweated, we never got thirsty or worried about fluid intake. It sounds astonishing today, but nobody was talking about the importance of water in those days, and if you weren't thirsty, what difference did it make? Finally, on that last eighteen-miler, when the sun was out, we did get thirsty. I saw a stream at the bottom of a muddy field and said I'd check it out. Arnie said to forget it, that the water was undrinkable because of the horses in the field, but I was over the fence by then, slopping through the mud and clumps of new spring grass, and when I got to the stream I pronounced it perfectly safe, as the water was moving swiftly and watercress was growing in it. It was a spring, and my dad had always said that the water watercress grew in was pure; watercress can't grow in a dirty stream. Arnie wasn't convinced, but when he saw me drinking so heartily he joined in, muttering that we'd probably get lockjaw or typhus or something. The water was numbingly cold and utterly delicious. We never got as much as a gut cramp, although years later I told that story to my dad, thinking he'd be proud of my remembering this bit of survival lore. He looked alarmed. "I never said that about watercress," he said.

PART II | BUILD-UP

After obtaining a good base, distance runners begin piling on the miles. Successful runners do this judiciously, making every mile count by running them at different tempos to add quality to the quantity. Beginners (like most of us, actually) usually don't have a choice— they have only one pace, so they just add more and slowly keep moving farther along.

Chapter | 6

"You can run the Boston Marathon!"

After the last eighteen-miler, Arnie said we'd go for the twenty-six miles the next weekend. Why he elected for us to jump to the full distance I don't know, perhaps because it was just a month before Boston. Maybe he just felt I was ready, but it didn't concern me. Arnie was calling the shots. But I can tell you I was excited. Really, *really* excited. It was my big moment, or more accurately, my big day, because we figured it would take most of the day.

We started in the morning, parking the car at Christian Brothers Academy on Randall Road, and planned to run a sixteen-mile loop into the country, then add on our Manlius Ten. That circled us closer to home without the danger of getting stuck in some kind of remote out-and-back course. Arnie never ever mentioned the incident when he'd had to flag down the car to get me home, but we didn't want to risk a repeat of that. We also didn't want to run the monster Pompey hills, which was a good thing; our course was rolling enough without our needing to be heroes. We always wanted a course that was as free of traffic as possible, provided some interest, and yet never passed by our own car or house. It was too great a temptation to stop when you passed Headquarters, that's for sure, and forcing yourself past home when you're tired makes you feel even more tired. That's one reason why I never was a good track runner; psychologically, the laps killed me.

• • •

The interest on the Manlius Ten route was always the nice houses along the way; I fantasized that someday I would have a nice house and yard like that of my own; sometimes I'd even imagine how I'd decorate them. Besides, Larry the Llama lived at one of the richer ones. Some slightly eccentric wealthy person had a nice estate we passed with a collection of what I would call "farmette" animals, one of which was this peevish llama that Arnie named Larry. I suppose all this sounds pretty lame on the entertainment scale, but believe me, when you are constructing a 26-mile, 385-yard route you are happy to have *any* pleasant diversions for the last ten miles.

At about six miles into the countryside, a black mongrel farm dog we'd seen before ran out snarling and barking at us and, as usual, we faced him and just ran backward until we passed the area of his domain. But instead of going back, the dog started wagging his tail and following us. After stopping and shouting "Go Home!" a dozen times, we gave up, and Blackie was our companion. Big Mistake, Blackie, I thought. My dad had told me that humans can eventually outrun most animals, including a deer, so I felt after a couple of miles Blackie would get tired and limp home, but the miles passed and Blackie hung in, tongue out, as loyal as if he were ours. After six miles, he began slipping back, limping, and would then try to sprint back up to us. "I know the feeling, you poor slob," I muttered and finally, after eight miles, Blackie just lay down on the side of the road and watched us go. It upset me; what if he died or something? But Arnie convinced me not to be sad, that dogs find their way home. Remember all those times Lassie did on TV, and besides, what could we do, carry him back?

Even though I never saw *Lassie* on TV, Blackie was as good a diversion as any, as we'd covered sixteen miles and were now starting on the last ten and hadn't felt the distance at all. The pretty houses went by, the overhanging trees had a very tiny hint of green, and Larry the scruffy apricot-colored llama walked up to the stone wall as we passed and looked at us with that sourpuss camel face. Ha! Except for having four legs, he looked just like some of the stone-faced people we passed along the way.

Sooner than I imagined, we were coming back up the hill on Randall Road and we could see Arnie's blue car in the parking lot in the distance, a half mile to go, 26 miles, 385 yards, the home stretch. It seemed we'd gotten there quickly, and at the same time it seemed it had taken all day. I didn't feel tired at all.

"You're going to do it," said Arnie. "I wouldn't have believed it. You are going to do it!"

I felt strangely disconnected, almost disappointed. This was supposed to be my moment of truth, victory, and validation. I had thought that coming into the parking lot on this gray afternoon would be like entering the Olympic Stadium. Instead, it felt so, well, anticlimactic.

"You look *good*, you look strong!" he was saying.

"Hey, Arnie, I do feel fine. So, maybe this isn't really twenty-six miles, maybe it's short, huh?"

Arnie got very agitated, almost steamed. "It *is* twenty-six, it *is*! It's *long* if it's anything; I measured it with the car!" (In the ensuing years, of course, we all discovered that measuring road courses with a car is notoriously inaccurate. For many years, hundreds of runners have been cheated out of records and accurate times on such wrongly measured courses, leading the legendary ultramarathoner Ted Corbitt and other conscientious souls to create methods of precise measurement and certification.)

"Okay, well, then why don't we run another five miles, just to be sure." I said. "You know, if we ran another five miles, then I would know *nothing* could stop us in Boston!"

"Can you run another five miles?" Arnie asked with wonder in his voice.

"Sure! I feel great! How do you feel?"

"Well, if you can do it, I can do it." He sounded uncertain, but he was willing to be part of an adventure.

We passed the car, both of us trailing our eyes on it for a long time. We turned the corner; committed again. Of course, just as soon as we did that, we both felt pretty leaden. It always happens when you pass home base. It was getting late in the day now, the sun had gone, and it seemed so lonely. And so damn gray! Wouldn't spring ever come? Now I was the one who tried to be chipper, making small talk as Arnie looked down in the dumps. This was my idea, after all. After about three miles, Arnie became strange, sounding cranky, talking nonsense, muttering profanity. I'd never heard Arnie ever use profanity! He was such a little Catholic saint, carrying a rosary, never drinking, getting embarrassed when somebody told a dirty joke. I'd often wondered how he ever got his wife pregnant, if you want to know the truth.

I became alarmed when Arnie drifted into the middle of the road. I pulled him back to the side and said, "Hey, are you okay? He looked surprised, like I'd woken him or something.

A car came toward us, passed us, giving us very wide berth. Arnie flew into a tantrum, grabbing a very big rock from the side of the road and hurling it after the car. "You bastard!" he screamed. "You goddamn son of a bitch! Trying to run *me* off the road! You goddamn bastard, I'll kill you!" He was standing there looking like a scarecrow with his wispy gray hair all standing on end and his eyes like pinwheels.

"Shit! Arnie, come on, it's okay." I tried to pull him out of the road, and he pulled back, eyes full of terror. "They. Are. Trying. To. *Kill*. Us." He hissed, as if he couldn't understand how I could be so stupid not to see that my life was in danger.

"C'mon, Arnie, one more mile, one more and we're there." I linked my arm through his, guiding him. He was as gray as his sweatshirt. His eyes were gone, blank. Still he ran and hobbled with me, legs like a rubber bendy toy, us linked at the elbows. Then there was the car, a block away. Honestly, I could hear the distant roar of the crowd in the Olympic stadium. "We're going to do it Arnie, we are!" I kept cooing, my heart filling. Then we were there by his old mud-spattered jalopy with the plastic Jesus on the dashboard and I flung my arms around him and pounded him on the back, "We *did* it, we *did* it, we're going to *Boston!*" and Arnie fainted in my arms.

I staggered a little under the sudden dead weight, clasping him tight under the armpits, and lowered him backward to a sitting position on the curb, where his head dropped between his knees. I tried to dance a little jig as I sang, "We did it, we did it," but I couldn't pick up my feet. I was like a drunk who could not really move but who could not stop smiling. I had never known such complete joy. It was if lying on the fender of that old car was my shiny gold medal. Arnie looked up, closed his eyes again, and said, "*You* can run the Boston Marathon."

• • •

Just about every student who lived along Comstock Avenue knew Arnie because he was our mailman, and almost everyone had at one time or the other picked up a houseload of mail from Arnie and had a cheerful exchange. He loved his job because everyone was happy to see him. College was just like the army that way; everyone is desperate for mail from a loved one. They'd call out, "Hey, Arnie, how are ya?" and Arnie would hand the mail through the door and give a cheery reply or a weather report.

On Monday, after our run, which I calculated to be close to thirty-one miles, a couple of guys in my English class said, 'Hey, what's up with Arnie?'

"I don't know, what do you mean," I answered.

"Well, he dropped off the mail today saying, 'Women have hidden potential in endurance and stamina!' right out of the blue."

I just laughed, and then when I came into my dorm between early classes, I overheard a couple of my housemates talking about the same exchange they'd had with him. One of them said, "He told me, 'She ran me into the ground.' What does that mean?"

I had this image of Arnie like Archimedes, leaping out of the bath, flinging open the doors of every house on Comstock and shouting "Eureka! Women have hidden potential in endurance and stamina!" Only it wasn't that funny to me, as now more than ever we had to keep this a secret. I was convinced that the surest way to fail was to tell everyone we were going to attempt Boston, because then they would expect things of me, and no matter what I did it wouldn't be good enough. I didn't want that pressure, and Arnie knew that, but he couldn't contain himself.

"I am just so proud of you I have to tell people how good you are," he said.

"Okay, but that's it, no telling anymore and no telling about Boston." He agreed.

After that, it was all business again, and Tuesday, instead of picking me up as usual in front of Huey Cottage, Arnie came in and made me sit at the desk in the lobby. We couldn't run anyway because we were still so sore. I could barely get down the stairs, and I had terrible blood blisters under four toenails. They were puffed up, purple and black, the nails raised, and they hurt like hell.

"Here, you have to fill out the entry form for Boston," he said, shoving under my nose the paper that said "American Marathon Race under the auspices of the Boston Athletic Association." Arnie had a dozen or so entry forms, since, as the longtime president of the mostly defunct Syracuse Harriers, he was on the Boston mailing list and received a bunch of entries every year to distribute to members of the club.

"I'll take care of the travel permit, but you need to fill this out, and you need to get down to the school infirmary and get a medical certificate testifying to your fitness. Plus you need to enclose three dollars. Cash. No checks; cash."

"Gee, Arnie, I don't know. Why do we need to register? Why can't we go and just run?"

"You can't do *that!* This is a serious race. You can't just go and jump into this race without a number. You're a registered member of the AAU; you have to follow all the rules."

"Well, that's what I mean, Arnie. What if I'm not welcome at Boston?"

"Of course you'll be welcome! You've done the distance in practice, that's a lot more than most of those dunderheads have done. Some of those rich kids from Harvard just think they can come out and run twenty-six miles—huh, some kind of fraternity prank; they jump in with no numbers and try to sprint with the leaders. Jerks! This is the most important road race in the world after the Olympics and you've trained for it, so you've got to do this right."

"Well, that Roberta girl did not wear a number last year."

Arnie got very solemn. "She should not have done that. This is a serious race, you must register for it, follow the regulations. Don't mess with those Boston people! That BAA, they are strict, and real hoity-toity, too. And you know the AAU!" Just the mention of the AAU gave me a shiver; you never knew who the Joe McCarthy was who was going to blacklist you for some insult or infringement you didn't even know about. Arnie and Tom had told me how great athletes got in trouble, like miler Wes Santee who was "set up" to take a prize whose value was beyond the AAU's acceptable limits and when he did they kicked him out, and he was an American hero! So you had to do things right.

"Yeah, but what if it's against the rules for a woman to run or something? I don't want to do something wrong. I'd rather just go up to Boston and be unnoticed."

"Ha! I was sure you'd ask that question, so I brought the AAU rule book with me. Look." He handed me the five-by-seven blue-and-white paperback book. Then he took it back and showed me, "Here. 'Rules for Men's Track and Field.' Here. 'Rules for Women's Track and Field. Here, look, the third section is just titled 'The Marathon.' Nothing about sex at all! Plus, look at the entry form, nothing on it says you have to be a male to run."

I looked through the book, lingering over the women's events, which I already knew well enough—the longest women's track event was 880 yards, and the length of the cross-country race was a mile and a half. The men had the additional events of mile, 3,000 meters steeplechase, three miles, and six miles. Their cross-county was 7.5 miles. Of course the AAU would never encourage women to run longer by offering any longer events, oh no; besides, your uterus might fall out.

But technically Arnie was right. In the separate section about the Marathon, there was nothing about gender. I looked over the entry form—it was neutral, too. But I knew that's because nobody could imagine a girl might want to run. Women just weren't interested, and they were afraid—they believed the myths that said long-distance running would de-feminize them. In fact, the only people who ran marathons were pretty nutty guys like Arnie. My total experience with runners was that the longer the distance a guy specialized in, the weirder he was. Not only weirder but also more interesting, in a quirky, not-stuck-up kind of way. So no girl in her right mind would even consider doing a marathon, and that, along with all the old myths, meant that the authors of this rule book and this entry form couldn't even conceive of women's participation. Not in a million years.

"I'm going to be noticed." I sighed, thinking of all the ballyhoo at Lynchburg when I wore official numbers in the men's mile race. That public reaction had surprised me, but it was over quickly. Plus, I had no doubt about finishing a mile! This was a marathon. Anything could happen over twenty-six miles. All I wanted to do was to keep my head down and run it.

"Yes, you will be noticed. But you are used to that. You're always the only girl no matter where we are." Arnie sounded proud when he said that.

I went upstairs and got my AAU number, limped back down,

and filled out the form. Where it said *Name,* I printed "K. V. Switzer" and signed the waiver at the bottom of the form the same way. I always felt good signing things K. V. Switzer; it felt strong and fast. "Three dollars, please." I handed over the three bucks. "Okay, go down to the infirmary and get a certificate stating you are in good health to run a marathon. We don't want to waste time standing in the medical line at Hopkinton High School to have someone listen to your heart. Plus, there are naked guys running all over the gym and you'd be embarrassed."

So Arnie went back to the post office, and I went down to the university infirmary. I felt cocky enough to tell the truth, that I planned to run a twenty-six mile event and that I'd done thirty-one miles in practice so I was sure I was very fit and capable. The doctor, a portly guy in his sixties, just beamed. He said he could remember the days of Clarence DeMar—"By golly, this is great!"—and he did heart and blood pressure checks. Then he asked me to run up and down the steps so he could listen again. "Fit as a fiddle!" he boomed out. He wrote out a prescription form with the exact information I wanted and used my patient name, Kathy Switzer. "Good luck, good luck!" he shouted as I left his office. I can't tell you how buoyed I was by this experience. Maybe he was, too. I was probably his first student patient in weeks who wasn't weeping over a nervous breakdown, a surprise pregnancy, or a mysterious case of the clap. Boston! I was going to Boston!!

I gave the certificate to Arnie at practice the next day; we were going to jog an easy five, normally so easy it was a vacation day, but today it was going to be excruciating. My quads felt like shredded beef. My hips, right at the connector at the top of the femur into the hip socket, had a deep, deep ache. I wasn't really hurt, just beat up.

But worst, even worse than the shocking blisters, were my toenails, which were now so puffed up with blood that I couldn't get my shoes on. I had to cut a triangle wedge out of the front out of my beautiful blue Adidas shoes, which had finally arrived from Germany. This broke my heart; they were the most expensive pair of shoes I'd ever owned, and the first I'd ever prized; now I had to mutilate them to even get them on my feet.

I had a growing sense of Function First, as if I were going to war or something. I was paring down and focusing, purging my life of all but the basic necessities, shedding appearances for the sake of utility. Well, with the exception of putting together a nice outfit for the race. This was not easy, as fashion was hardly a consideration in sports, and what looked good also had to work well if you're running a marathon. One scratchy piece of lace for the sake of looks could finish you off.

I'd spent a lot of workouts on the warmer days trying different shorts, most of which were hopelessly chafing, and for a simple reason: they were all cut for a man's body, of course. Women didn't run, so shorts would not be cut to take a woman's rounder hips and fleshier thighs into consideration. That uniquely female fatty bit at the top of the inner thigh was especially vulnerable to chafing—add salty sweat to raw skin there and you got stopped in your tracks. Arnie had a stash of stuff in the trunk of his car that he'd pilfered over the years from various locker rooms, and by golly if one pair of gray shorts with kind of skirty legs didn't work for me. Burgundy was the "in" color that year, and I had a burgundy knit shell that I'd run in that worked and looked great, so I dyed the shorts to match. It ruined the old porcelain sink in Huey and completely outraged the house matron, but nobody blew the whistle on me, and that sink remained rosy pink until the day they tore Huey down about fifteen years later.

Aside from the holes in my shoes, I was going to look great, and that was important to me. Nobody who saw *me* was going to go home and say those female athletes all look like dogs. I was sick of that stereotype and knew that while running the race I could at least do my part to demolish that old notion. Arnie said we would bring our oldest, crummiest sweats to Boston. We'd wear them for loosening up and at the start of the race, and when we got warmed up, we'd throw them away as we went along. "Those people at Boston can never manage to get your sweats back to you at the finish, so you might as well bring something you were going to dump anyway," he said. I thought, Good, I'll get rid of this old stuff at the same time, and when it comes off, voilà, I'll be a vision in burgundy.

John Leonard was at practice. He had fairly recently decided to come to Boston with us and run also, an alarming decision, in my view, since he'd done lots of our base midweek runs but almost none of the really long ones. I couldn't imagine running twenty-six miles "in public" without having done the distance first, but Arnie assured me, sniffing a bit as he said this, that most people don't, and added John to the travel permit.

Later, when we were alone, I told Arnie that I liked John fine but we were not the Three Musketeers here; if he started to fade and held us up, we had to go on. I was feeling more and more like a soldier at the Normandy landing or something; we were companions, but we had to take that beachhead at all costs! "If one of us can't do it, Arnie, the other must go ahead." Arnie agreed to this, but astonishingly we never had a plan for what we would do if that happened. Years later, knowing how very unlikely it is that two people, much less three, will make it to the finish line of a marathon together, it is simply incredible that we did not have contingency plans. I didn't even think of it because I was so ignorant, so that meant either Arnie had no intention of honoring the agreement, or he was as naively optimistic as I was.

Anyway, Arnie sent in all our papers together, entering us as a team from the Syracuse Harriers. I didn't know what a harrier was, I figured it was some version of always being in a hurry, and I could tell the way Arnie pronounced it he didn't either: "HaaarYerrrs." But we were a real team; the die was cast, and we were on countdown. Three more weeks: two of training, two more semilong runs, and then one week of hardly running at all. I couldn't believe that we got to take time off, but Arnie said we needed to rest up that last week: "If it's not done by then, there's nothin' else we can do. Might as well get some sleep." This was a revelation—I thought we had to run hard right up to the day before, and it was a good lesson in other ways, like my studying for exams. I felt stupid; all the books on how to study told you that, and I never believed them. I began to look forward to the last week as a vacation break.

We finished the five-miler at the field house, which was practically empty now that it was getting on to springtime. The board track had been taken down and the runners were out on the track at Archibald Stadium, on the other side of the campus. Coach Grieve was out there with them but the ground was still too mushy to accommodate repeated tosses of heavy field implements, so Tom was still coaching the throwers inside. While I waited for Arnie to shower, I stretched and watched Tom, an endless fascination. Today he was working with the javelin throwers on how best to drop the arm back and pull through. I would never tell hammer-throwing Tom, but I loved the javelin the most of all the throwing events because it was so

Greek, so Olympian, so true to its origins as a spear. Every year we'd read about some poor sucker, usually a dedicated but momentarily dozy official, walking across a field somewhere and getting speared through. "Just shows how fast that javelin flies," we'd all cluck.

Arnie was just coming out of the locker room as Tom walked over to me.

"Hiya. Catch you for a beer later, about eight?" Sure, I said. What this truncated conversation meant was that we'd both go back to where we lived so we could get something to eat, since we couldn't afford to buy a meal out. But sometimes we could afford a beer at the Orange, the college bar. Even though it was a grungy place, it felt like a date; it salvaged Tom's pride at being unable to afford anything fancier and was a less obvious way of just taking me over to his apartment for the night. Plus, I got to put on a skirt and sweater, which made me feel feminine and even sexy, a huge relief after days of neutral sweats in practice and jeans in class.

Later, at the bar, Tom was having one of his "remote" moods. Perhaps he was worried about money or studies; we all did, but I thought how weird it was that two people who had so much in common and had been sleeping together for four months often had so little to talk about. His moods were always a mystery to me. Sometimes I thought that Tom was just not a very good conversationalist, but then I felt this was unkind, since he was such a talented guy in other respects. Maybe he was just bored with me. Tom always acted oh, so cool, making me feel that I was not. Certainly, when you are sitting with someone who is quiet and seemingly judgmental, you feel like an idiot yammering on and on; either that or like you're playing Twenty Questions. I knew I should not feel uncomfortable with someone I was sleeping with, but I shoved it to the back of my mind.

Finally, he broke one of the silences with, "So. How's the *jogging* coming along?" There was that sarcastic emphasis again, this time on the jogging, and hell, that just did it. No matter how untalented I was, no matter how slow I was, I was a *runner*, dammit, not a jogger.

"The *running* is coming along just great," I said, with double the sarcasm. He'd seen me out there on Saturdays and Sundays doing those long runs. In fact, he often dropped me off at Arnie's car the morning after we'd spent the night together, something we used to joke about, imagining how shocked Arnie would be if he knew. Tom hadn't a clue about our going to Boston, and I knew vaguely that I should tell him, but I kept putting it off. I just didn't want pressure from anybody, but now Boston was only three weeks away. Plus, I wanted to come back with a good retort. I took a sip of beer, trying to act nonchalant.

"In fact, Arnie and I are going up to Boston in a couple of weeks to run the marathon." I made it sound light, like we were going shopping.

At first, Tom looked startled, then quickly recovered, assumed a look of tired condescension, and whined loudly, "A marathon is twenty-six miles, three hundred—" I cut him off.

"I know how far it is Tom, I've run it. Arnie and I ran the distance last Saturday." I felt great. Instead of icy cold nervousness, I felt covered with warm perspiration. It was the first time I'd come out on top of him and he knew it. There was a long silence. I smiled.

"Okay, I'm coming to Boston, too," he finally answered.

"What do you mean?"

"I'm going to run the Boston Marathon, too. Really, if any *girl* can run twenty-six miles, I can do it, too." I was more incredulous than insulted, especially by the words "any" and "girl."

"Tom, you are a talented athlete. I have no doubt you could do it. But even you would have to train. Twenty-six miles takes a lot of training."

"Like I said, if any girl can run it, I can run it."

I tried again: "Tom, consider height-weight ratio. Nobody who weighs 235 pounds runs marathons! It's stupid even to consider." At this he got angry.

"I could go out that door *right now* and run twenty-six miles," he said.

"Boston's only three weeks away, Tom." I sounded defeated and I knew it.

"Plenty of time to get ready," he said, gulping down his beer. We went back to his apartment because I was too gutless to say I'd sleep at my dorm that night, and he was too stubborn to suggest that I not come home with him. We just didn't say anything, got into his foldout sofa as we always did, but this time we didn't make love. He turned on his side away from me in a huff and I spent most of the night looking at the ceiling, upset at losing a night of both sleep and study, and chastising myself for telling Tom about Boston. "See, I was right, just don't tell anybody big dreams because they mess them up for you. I should have waited until we got up there and called him or some-thing, but you can't treat someone you are sleeping with that way," I thought. I debated it back and forth in my head until it was time to get up and drag myself to class.

The next day at the field house, Tom wasn't there when Arnie, John, and I went out to run, and he still wasn't there by the time we got back. Then, just as I was leaving to go back to my dorm he made a bombastic entrance. It was dark by now, and Tom was all flushed, sweating and defiant. I could tell he had been working hard, I could smell the cold night air all around him; it's a smell you don't get from being outside just a few minutes.

"Nine miles, that's enough to do it," he said.

"Wow, Tom, you just ran nine miles?!" I was flabbergasted that he could just go out and go that far.

"Yes, so you see, I can run Boston." I didn't say anything, as I was more amazed by what he could do than by what a chasm there was between nine and twenty-six. And that was that. Arnie and I told him the plan: We'd start together, but if anyone faltered, the others would go on. Since our applications had long since been mailed, Tom sent in his own paperwork, but because he was late in applying, he would have to take the physical at the high school gym in Hopkinton. This ticked me off; it meant just another delay and complication at the start for us. First John, now Big Tom: not even invited, not well trained. There were too many variables.

CHAPTER | 7

"GET THE HELL OUT OF MY RACE AND GIVE ME THOSE NUMBERS!"

The 1967 "American Marathon Race, under the auspices of the Boston Athletic Association," better known as the Boston Marathon, was on Wednesday, April 19, Patriot's Day in the State of Massachusetts. (A few years later, when the federal government moved major holiday observances to Monday, the Marathon was run on the third Monday in April.) I thought it was neat that folks in Massachusetts got a special holiday commemorating the young American patriots who fought the British in the first battles of the American Revolution, at Lexington and Concord in 1775. The marathon was made a part of Patriots Day in 1897, the year after the revival of the Olympic Games in Athens.

Several young men from the BAA participated in the Athens Games and returned home fascinated with a romantic new event called the marathon. Since the marathon in Greece commemorated the historic run of a messenger, the BAA Marathon would commemorate the historic midnight ride of the messenger Paul Revere. For a long time I thought the Boston Marathon course must have been the same route as Revere's ride but Arnie said it was not. In any case, the revolutionary history was significant to me and I felt proud to be a part of it. Every American school kid can tell you about "the shot heard round the world" and quote some of Longfellow's poem, "Paul Revere's Ride." We had visited the main historic sites on a family vacation to New England when I was a kid and here I was going back to them, and to being a part of the oldest American race, the biggest one, and the most famous. I was going to be a part of history!

Still, I told no one else until the day before, and then only under duress. I'd decided to cut all my Wednesday classes with no explanation, but I had to tell Dr. Edmund Arnold, my graphics arts professor, as we were having a test on Wednesday and I needed to request a makeup. Since honesty worked best with the doctor at the infirmary, I decided to tell Dr. Arnold the truth, swearing him first to secrecy. I did not want this spread all over campus and Dr. Arnold was a chatty guy, quite an enthusiast about everything. I was pleased with his unequivocal support, and then he said, "Well, I remember the days of the great Clarence DeMar!" Boy, this guy DeMar must have been something, I thought.

As I was packing up my stuff on Tuesday afternoon, I decided to tell my roommates, who were wondering where I was going anyway. Since I didn't actually know what might happen to me—I mean, we could have a car crash or something—I thought *somebody* should know where I was. Jane, Kaye, and Connell had all moved on from the first days of my running in October, when they'd mildly ridiculed me and called me "Roadrunner," to a kind of acceptance as a good-natured eccentric. I was incredibly independent and not totally uncool after all, and as these were all women who abhorred conformity at all costs (with the exception, of course, of turtlenecks, jeans, and Winston cigarettes) they had all rather come to like me. I had to explain what a marathon was, trying to be offhand when I told them that I might be the only woman. I begged them for secrecy, as I didn't want any fuss at the last minute. They sat on their beds, smoking, thinking, and then just said, "Okay, cool," as if, who could we tell even if we wanted to?

Arnie picked up John, Tom, and me, and we hit the road at about three in the afternoon for the five-hour drive to Boston. It was a blast of a trip, mostly because Tom was in a great mood; he told jokes and we all acted silly. I'd noticed that when Tom was grumpy it made everyone around him tense, not just me, and when he was pleasant, we'd all be so relieved we would fall into a kind of silly glee. I felt confident enough to ask Arnie who Clarence DeMar was in front of Tom, and for a moment the fun was almost over. Before Arnie could answer, Tom smacked his head in disbelief. "How can you not know who Clarence DeMar was? Hell, he was the *greatest*. He won the Boston Marathon seven times!" Even John knew who Clarence DeMar was. Then Arnie said kindly, "Yeah, but he ran a million years ago," which meant that Arnie, like so many people, only go on and on about those heroes of their own generation. Anyway, you had to hand it to Tom, he knew about every sport and just about every athlete in it.

That was the mood in the car and it was great. We shared the driving and the costs for gas and dinner, and we found a motel with a vacancy sign in Natick, about nine miles east of Hopkinton, where the race was to start. I thought it was amazingly chivalrous that the three guys took one room and gave me one by myself and we still split it four ways. After dinner, Arnie insisted on showing us the course even though it was already nearly ten at night—it was freezing cold and rainy outside, pitch black, and as we drove along in Arnie's old rattletrap with bad windshield wipers, we couldn't see a blessed thing.

Arnie was all excited at every landmark, saying things like, "Now here's Wellesley College! Here are the Wellesley hills!" The windows were completely steamed up, there was nothing to be seen, and the ride seemed to last an eternity. I had a feeling of impending doom. Here we were, driving at forty miles an hour, and it was taking *forever*. Finally, we all said it was hopeless, what did it matter, we had to run it anyway, let's go back and get some sleep, and Arnie reluctantly turned the car around for the journey back to the motel, which seemed to take most of the night. Ever since then I've never driven over a marathon course the day before the event. It is demoralizing when you see how far twenty-six miles actually is.

I was spooked by this experience, and when I called my parents it was late, but they were always up. As I had to my roommates, I had to explain first what a marathon was, and then why I was in Boston, ending with, "I am nervous about being able to finish. It is important for me to finish the race." My dad was acute when it came to any anxiety on my part; I never reached out with a lack of confidence unless it was serious. And he delivered perfectly. "You go get 'em, kid, you can do it!"

"It's twenty-six miles, Dad."

"Aw hell, kid, you can do it. You're tough, you've trained, you'll do just *great*."

It was exactly what I needed to hear. My dad knew I didn't jump into things untrained; he'd watched the running progress in high school, and although this marathon thing was a surprise, he had no doubts. I knew he had no doubts, and I felt good but just a little sad when I hung up. What I couldn't explain to him, what nobody knows unless they've done one, is that the marathon is unpredictable, anything weird could happen, and anything could happen to *me*! I could get diarrhea! I could get hit by a dolt opening his car door. Arnie had told me about that happening to a guy once. Eventually, I got too tired to worry about the kinds of things I could not control. The thing I worried about most was courage. Would I have the courage to keep running if it really hurt, if it got harder than I was used to, if Heartbreak Hill broke me? Yep, that was it, I was worried about maybe not having the courage if it got awful.

So I decided to have a word with God, for whom I felt I'd shown plenty of respect and appreciation well in advance of this race, so this was no last-minute panic plea. I thought it was selfish of runners to ask God for things like, "Please make sure I finish," or "Please don't make it hurt." If you've done the work, I don't think God is up there making those kinds of decisions anyway. But I do think he (or she) does help us out if we ask for things to better our character, so I felt it was fair to ask for the courage to make the right decision when it got hard. Because it was going to get hard. The marathon was always hard. It took me a long time to boil down my fears to this, but once I realized what my fears were really all about, I slept soundly.

I also thanked God that the Boston Marathon starts at noon, as we all got to sleep till eight and were eating breakfast at nine. Arnie said to chow down, we really needed a lot of fuel because it was a long day and cold outside. He wasn't just kidding—it was freezing rain, really pelting down, with sleet and wind. So we ate everything: bacon, eggs, pancakes, juice, coffee, milk, extra toast. I was excited to see other people in the little roadside restaurant wearing gray sweat suits just like us.

In addition to allowing us a great breakfast, the noon start gave me time for a significant poop, which was always an issue on early-morning long runs that started before breakfast. Today the system never felt better; I crossed "getting diarrhea" off my worry list. No period, no diarrhea, there were two of the big ones. Oddly, the weather didn't concern me; we'd trained for months in weather like this. It was annoying, though, as I had wanted to look nice and feminine at the start in my newly ironed burgundy shorts and top. Now that would have to wait until later, when I'd warmed up and chucked off my sweats, as Arnie said we would.

We went back to our rooms, packed our stuff, and I carefully put on makeup and gold earbobs, and coated my feet in Vaseline. For what it was worth. My feet hadn't totally healed from our trial marathon run and I just hoped this Vaseline would protect them for as many miles as possible. Tom banged on my door, holding out a sanitary napkin bag from the back of the toilet and a big safety pin. "Here, we're pinning these on the back of our gloves. They're perfect for holding dextrose tablets. See, you put four tablets in the bottom of the sack, rip off the top, fold it over, and pin it to your glove. Then when you need the dextrose, you rip it open."

"Why do you need dextrose?" I asked.

"It's sugar, for energy, get it?" he said in that tone that made me feel stupid again. Tom always had a system, knew there was a vitamin or something magic that would make you better. I had no idea that sugar per se would give you energy, I mean any more than, say, a piece of bread. I'd been hungry and tired plenty of times on a run, but I never craved sugar or equated it to energy.

"I don't need sugar, we never needed it before," I said. It was just another complication. I hated fussing with equipment anyway; we had enough to worry about.

"How do you know? Just pin it on, already." I shrugged my shoulders. It was easier to do it than argue. Besides, Tom was now assuming his experienced-athlete-and-coach role and was acting bossy. He was starting to get hyped; I'd seen him before competitions as he stomped around and snorted, and this was no different. Still, I felt idiotic, but when I got to the car with my suitcase I saw that Arnie and John had the sanitary napkin bags pinned to their gloves, too. What a team!

As we drove to Hopkinton, the rain at times turned to snow, with giant flakes that splashed into slush on the windshield and onto the pavement. It wasn't cold enough to be icy slick, but it was penetrating. The temperature was 34, and I knew there was no way I was taking off my sweats. It was plain awful outside, even by Syracuse standards, and inside my sweats, which had been worn down to soft flannel over the hundreds of miles of training and laundering, I felt as cozy as if I were wearing pajamas. To hell with looking great, I thought, I've got to keep warm and loose to run, that is my first priority.

We got to Hopkinton High School and parked right beside it, an unthinkable thing nowadays, where there are thousands and thousands of people who have to come in streams of special buses just to sit around for hours to wait for the start of the race. Arnie told John and me to wait in the car where it was warm while he got the envelope with our numbers and pins. Since we'd preregistered as a team and sent our papers in together, the race organizers would put all our stuff together for pickup by the team coach or captain, just as they always did for a track or cross-country meet. Tom went in with Arnie, since Tom had to take the physical. A few minutes later, Arnie came out with the envelope and two number bibs each to pin on our fronts and backs; they looked like cardboard license plates. We looked up our names in the printed start list and smiled at each other nervously; seeing "K. Switzer" in print beside "261" gave me a little frisson. There were 733 people listed on the program, a huge race. Arnie grumbled about it getting out of control.

I pinned my numbers on my sweatshirt and not my burgundy top. It was the final commitment to wearing that sweatshirt for the whole race and I was pleased; the sweatshirt had been a buddy in Syracuse for a few hundred miles and would live on another day rather than dying at the roadside on the way to Boston. Not so for the big hooded warm-up sweatshirt, however, that I'd worn during blizzards in Syracuse. This was the one with "U.S. Naval Academy, Annapolis" on the front. Dave had given it to me at my request for Christmas three years ago and it had been my pride and joy. Now it was going to get jettisoned forever—like Dave. That made me glad, too.

We got out of the car and started warming up as we waited for Tom. Everyone was darting about in different directions, all in gray sweat suits, some with hoods up, some with nylon windbreakers over them, some barelegged, and some with shorts over the pants, a method of wearing sweats I never could understand. If you had cast your eye over the whole scene, we all looked alike, like ragtags.

As runners jogged past us, most kept their slightly nervous eyes ahead, lost in pre-race concentration, but plenty did double takes, and when they did I'd smile back or wave a little wave. Yep, I'm a *girl*, my look back said. Many of these guys turned right around and jogged over to me, all excited. "Hey! Are you gonna go the whole way?" "Gosh, it's great to see a girl here!" "Hope you know there are hills out here—are you ready?" "Can you give me some tips to get my wife to run? I know she'd love it if I can just get her started." Arnie was kind of holding court, saying, "Sure she's going all the way!" Then he'd start on his "This girl ran me into the ground!" routine. He was shining. "See? I *told* you you'd be welcome at Boston!" he said. And indeed, I felt very welcome. I felt special and proud of myself. I knew something other women didn't know, and I felt downright smug.

It was getting close to noon and Tom had not appeared. We still had to park the car for the day and get to the start. Suddenly he burst out of the doors of the high school in his bright orange Syracuse track sweatshirt and ran over to us, practically punching the air. "Stupid jerks!" he said. "They weren't going to let me run, said I had higher than normal blood pressure! Of course I have higher than normal blood pressure! I am getting ready to run the goddamn Boston marathon, what do you *think*, you asses! So I had to sit down and get calm and convince them I was okay to run and they took it again and said it was entirely up to me but they wouldn't recommend it." Arnie said, "C'mon, c'mon, let's get the car parked," and he drove around the village square and over to St. John the Evangelist Catholic Church and parked in the lot there, apparently his regular place. It was a two-minute walk to Hayden Row, where the race started.

Incredibly, with twenty minutes to the start of the race, Tom and Arnie decided they had to go inside to pray. John and I wailed to the sky. "Oh come *on*, why didn't you pray last night when you had time!" I implored. I wanted to say it doesn't count if you wait until the last minute like this, but not really being an authority, I said, "Come on, just pray as we walk, you don't need to go into a church for heaven's sake, God hears you no matter where you are!" I was frantic and it was useless. I wasn't Catholic so of course I wouldn't know that maybe it counts more when you're down on your knees with a crucifix and all. John and I jogged in circles around the parking lot and I swear to you Tom and Arnie were in there ten minutes if they were in there a second.

When they came out Tom was pumped. "I'm ready! I'm psyched! Hey, where's Bikila*? Bikila, ha!!" And he spat in joking contempt.

"God, you are wearing lipstick!" he said to me as we jogged over to the start.

"I always wear lipstick! What's wrong with that?"

"Somebody might see you are a girl and not let you run, take it off."

"I will *not* take off my lipstick," and that is how we arrived at the start. There was a mob of runners in every getup imaginable funneling into a penlike area that was a block off Hayden Row surrounded by snow fencing. At the gate of the funnel were clipboard-holding BAA officials wearing long overcoats with blue ribbons on the lapels, and felt dress hats. Everyone was sodden, and hats were gathering snow, as were the shoulders of the runners who had been standing in the pen a while. It was pretty disorganized and the officials were agitated. They were checking off the bib numbers of the runners as they came through the gate. I lifted up the big outer sweatshirt so they could check off my number and the official put his hand on my shoulder and gently pushed me forward saying, "C'mon runners, let's move on in, just keep it moving here!" We worked our way into the back of the field, and Arnie said, "See? No problem!"

All around us the men were excited and pleased to have a woman in their presence. I tried to stay low key. I didn't want any attention especially at this moment, but I tried to be accommodating, even when one runner insisted on having his wife, who was on the other side of the fence, take our photo together. Then the crowd quieted,

---

*Abebe Bikila was the legendary runner from Ethiopia who won the Olympic Marathon barefoot in 1960 and then returned in to win again in 1964, in a world record, this time in shoes.

someone up front must have been making announcements. We moved close together, and the smell of liniment was so strong my eyes stung. I pulled off the heavy top sweatshirt and threw it over the fence, the gun went off, and we were away at last. At last!

Boston was always a Mecca for runners, and now I, too, was one of the anointed pilgrims. After months of training with Arnie and dreaming about this, here we were, streaming alongside the village common and onto the downhill of Route 135 with hundreds of our most intimate companions, all unknown, and all of whom understood what this meant and had worked hard to get here. More than ever before at a running event, I felt at home.

When you are a slow runner like we all were, the first few miles of every marathon are fun, when the running is easy, the crowd noise exciting, and your companions conversational and affable. You know it's going to hurt later, so you just enjoy this time. So it was with us as we stayed in our little group, running four abreast, joking and saying thanks to the many well-wishers who passed us with encouragement. Arnie and Tom were in their element hearing all the positive encouragement directed at us; running with me—a girl!—was giving them attention they had never had before. Tom ran with his chest stuck out and Arnie pranced; it was nice to see.

Then there came a honking of horns and someone shouting, "Get over, runners move to your right!" There was a lot of shuffling and some cursing as a big flatbed truck lumbered by on our left, forcing us all to the right side of the narrow road. Following close behind the truck was a city bus. The truck was the photo press truck; on the back of it were risers so the cameramen could each get a clean shot of the race as the vehicle pushed up to the front of the field. I thought at the time that it was incredibly poor organization, dangerous even, to allow moving vehicles behind a pack of seven hundred runners, especially in a world-class competition like this one. We were pretty slow, but up front were good guys and it's pretty risky to beep at Olympic athletes in full flight and expect them to move over. I was thinking this when I realized the press truck had slowed to be right in front of us and were taking our pictures. In fact, they were getting pretty excited to see a woman in the race, a woman wearing *numbers*. I could see them fumbling with their programs to look up my number and name, and then shoot again. We all started to laugh and wave. It was our "Hi Mom! on the nightly news" moment and it was fun.

Then suddenly, a man with an overcoat and felt hat was in the middle of the road shaking his finger at me; he said something to me as I passed and reached out for my hand, catching my glove instead and pulling it off. I did a kind of stutter step, and we all had to jostle around him. I thought he was a nutty spectator, but when I passed I caught a glimpse of a blue and gold BAA ribbon on his lapel. Where had he come from?

Moments later, I heard the scraping noise of leather shoes coming up fast behind me, an alien and alarming sound amid the muted thump-thumping of the rubber running shoes. When a runner hears that kind of noise, it's usually danger—just like hearing a dog's claws on the pavement. Instinctively I jerked my head around quickly and looked squarely into the most vicious face I'd ever seen. A big man, a huge man, with bared teeth was set to pounce, and before I could react he grabbed my shoulder and flung me back screaming, "Get the hell out of my race and give me those numbers!" Then he swiped down my front, trying to rip off my bib number, just as I leapt backward from him. He missed the numbers but I was so surprised and frightened that I slightly wet my pants, and turned to run. But now the man had the back of my shirt and was swiping at the bib number on my back. I was making little cries of aa-uh, aa-uh, not thinking at all, just trying to get away, when I saw tiny brave Arnie bat at him and try to push him away, shouting, "Leave her alone, Jock, I've trained her, she's okay, leave her alone!" And the man screamed, "Stay out of this, Arnie!" and swatted him away like a gnat.

Arnie *knows* this maniac, I thought wildly, as I tried to pull away. The only sound was the clicking whirr of motordrive cameras, scuffling sounds, and, faintly, a Japanese cameraman yelling, "eeechai yawoow" or something. The bottom was dropping out of my stomach; I had never felt such embarrassment and fear. I'd never been manhandled, never even spanked as a child, and the physical power and swiftness of the attack stunned me. I felt unable to flee, like I was rooted there, and indeed I was, since the man, this Jock guy, had me by the shirt. Then a flash of orange flew past, and hit Jock with a cross-body block. It was Big Tom, in the orange sweatshirt. There was a thud—whoomph!— and Jock was airborne. He landed on the roadside like a pile of wrinkled clothes. Now I felt terror. We've killed this guy Jock, it's my fault, even though Tom that hothead did it, my God we're all going to jail. And then I saw Arnie's face—it was full of fear, too; his eyes were goggled and he shouted, "Run like hell!" and boy did we! All the adrenaline kicked in and down the street we ran, flying past the press truck, running like kids out of a haunted house.

I was dazed and confused. I'd never been up close to physical violence; the power was terrifying and I was shocked at how helpless I, a strong woman, felt against it. Tom's precise execution, the way he took out Jock and only Jock, was sublime athleticism but I was not grateful for the save, I felt sick at heart, it was awful; it had gone too far. I wished Tom was not there; I wished I was not there.

Everyone was shouting. I could hear the journalists on the truck behind us yelling to the driver, "Go after her, Go after her!" The driver accelerated, popped the clutch, and I heard the truck buck and what unfortunately sounded like photographers, tripods, and crank cameras crashing down in a cursing melee.

Everyone was cursing, most loudly Arnie, the mild-mannered sweetheart, who proclaimed he was going to Kill That Jock Semple Who Should Know Better Being a Runner Himself! (Arnie actually *ran* with this maniac?) Tom really looked as if steam was coming out of his ears. He was still in full bombastic mode, and each of his curses was accompanied by a jab or a challenging look over his shoulder. John looked bewildered. I felt puke-ish, afraid that we had seriously hurt this guy Jock Semple, and maybe we should stop and get it sorted out. But it was clear that Jock was some kind of official and he was out of control, now he's hurt, we're in trouble, and we're going to get arrested. That was how scared I felt, as well as deeply humiliated, and for just a tiny moment, I wondered if I should step off the course. I did not want to mess up this prestigious race. But the thought was only a flicker. I knew if I quit, nobody would ever believe that women had the capability to run the marathon distance. If I quit, everybody would say it was a publicity stunt. If I quit, it would set women's sports back, way back, instead of forward. If I quit, I'd never run Boston. If I quit, Jock Semple and all those like him would win. My fear and humiliation turned to anger.

The press truck caught back up to us and hovered alongside with its engine droning only about three feet away. Off the back and side of the vehicle the journalists began firing aggressive questions and the photographers hung out very close to us to get face shots. It felt very weird to try to answer someone's question when there was a clickety-clickety apparatus practically up your nose. And oh, how quickly their tone had changed! Now it was, "What are you trying to prove?" and "When are you going to quit?" Consequently, my tone changed, too. I was polite but no longer friendly. I made it clear that I was not trying to "prove" anything except that I wanted to run, I'd trained seriously for the distance and I was not going to drop out. They wrote down what they wanted to write. Clearly, they didn't believe me, as they stayed alongside us even when I stopped answering their questions and tried to ignore them. They thought it was a prank and didn't want to miss the moment when I'd give up. This only strengthened my resolve. In fact, it actually infuriated me.

Then the bus came by. Standing on the floorboards and holding on to the outside door rail was Jock Semple! My God, he's alive! I thought. I was so relieved! But the bus slowed as it came alongside us, and Jock, teeth bared again and shaking his fist, screamed in a Scottish brogue, "You all ere een beeeeeggg troooouble!" All around us, men gave him the finger and shouted obscenities back at him, And Arnie shouted "Get out of here, Jock! Leave us alone!" I put my head down—I was not going to say a word. My mom had always told me not to say *anything* to unreasonable or aggressive people, and she'd been right so far. And with that, the bus accelerated with a huge cloud of stinking exhaust in our faces and sped away, blaring its horn for the runners to get out of its way.

Eventually, after fifteen minutes or so, the press truck gave up on me when they saw I was not talking anymore and was not going to give them the satisfaction of dropping out to suit their photo ambitions. With a smoother shift of the gears, it accelerated and drifted up toward the front of the race, where it should have been anyway. Our chatter died down, and without the sound of the truck motor and cameras, it seemed very quiet. It started to snow again. We were all deep in thought, and mine were moving all over the place, including wondering why girls first get embarrassed over confrontational situations and only later get angry, and guys can react instantly. I was a little envious of that and glad to feel anger now, because I believed that this was not over, not by a long shot. I said quietly to Arnie, "You know that guy Jock has gone up ahead and is probably arranging for one of those big Irish cops to arrest us when nobody is looking." I'd never seen such big, burly policemen. They made even Tom look small. "So, if it happens, I am resisting arrest, okay? And something else." I turned to Arnie and looked him in the eye. "Arnie, I'm not sure where you stand in this now. But no matter what, I have to finish this race. Even if you can't, I have to, even on my hands and knees. If I don't finish it, people will say women can't do it, and they will say I was just doing this for the publicity or something. So you need to do whatever you want to do, but I'm finishing."

"Well, the first thing we're going to do is to slow down, then. Forget about time, just finish!" Arnie was now the army sergeant. "Okay everybody, listen up!" he said to everybody in hearing range. "Let's get it together. Slow it down, just relax, we've got a long way to go. Shake it out, shake it out!" We dropped the pace down, dropped our arms, shook our hands. My left hand was wet and freezing; losing that glove was bad. You can have a lot of your body uncovered while you are running and be okay, but if your hands are cold, you are miserable all over. I pulled at the sleeve of my sweatshirt and tried to cover my hand but the sleeve wasn't long enough.

We were just falling into the rhythm of Arnie's stride and beginning to relax when Tom, still fuming, turned to me and blurted out, "You're getting me into all kinds of trouble!"

It was out of the blue.

"What are you talking about, Tom?"

"I've hit an official, and now I'll get kicked out of the AAU. I'll never make the Olympic team and it's all your fault."

I felt really sad, but I was angry, too. "I didn't hit the official, you hit the official, Tom." I said it quietly. It was pretty embarrassing having an argument in front of Arnie and John, and for that matter anybody else running near us. I thought it extremely crass of Tom to pick a fight in public with me, his steady girlfriend. Everybody looked embarrassed.

"Oh great, yeah, thanks a lot for nothing. I should never have come to Boston," he answered loudly.

"I told you not to come to Boston! It was your idea to come to Boston!" I was whispering now, trying not to go on in front of all the people who couldn't help but hear us, and feeling sickish again, as if I were swirling out of one nightmare into another.

"Just stop it, you two," said Arnie.

Tom ripped the numbers off the front and back of his sweatshirt, tore them up, threw them to the pavement, and shouted, "I am *never* going to make the Olympic team and it is *all your fault!*" Then he lowered his voice and hissed, "Besides that, you run too slow anyway." And with that, he took off and disappeared among the runners in front of us.

I couldn't help it. I felt so ashamed I was crying. Once again Tom had convinced me I was just a girl, a jogger, and that a no-talent like me now had bumbled the Olympic Dream out of his life. I thought I was a serious girlfriend to him, and so I guessed that was over, too. It was a helluva race so far, that's for sure, and we still had over twenty miles to go.

"Let him go. Just let him go. Forget it, shake it off!" scolded Arnie. Dutifully I dropped my arms like I'd done a million times in practice and shook my hands. I kept my head down. I didn't want to see anyone, as this was the only way I could lick my wounds in public. I felt myself go into a deep trough of fatigue; actually, the three of us began to go under together, I could feel the downward pull. Even I knew the adrenaline had gone. God, what I'd give to just go to sleep for a while, I thought. We had such a long way to go, but I didn't care anymore, not about Tom, not about anything but finishing. I didn't care how much it hurt or how long it was going to take or if I got put in jail or even if I died. I was going to finish no matter what. We were all quiet for a long time.

A couple of miles later, we slowly began to notice things, the way you do when you first come out of anesthesia. The energy was coming back; by letting ourselves go into the trough we had rested and now we were getting strong again. It was an amazing sensation. First we heard a few feeble cheers; this was really nice and we waved back. There were hardly any spectators. It was such a rotten day that nobody was waiting around for the back-of-the-packers like us. I felt I was still going so slowly, that my soggy long pants must be dragging me down, so I went over to the roadside, pulled them off, and tossed them away. As I did this, a boy of about eight ran for the pants and grabbed them up, swung them around his head, and screamed in glee at his souvenir. The three of us looked at one another and made a face as if to say, "Can you imagine what his mother is going to say when he brings *that* home!?"

We came upon a great scattering of orange peels in the road, a sight incredibly weird to me. When I asked Arnie, he said "Oh those are for the elite runners."

"You mean, the elite runners get *orange slices?!*" I was astonished at this privilege. "Why don't they have orange slices for everyone?"

"They are only for the guys up front, the *real* competitors."

"So, when you were racing in the fifties, you got orange slices?"

"Yep. And sponges and water, too."

"Everyone should get those things. If I ever organize a race, I'll make sure of that."

"Well, everyone does get beef stew at the end," said Arnie.

John and I both laughed. "Why do I think we will not be getting beef stew, Arnie?" I said.

He grinned sheepishly. "It's not very good anyway. It's Dinty Moore's, out of a can."

"Oh yuck, I hate beef stew out of a can!" said John.

"Who wants beef stew at the end of a marathon anyway?" I said. "I wonder where they got that idea."

"It's some kind of old tradition," said Arnie. "And you're right. Plenty of guys on a hot day just get kind of sick when they eat it."

There was a lot about this great race that was just plain wacky to me.

In Natick Center, at about ten miles, we were comfortable again, even telling jokes and stories. I saw a truck parked along the road with a big sign on the side: Snap-On Tools. For some smutty and very childish reason, this was just hilarious to me, and I got John laughing so hard we both got side aches. Arnie didn't get it, which made it even funnier. From the crowd on the sidewalk a youngish man came running toward us shouting, "Arnie, Arnie!" and jogged alongside us in his raincoat and street shoes. It was Jimmy Matthews, one of Arnie's former running pupils from a few years before, when Jimmy was studying at Lemoyne College in Syracuse. Jimmy was now living in nearby Wayland, and the way he treated Arnie you'd have thought Jesus himself was strutting down Natick's Main Street. After chastising Arnie for not telling him we were coming to Boston, Jimmy proposed that he pick us up at the finish and get us back to our car. By any stretch, this was a generous offer, and we readily accepted, especially since Arnie apparently didn't have any kind of plan to get us back to Hopkinton. Then Jimmy ran ahead of us, turned around, and took a fast photo.

Now we entered the famous Wellesley Hills, where, in one of Arnie's theories, "the race began." I was wondering how I'd do on the hills—if the girls at Wellesley would cheer for us and what they would make of me—when I saw a flick of orange go over the top of the next hill in front of us. No, it couldn't be . . . could it? For a while on this stretch, we could see the road ascend, descend and ascend again, and the tableau was so gray, and so wet that the only color was in store signs or in odd bits of spectators' clothing, and there weren't many spectators. Orange anywhere was definitely eye-catching. I couldn't think of anything else but what was going to happen when I got to the top of the next hill, and before I knew it, we were there. We looked down and saw runners running away in front of us, and one big one, in an orange sweatshirt, walking.

Shoot, another disaster, I thought.

"Hey! Is that Tom up there?" chirped Arnie.

"That sure looks like Tom," John added, all singsongy.

I didn't say anything. Of course it's Tom, you jerks, I saw him a long time ago.

Because I said nothing, Arnie then said loudly, as if I were deaf or something, "Hey, I'll bet that really is Tommy!"

Jesus, Arnie! I wanted to smack him. Still I said nothing. Getting the message, the guys went quiet. Tock tock tock went our feet. The orange sweatshirt got closer and closer.

Arnie couldn't stand it. He finally declared, "Yep. That is *definitely* Tom." I slowly looked over at Arnie and gave him a look that said, "Oh, puh-leez," and he said, "Okay, okay!" We ran the next half mile in total silence, and then we were upon Tom, passing him.

"Hey, Tom, how ya doin'?" we all said, trying to be casual.

Tom jumped as if we'd stuck him with an electric prod. Then he started to run, pretending he'd been running all along. I almost laughed out loud at his not knowing we'd been watching him walk for the last mile.

Then he sputtered to back to a walk, saying, "Whew! I'm tired! I just need to walk a little."

"It's long way," I said dryly. The guys didn't say anything. Since we kept running, Tom had to jog again to try to catch up.

"Hey!" he said breathlessly, "Walk with me. I'll be okay in a minute."

"Don't walk! Don't you walk!" Arnie whispered to me furiously.

"I'm *not* going to walk, Arnie, for heaven's sakes!" I whispered back. Tom was walking again. I was drifting ahead.

"Hey, Tom, I can't walk with you," I said apologetically.

"Oh, c'mon, I'll get it back!"

"Tom, I can't walk! As slow as I'm going, I have some *momentum* here." Since I said this last thing quite sarcastically, I added a bit more kindly, "You're a talented athlete and you can get it back. If I walked I'd *never* get it back again." Even this sounded patronizing, and it was. Frankly, if you are walking at the thirteen-mile mark in a marathon, you should call a taxi. You're never going to get it back.

Tom tried to run again and then just went "pffffft." I was running backward now, still talking to him, and said, "Look, there's a sweep truck that comes along and picks up the wounded and the lame. Now, since you are a talented athlete" (I couldn't resist saying that again), "you will probably get it back and pass us again. But if you don't for some reason, catch the sweep truck and we'll see you at the finish!" And I turned around and caught up to Arnie and John. I looked back over my shoulder and Tom was walking along like a petulant child. Then presto, we were gone. A while later, I heard him shout from a long echoing distance, "I'd never leave yoooouuuu!!!"

The rest of the race came in remote vignettes, as I was deep in thought, lost in the rhythm of the long run. This had been an eventful day, and I had a lot to think about and needed the miles to work it all out. I could feel my anger dissipating as the miles went by—you can't run and stay mad!—and, as always, I began tumbling it all over, reliving the moment, trying to twist it this way and that until I got an answer. Why did Jock Semple pick on me like that? Just because I was a girl or because he was tired and overreacted? Naw, it was because he thought I was like one of those goofy guys pulling a prank, making a mockery of his race. Well, he should have known better, I was running there, not wearing a sign that said Eat at Joe's or something. So he's all furious, huh? We're probably going to get nabbed by one of those cops just at the point where we're too tired to fight. He'd know the spot. Got to keep a sharp eye out. So I wonder why I am the only girl in this race, anyway. Girls just don't *get* it! Girls just aren't interested, that is why there are no girls' intercollegiate sports at Syracuse and other big schools. And that is why there are no scholarships, no prize money for us. God, they drive me crazy. So if they aren't even interested in basic fitness, they sure aren't going to be interested in running marathons! Well, if they only knew how good they would feel running they would do it. And if there were enough of them, we could have our own race! Yeah, right. So how come I am interested, how come I want to push my physical limits, and they *don't*? Why am I so doggone special? I don't feel very special today, that's for sure.

We'd just gone over the hill at sixteen miles that crosses Route 128. It shook me out of my thinking because it is a sharp hill, and I said, "Shoot, that's not even Heartbreak Hill," and Arnie said, "No, not by a long way."

Often, we'd pass or be passed by men with whom we chatted amiably for a while, all of them happy to see us, even if they were having a bad day. Sometimes we'd run together for a mile or two; mostly we'd just exchange words of motivation. Each one gave me a special word of encouragement; their positive sincerity was very touching. All these guys felt like my best friends; there wasn't one of them I wouldn't trust with my life, that is how strongly I felt. They *understood*. Maybe this is what war is like, only we're not hurting anybody. Better, this is what a quest is like, that's it, we're in search of a kind of Holy Grail. I couldn't find the exact words that would fit. I still can't, but all of us who do it understand.

Occasionally a die-hard spectator would cheer outrageously for us, and this would shake me out of my reverie. Very occasionally it would be a woman, screaming, "C'mon, honey, do it for *all* of us!" Most often though, the women who saw me looked stunned; they didn't know how to react. Almost always the men they were standing with would cheer heartily, but the women would stand there, hands suspended in midclap as if they were afraid to voice an opinion. I wanted to say, "Yes, it's eighteen miles and I've run that far, and yes, I will go twenty-six. Women *can* do this." But why weren't they here running, too? Those women's faces covered a sweep of emotions—fear, anger, propriety, disbelief, joy, inspiration, hope—and I got lots of messages. A light went on. Those women weren't in the race because they actually believed all those myths about women's fragility and limitation, and the reason they believed them is because they had no opportunity to experience something else. That is why I seem like a creature from outer space to them; I represent something unimagined. And yet, I look just like *they* do!

Gosh, I wasn't special! How stupid of me to ever think that, how totally, utterly stupid. I was just lucky! I was lucky I lived in America and not some place where women have to cover their faces and bodies! I was lucky that my dad encouraged me to run and my mother had a career. I was lucky that my high school had a girl's field hockey team. I was lucky to be asked to run the mile in Lynchburg. And boy, was I lucky to find Arnie. When most girls got to be twenty years old, it would never occur to them to do something so physically challenging, because when they were eight, they were told not to climb trees anymore, and when they were twelve, somebody would whisper stuff about how they'd get damaged if they exercised, and then somebody else would tell them it was more cool to fawn over the guys than do something for themselves. All they needed was an opportunity to actually *do* it. To understand this freedom and power, they had to feel it, they had to feel the Secret Weapon, it doesn't work just talking about it, you can talk until you are blue in the face but you can only *feel* this kind of victory. If they could just have a running opportunity that was welcoming, acceptable for women, not intimidating, regardless of how slow they were to start, that would do it. I've got to do that, I thought.

Running has done a lot for me. I've got to tell them all about it! It is important to pass on this discovery. Dad said that to pass good stuff on is the best way to say thanks. And besides, I feel obligated, responsible. There will be a little noise from this. I didn't intend for that to happen but it turned out that way, and now I will have to make good on this by finishing this race and creating opportunities for women to run. It won't be easy, since the women don't yet know they need the opportunities; they are talking about them in other areas—like jobs—but running is a surefire way of really getting it quickly at a gut level. I'll have to be a kind of Johnny Appleseed, going around and spreading the word, putting together races and other things.

Even though my body was beginning to grind, my mind was just whirling, as if I'd drunk a gallon of coffee. For so many hundreds of miles in training, I was always amazed at how pieces of my past, long-forgotten memories of childhood, or some imaginary scenario, would flash in front of me like a slide show. Today it was all different. As I dissected the day, my mind threw back new images: of the future, of possibility, of an astonishing sense of destiny. I could see my life spread out ahead of me, like a road map.

I felt both light and very old. Finding the solution was wonderful, but I knew I had a lot of work to do. That included becoming a better runner. Nobody was going to take me seriously as an athlete at this pace, and there would have to be a lot of training to bring the time down. Arnie always told me I could be really good, but that was just Arnie giving me a pep talk. I didn't think I could ever be good, but I knew I could be better, and dammit, I was going to try. I was already twenty, and people were telling me I was too old to start serious running. Although I didn't believe that for a minute, I knew I didn't have a lot of time, either.

Jimmy Waters rushed onto the course again with his camera, took our picture, and gave us a big cheer. We laughed and waved. I was back in reality again, realizing that my hips were beginning that deep ache. I could feel the jelly wateriness in my arches and knew some very big blisters would soon have to burst. But I could handle that, pain was nothing. *Nothing.* It was part of what made you a hero, doing this, overcoming it, relegating pain to the incidental for a higher purpose. Arnie said Emil Zátopek, the legendary Czech runner, would keep going until he passed out. Now that's something, but I'm not sure what. Crap! How much longer? I didn't want to ask, it sounded sissy, so I said, "Arnie, when are we going to get to Heartbreak Hill?" Arnie looked startled. "Why, you passed over Heartbreak a long time ago!"

"We *did?* Gosh, I missed it. Why didn't you tell us?" I actually felt disappointed; I thought there would be a trumpet herald or something at the top. In fact, nowadays there is a guy who is a self-appointed archangel on a megaphone telling you "You've done it! You're at the top of Heartbreak Hill!" but on that day it was so unremarkable I didn't know it from any of the other hills.

Arnie was smiling and shaking his head. "You've got to be the only person not to know they just ran over Heartbreak Hill!" He sounded very proud of me, but in fact wherever it was, Heartbreak was a piddly hill compared to those we ran over in Pompey in our workouts or, for that matter, compared to the one here at sixteen miles.

We turned from Commonwealth Avenue onto Beacon Street and now it really did seem endless. There was block after block of identical row houses. There must have been a hundred sets of trolley tracks; I was afraid I'd catch my foot in them and break my ankle, and every time I broke stride to mince over them my blisters squished and stung like hell. The cops had let traffic out on the course, and although they were monitoring it, and although there were plenty of runners behind us, I felt like we were holding up the show. It was another disappointing organizational detail about Boston. I had heard the road was closed for the race and it really wasn't. "I can stay home and run in traffic," I carped. We were frozen. John groaned and rolled his head. Together Arnie and I said, "C'mon John. You can do it." I was amazed at John. What a guy, to hang in like this!

On a street corner, a boy with a stack of newspapers held one up and cried out, "Read all about it! New Zealander wins Boston Marathon!"

"Do you believe *that?*" I said. "Jeez, just imagine. He finished hours ago! He's had a hot shower! He's had a press conference! Shoot! He's on his second beer *right now!*" We had a good laugh, but it was pretty eye-opening. I couldn't even imagine how fast that was. But hey, it was also inspiring. A year ago I couldn't run more than three miles, and here I was at Boston, running twenty-six. I couldn't ever be like those guys, no matter what Arnie said, but I bet I could be better. Those guys are my heroes!

Someone from the sidelines shouted, "One mile to go!" And Arnie snapped quickly, "Don't listen to them, they are all wrong. We have at least three miles to go." John groaned again. I tried not to think about it, but it was hard, because for twenty-five minutes along Beacon Street people kept shouting, "Only one mile to go!" Finally, even Arnie wanted to believe them. A nice cop directed us up Hereford Street, and Arnie got agitated. In his day, the finish had always been up Exeter Street, and he began to protest; I think he and I were both worried that maybe we were getting misdirected at the last minute on purpose. But up at the top of Hereford, we rounded the corner onto Boylston, and there it was, the long slope down to the front of the Prudential Building to a line painted on the street: FINISH. Nobody had misdirected us, nobody had arrested us, and we were going to do it.

John said, "Let's let Arnie finish first," and Arnie said, "No, we'll all finish together," but John winked at me, and at the last moment we slowed and pushed Arnie in front of us. We three had run every step together, we never walked, and we never doubted. Then we hugged, but only briefly, as we didn't want to get all gooey about it. Golly! We'd just run the Boston Marathon!

The finish line crowd consisted of about a dozen water-logged people, none of whom clapped for us. Half of this group converged on us, a few kindhearted souls throwing army blankets over us and the rest peppering us with questions and writing down stuff in their reporter's notebooks. They were very crabby, which is what I would have been if I had had to stand out in this freezing wet for four hours and twenty minutes, which is what one of them said our time was. And they were crabby at *me*, since it was my fault for keeping them waiting so long. Plus, I could tell, they felt indignant at having to cover a *girl*. Being a journalism student, this amused me most. Here you are a big shot sports reporter and your editor tells you to wait for the *girl*. *Na na-na na na.*

"What made you do it?" (I like to run, the longer the better.) "Oh come *on*, why Boston and why wear numbers?" (Women deserve to run too. Equal rights and all that, you know.) "Will you come back to run again" (Yes.) "They will ban your club if you come back." (Then we'll change the name of our club.) "Are you a suffragette?" (Huh? I thought we got the right to vote in 1920!) All of the questions were asked in such an aggressive way that it put me off to be suddenly challenged again. After all the miles, I'd worked out the anger and was now quite mellow. Plus, I felt so *great*. Really, except for the blisters, I felt like I could have run all the way back to Hopkinton. There was only one journalist who asked interesting questions, and asked them politely. He was a young man, about my age, covering his first Boston Marathon. His name was Joe Concannon.

A BAA official came over insisting that I report to the ladies' locker room and have the podiatrist check my feet. This "locker room" was in the garage of the Prudential building; it was freezing cold and damp, devoid of towels, heat, water, or anything that would actually constitute a locker room. The podiatrist was real, however, but very grumpy at pulling this detail, and when I took off my shoes he nearly fainted. My socks were blood-soaked. He lanced and bandaged and lanced and taped and then left. Now what am I supposed to do, I thought? I waited a while, no one came, and I certainly could not get my shoes back on. So I pulled the socks over the bandages and I hobbled back upstairs to the finish line area. I was now really frozen, chilled through, and I had to walk in my socks and bandages through the icy rain puddles. Arnie was frantic wondering where I'd gone. "I think I was removed from the press guys," I muttered.

Jimmy Waters was there to take us home, but there was no sign of Tom. We huddled in our blankets waiting. It had already been over half an hour and we began asking around. Where would official vehicles drop people off? Nobody knew anything. We waited another fifteen minutes, and Arnie kept saying, "Where could he be, where could he be?" If he's smart he's someplace warm and dry and probably gave up on us thinking we'd never finish anyway, I thought. God, now we're just dead frozen and we're gonna have to spend the whole evening looking all over Boston for Tom. We weren't accomplishing anything now, we decided, and got ready to leave when John shouted, "There's Tom!" And sure enough, up at the top of Boylston Street, we saw a figure in an orange sweatshirt, lumbering and lurching forward in a shuffling walk. At first, I didn't even recognize him except for the orange shirt. All recognizable body movement and body type had changed. He looked so, well, *thin!* But it was Tom, and for a moment we were all motionless, thinking the same thing: He had actually finished the Boston Marathon! Then we croaked out our cheers, as loud and long as we could. Honestly, it was one of the gutsiest things I'd ever seen. "C'mon Tom, you're gonna do it, way to go Tom, all the way, all the way!" and hearing us he burst into a little jog to the finish, crossed the line, bent over gasping, his hands on his knees. He sounded like he was having an asthma attack, but we rushed him, clapping him on the back. "You did it, Tom, you really *did* it, gee I'm proud of you!" I shouted. Tom kept gasping and then spit out, "The goddamn sweep truck never came!"

We went back to Hopkinton to get Arnie's car, and on to Jimmy's house, where we took wonderful hot showers, and his wife made us a superb steak dinner that we just inhaled, we were so hungry. How she managed to find a grocery store open on a holiday I'll never know, but I'm grateful to this day. We laughed ourselves silly, drinking beer and telling and retelling stories of the day's adventures, and then it was past ten and time to begin the long drive back to Syracuse. With our spirits at an all-time high, it didn't even occur to me to phone my parents to tell them how I did. In hindsight, I can see how children by their very nature drive parents crazy.

Arnie did the driving and we took turns talking to him to try to keep him awake. In the backseat, Tom was ebullient with his new athletic success—after all, running a marathon is not something too many hammer throwers can do!—and he got all lovey-dovey with me, whispering endearments. I felt pretty darn good. We'd had a tough time, but in the end we'd done it, did it as a team and lived to laugh about it. In this endorphin high, neither Tom nor I had a memory of any hard feelings, and somewhere on the Massachusetts Turnpike, in the darkness around Pittsfield, we decided to get engaged. Surviving your first marathon together is as good a reason as any, I guess.

Albany was halfway home, and it was around midnight when we stopped along the New York State Thruway for gas and coffee. We were so stiff we could barely unfold ourselves from the car. In the restaurant, there was only one person at this hour, a man sitting at the U-shaped counter, reading a newspaper. We sat in a row opposite, yammering away, when my eyes became fixed on the man's newspaper. "My God!" I shouted and ran over to the man, babbling, "Excuse me, sir, excuse me, please let me look at your newspaper!" I was so frantic that he thrust it at me like it was on fire.

All over the front and back covers were our photos. The three of us—and the man, too, who suddenly realized it was us in the photos—gathered around gasping as we went from page to page. Everywhere it was girl running, girl being attacked, girl being saved by boyfriend, girl continuing to run, angry officials and race director, bedraggled girl in rain in socks. Sandwiched in between were photos of the front runners, the winner, Dave McKenzie, and Roberta Bingay (now Gibb), who had also run the previous year. We hadn't even known the name of the winner or that Roberta had run until that moment. When had they taken so many pictures? Finally, we just looked at each other and I handed the man his paper. "Keep it! Oh please, I insist, keep it!" he said.

There was surely no danger of anyone falling asleep at the wheel after that. The guys were in heaven; they sounded like roosters in a barnyard, crowing all the way back to Syracuse. I laughed at their jokes, but my revelry had turned into quiet musing. I've stepped into a different life, I thought. To the guys it was just a one-time event. But I knew it was a lot more than that. A *lot* more.

Chapter | 8

The Aftermath

If you want to run, run a mile. If you want to experience another life, run a marathon.
—Emil Zátopek, three-time Olympic gold medalist

By Thursday morning everybody on campus and just about everywhere else knew about our run. The phone in Huey Cottage rang so often that my housemates became adept at answering, "Yes, but can she call you back *collect?*"

At first, there was a lot of confusion. While most of the Boston papers and the late editions had the full story of my coming across the finish line, the first editions said I did not finish the race. This upset me greatly, as that was the whole point of going to Boston! Obviously, those news outlets had filed their stories while I was still running, but to me that was no excuse, as in journalism school we were taught *be sure* before you print. They at least could have covered it by writing "By press time, she had not yet finished," but it was clear that some of the reporters, like the population in general, didn't bother to check because they so expected (or wanted) me not to finish. The depth of disbelief in women's capability was worse than I thought.

Especially galling was when the Associated Press (AP) and the

New York Times misreported my finish. The AP story went out all over the United States, probably even the world, and that was all my relatives! But the big one was the *Times*. Unequalled in the world of journalism to all of us students at the Newhouse School, it was unthinkable that they would get it wrong. My story was by a guy named Frank Litsky; I had to set him straight, so I phoned him and politely corrected him. He was really good about it—nice, even—and asked a lot of questions. I could hear him typing, so I hoped the *Times* might run a correction. AP called on their own to do a follow-up.

I was also hurt. I knew that a 4:20 time was a jogger's time and I felt that was part of why they were dismissing me, although it was news to us that suddenly there was a four-hour cutoff time for recording finishers. I vowed quietly to run faster the next time, and hoped I could do it without a gorilla jumping on me.

The press weren't interested in performance anyway; their emphasis was in propriety. Roberta Gibb, again not wearing a number, finished in 3:27 and they didn't talk about the quality of that, only the issue that we were "girls." One journalist humorously described me as "the well-built Mata Hari of running that any American boy would lunge for." The journalist Jack McCarthy was not as kind when he declared that we were posing an "unnecessary problem" for the race organization and also said that if he "didn't abhor women golfers so much, women marathoners would be number one on his list." Jerry Nason, the dean of marathon reportage, made a crack about my unflattering warm-up suit. Although most of the coverage wasn't so visceral—one journalist favorably compared us women to Gandhi and Thoreau, who try to change a bad rule through civil disobedience—it was all centered on whether it was right or wrong for us as women to run. Pretty soon, everyone—the race codirectors Jock Semple and

Colonel Will Cloney, my mom, even the author Erich Segal—weighed in with an opinion, and the debate raged on.

Meanwhile, back on campus the next day, I was unaware of these gathering media storm clouds. True to his word, Dr. Arnold hadn't told anyone about my Boston run until noon the day of the race, when he announced to the class that at that very moment I was answering the starter's gun to run the Boston Marathon. The sports editor of the *Daily Orange* (*DO*) was in my class and he nearly jumped out of his chair. This was a campus scoop! Like a lot of my friends, he was disappointed that I hadn't told him in advance, but when I got back from Boston, he insisted I sit right down and write a first-person story. The *DO*'s photographer, Teddy Horowitz, shot hundreds of pictures throughout the day of me with Arnie, Tom, and John; it was like having our own paparazzi, and out on the training track that afternoon with the cameras clicking, Tom was very hot stuff among his undergraduate charges. He'd told them he was a natural athlete and now they had to believe it; after all, how many hammer throwers can run a marathon?

Tom was brandishing a fifth of whiskey; he'd won it from Coach Grieve, who had bet Tom that I wouldn't finish Boston. Now I was annoyed at the coach for his lack of faith, and at Tom, too, since he had blabbed our plans in advance. Tom saw my look. "Hey, at least I bet *for* you!" he said. "Besides, we can drink it together."

As Arnie and I ran our regular route alone, it gave him an opportunity to blow off steam about Colonel Will Cloney and his former friend Jock Semple. Colonel Cloney was a kindly, intellectual nonrunning guy who had taught journalism and now worked in public relations for a financial company. He was the first guy off the bus, the portly one with the blue ribbon who caught my glove, and I also remembered him as the one who checked me in at the starting area.

"Jock" was the Scottish nickname for John, and he and Arnie ran races together in the late '30s and '40s. Jock had been a top marathoner and had been favored to win the Boston Marathon in 1934; failing to do so was his greatest disappointment, although he did make the Pan-American Games team in 1937. He and Arnie shared a tough working-class background where there was no money for shoes, training, or transportation; Arnie told me how he and Jock hitch-hiked to races and slept on floors. I was inclined to feel sympathetic now toward Jock since these were the stories that had inspired me to run Boston in the first place.

Arnie continued: Jock eased from his own running into coaching and physical therapy; he had a small clinic in the Boston Garden and worked his magic massage on the Bruins, the Celtics, and his beloved Boston Athletic Association runners. The BAA Marathon was Jock's passion; when it started to lose prestige over the years, he jumped in to help and eventually, with a minimal budget, wound up as race codirector with Will Cloney. Jock did all the clerical work through the '50s and '60s, and his steamy, liniment-smelling clinic became Marathon Central.

"The race probably would have folded if it hadn't been for Jock," Arnie told me. "He has a big problem though, and that's his temper! There are lots of stories. I saw him slug a runner once because he was wearing a high bib number and was on the starting line with the low-numbered elites. Everyone says Jock's a diamond in the rough, ya ya, well, he's a hothead, plain and simple. He shoulda known better when he saw me with you!"

Naturally, over the coming days, the press made a real feast out of

Jock's legendary fury and pushed the storm clouds along by dredging up past escapades and comparing them with mine—like the time Jock tackled a guy in the race for wearing swim fins. They embellished them and made them hilarious, and Jock got angrier at being made fun of. He'd retaliate by saying things that only fueled the fire, like, "My wife is so mad at me over this she gave my roast beef to the dog and made me buy my own Swanson's."

I didn't think what Jock did to me was funny at all. While I was somewhat sympathetic and wanted both him and Will Cloney to believe in my sincerity, I also thought he was dangerous and I wanted to steer clear of him. There were a few press calls slyly asking if I planned to sue Jock Semple. Sue him! This was the last thing on my mind! That really would have made everyone in the running community and in Boston angry and set women's running back forever. I was trying to win people over, not alienate them!

But it was Jock who was determined to alienate me. For a guy who supposedly had a short fuse, Jock sure kept sizzling. Within thirty-six hours, I'd already gone more than halfway by saying in an interview that I was sympathetic since I knew he had a lot on his plate that day, and that I, too, felt Boston was special and that was why I wanted to run. "Marathon Girl Forgiving" was that headline, but Jock had only started on me.

Two days after Boston I got a Special Delivery letter from the dreaded AAU—the Amateur Athletic Union—expelling me. In my entire life, I'd never known the U.S. Post Office to deliver a letter that fast. What it meant was someone had to be determined enough to make a long-distance call to the AAU headquarters even before I finished the race on Wednesday in order for me to have a letter on Friday. Who could have been that vicious but Jock Semple?

The reasons for my expulsion were that:

1. I had run a distance of more that one and a half miles, which was the "longest distance allowable for women."
2. I had fraudulently entered the race by signing the entry form with my initials.
3. I had run the Boston Marathon with men.
4. I had run the Boston Marathon without a chaperone.

What kind of after-the-fact made-up rules were these? Some men had entered the race with their initials, and nowhere on the entry form or in the rule book did it say it was for men only. The mile-and-a-half rule was taken from the distance of women's cross-country; presumably this meant anything more was dangerous to me. So I suppose I needed to be protected from myself. Running without a chaperone was just downright funny, but banning me for running with men was insidious. These men were my friends, and saying it was wrong to run with them had a sexual tone that I thought was hateful.

The letter was signed by Ollan Cassell, executive director of the AAU. The name was slightly familiar to me, but not as an official. Sure enough, Cassell was on the gold medal 400-meter relay team in the 1964 Tokyo Olympics. I remembered him, in fact, warming up in a blue USA warm-up suit in a meet I'd run in just the year before. It couldn't be the same guy! No athlete would write this letter; athletes support each other! So now I was disgusted with this Cassell guy and the AAU, and really furious with Jock.

While I was steaming, the Sunday *New York Times* came out with Frank Litsky's "correction," which in fact was the main sports feature, complete with a glamorous photo of me in an evening gown.

I was delighted with the photo, as I thought it might inspire some girls to run; it sure wasn't Tamara Press in the shot put! The article also had some quotes from Will Cloney, a more articulate and temperate man than Jock Semple. Among other things, however, Cloney said, "We have no place in the marathon for any unauthorized person, even a man. If that girl were my daughter, I'd spank her."

With that, the full storm was upon us. My normally generous and diplomatic mother was explosive and sputtering, saying, "I am just going to tell that man that *I* reserve the right to punish my own daughter!" Apparently the Boston press got all over the hapless Cloney about it, too, and cornered him into saying hilarious things like, "No girls ran the Boston Marathon. They merely ran on the same course at the same time as the men," or "Unless we have rules, society will be in chaos." The author Erich Segal retorted that he approved of women running in the marathon, and "if we have to preserve male superiority through legislation, we are in trouble." It was almost inevitable that the *Tonight Show* would invite me to be on TV with Johnny Carson; it was his kind of story.

I'm sure Carson and his staff were hoping for a funny show. But when I was on the air, I didn't want to castigate anyone as a fuddy-duddy or make light of the marathon race. I felt—and still feel—in my interviews that I had a responsibility to educate the public about women's capability. Carson could tell I was serious and changed the tone to one of informed support. He had been a track athlete himself, I could tell he understood, and that was great. Although I had been covered by TV before, this was my first actual TV interview, and what I remember most vividly was not the conversation but how disorienting Carson's stage makeup was to me. I'd never seen a man wearing lipstick before.

Despite feeling whipsawed at times, the whole news process, particularly the biased conjecture, was fascinating and provided me with the best journalism class I could ever have taken. The papers also provided news details that I didn't know about even though I was there. For instance, "Col. Cloney and the motorcycle police patrol had every intention of removing [Switzer's] fleet feet from Rt. 135 near Framingham." So my paranoia was not idle imagination. I also read in depth for the first time about the winner, Dave McKenzie, from Greymouth, New Zealand, who set a course record of 2:15:45. He said he was used to the bad conditions because it rained 100 inches a year in Greymouth. Coming from Syracuse, I had an affinity with that. I was happy to read that it was so cold and miserable that the fifty-nine-year-old Johnny Kelley considered dropping out for only the fourth time in his life. He didn't, and finished in an impressive 2:58. Also impressive was Tom Laris, who finished second in a new American record of 2:16, breaking up the top foreign finishes in recent years.

I was surprised to see that Roberta Bingay also ran in Boston, only because I hadn't thought of the other people there at all. Arnie and I were just going there to run, not to compete or make a statement, and were wrapped up in our own little world. I didn't see Roberta at all, but I wouldn't have, since she didn't register for the race and started down the road in the bushes, jumped in ahead of me, and ran an hour faster. This year, however, BAA officials would not let her cross the finish line, which to me seemed very petty and ungracious. At least by the time I got there I got to cross it, but by that time nobody cared anyway.

There was news in a different sport that also resonated with me. The day I ran Boston was the day the world heavyweight boxing champion Cassius Clay (who later changed his name to Muhammad

Ali when he converted to Islam), refused induction into the army on religious grounds and in protest against the war in Vietnam, even though it meant forfeiting his title. I was an apolitical kid then, but this impressed me.

Finally, it all settled down, more or less. I thought it was supremely ironic that I'd gone to Boston just to run and came away regarded as both a saint and a pariah; that I took pains to look feminine and got accused of disguising myself as a man; and, after following the rules of the AAU, that I got kicked out of the organization.

Arnie, Tom, and John got kicked out of the AAU, too, and ripped up their letters. Tom said, "There goes the Olympics!" and Arnie vowed never to speak to Jock Semple again. He never did, either, which reassured me that even the pious Arnie could have a black spot on his human heart.

We accepted invitations to race in Canada, making lots of friends and feeling like AAU draft dodgers. In one race in May in Toronto, thirteen-year-old Maureen Wilton was paced through a 3:15 marathon; it was cited as a world best.

I went into a six-week overdrive and somehow passed all the courses I'd slept through that semester, and then decided to stay in Syracuse for the summer and train and live with Tom. Every weekend, Arnie and I and a carload of runners would go to another race—race directors wanted us for the publicity and didn't care if we had to run as "unofficial" due to our banned status; they gave us "unofficial" numbers and if we placed, "unofficial" trophies; it was hilarious. The Grape Race, the Beet Race, the Onion Derby, county fairs and small-town carnivals—all were on our riotous itinerary. We got adept at changing in the car together with no one peeping before the race and jumping in people's plastic swimming pools afterward to wash off.

Every Tuesday, Tom, Arnie, and I organized an evening track meet with field events and a six-mile road race and formed the Syracuse Track Club. The events became an institution in upstate New York, attracting clubs from neighboring cities. I wrote the weekly newsletter, got trophies donated from used-car dealers, and sent news releases to the papers. The club grew to be the biggest in New York State outside of the Road Runners Club in New York City, and my work that summer became the basis for my eventual career in sports organization and journalism.

By the end of the summer, Tom and I decided to get married the next year, after my graduation. Tom reminded me that he, not I, was the truly talented athlete, so our focus would be on his making the 1968 team for Mexico City. Tom asked me not to run Boston again and risk getting him in trouble. He asked me to eat a little crow along with him and get reinstated into the AAU, too. He asked me to live with him during my senior year, so we could split his rent. He asked me to convert to Catholicism. We were a team. I was in love. I said yes to everything except becoming a Catholic.

CHAPTER | 9

"WHERE HAVE YOU GONE, JOE DIMAGGIO? A NATION TURNS ITS LONELY EYES TO YOU."

After having successfully negotiated the summer without my mom and dad noticing that Tom and I actually lived together, I needed to continue the charade for my entire senior year. So in exchange for free room and board—my parents were so proud of me for saving them this hunk of money—I became the ten P.M. to six A.M. housemother for a group of reform school girls. I had to be on call all night long and tidy up the central living space while they were in bed. Except for having to scrub and wax the huge downstairs floors every couple of weeks (from which my hands have never recovered, even forty years later), the only hard part was trying to stay awake or trying to sleep on the sly. Then, at six A.M., Tom (who was working across the courtyard in the boys' house) and I would go home. I would sleep for a couple of hours, then get up to drive to class by putting the Volks in neutral, sliding down the icy hill outside our apartment, and popping the clutch to jump-start it as we couldn't afford to get the starter fixed. I had to do it in one go or I wouldn't get to classes that day, and once on campus I had to find a parking spot with the car facing downhill and then get it back to Tom by two P.M. He didn't have to go to class, as he was supposedly working on his thesis, so he got to sleep in every day.

All of this was a ridiculous way to live, and I knew it at the time, but there was simply no way I could tell my parents I was living with Tom or they would have hit the roof and would certainly have cut me off. Being without tuition senior year is not what frightened me, however. What scared me more than anything in the world—scared me witless!—was disapproval from my parents. After all these years of being a model child, after all their pride, and after all this new, determined athleticism, for which they gave me such love and support, if they found out I was living with a man, it would have been a slap in their face. They would have disowned me, and we would all have been miserable. The plan had always been for me to get my college degree, have a nice wedding, start my family, and live happily ever after. All my life, my parents would mutter and cluck over someone who'd "blown it" by getting pregnant and having to drop out of school. There was no forgiveness for this. I was their pride and joy. I couldn't blow it.

So here I was, living a lie, and a very expensive one, as I was not getting paid to do this job every night, I only was getting room and board, which, outside of raiding the refrigerator as much as I could, I didn't use. On top of this, we still had to figure out how to pay the rent on the apartment, which was a real circus every month, especially for me coming up with my half, which of course I was determined to do since I was absolutely principled about pulling my weight. Tom's fellowship wasn't enough for both of us, anyway. Midway through the year, the summer savings ran out, so I started working at the reform school on the weekend nights, too, for minimum wage. This just about covered my half of the rent, but gas, food, electricity, and the sofa payments were always dicey. Sofa payments! Imagine buying a $115 sofa and needing three years to pay for it! I even volunteered—for $4 an hour—to be a psychological "test subject" for the Upstate Medical Center. Any decent test would have proved me certifiable.

We got to the point where there just wasn't any money for anything. Tom was mending the bottoms of his hammer-throwing shoes with athletic tape he pilfered from the field house, and I did the same for my running shoes. One of our neighbors gave us a pumpkin at Halloween and we carved it up as a jack-o'-lantern and had a good laugh, which was big-deal entertainment, that's how bad it was. We didn't really have any time to go out since we worked all night, but I was just longing to go to the movies. That was a perfect escape, and I'd been living off our seeing *A Man and a Woman* since the previous summer, the theme song of which even became "our song." We also saw *The Graduate*, which stunned me so much that I even took an elective in cinematography. Of course, Tom didn't think it was such a big deal, which annoyed and worried me—how could he not see that *The Graduate* was a masterpiece of filmmaking and a commentary on our generation? Tom would argue that a film should be good, solid entertainment; you didn't have to think about it, like *Seven Brides for Seven Brothers*. Anyway, I was longing to see a film and decided that it had to be *Blowup*, supposedly the next great film, which a year later finally made its way to Syracuse. It's all I could talk about. Somehow we saved up the three dollars apiece, and of course I loved it and Tom hated it, so I was criticized for having screwy taste *and* of wasting six dollars. Not only could we not discuss our differences (I thought he was incapable of exploring new artistic horizons, anyway), I could see that even a simple thing like going to the movies was always going to be a fraught experience.

I hated being poor. I hated it more than anything that had ever happened to me. Somehow I was convinced we'd always be worried about money and that it would never end. Sometimes I'd feel very self-righteous and think, "I'm doing this for love and out of principle." At other times, I'd be scrubbing the floor on my hands and knees, worried as hell about an essay that was due. I'd look up and see Johnny Carson on the TV in the corner of the tacky reform-school living room, and I'd think, six months ago I was ON that show and here I am scrubbing floors. Mostly though, I'd tell myself I was lucky if the only really bad thing that happened to me was that I was poor. I would go through my gratitude list, saying at least I had my health and that no matter what, I could hold on for another six or seven months and then I'd graduate, get a real job, we'd have a big wedding, and get lots of nice presents—beautiful crystal and china and table linens and everything!—and live happily ever after.

Running seriously or regularly was just out of the question, and occasionally I would see Arnie and we'd take a little run together. He complained about missing me and how I was losing conditioning, and I took his feelings not as sympathy for my exhausted state but as whining. Then I'd feel bad because Arnie would give me a stack of really neat magazines that I could never afford—*Vogue, Saturday Review, Sports Illustrated*, from which the mailing labels had supposedly fallen off—and later I'd find, tucked inside, one of those sappy Hallmark greeting cards about what a great friend I was, signed "Arnie." He always signed his name in quotation marks for some reason.

It was almost better not to run; I was so slow and shuffling, and it meant it would be hard, if not impossible, to keep awake on the job that night. I'd fight the sticky eyes and bobbing head, try to study, and then be doubly tired the next day, and the cycle would begin again. It was torture getting through classes, and then I'd get really fearful about graduating on time, and on it would go. Now I had a new goal, a new focus: Instead of adding up miles with my sights on the Boston Marathon, it was having to graduate, because everything was on a neat time line from that moment. No, it was more than that! I knew I couldn't live another year like this. I began to fantasize about having a job where you put on stockings every day and went to work and got a paycheck and then could come home and eat dinner and sleep at night like a normal person. For someone who had dreamed of running the Boston Marathon, of sailing beyond the bounds of safety and discovering that the earth was not flat, it was a dream that at times seemed every bit as far-fetched.

Part of the reason for this is that Tom never offered a joke, a consoling word, a sense that it would get better, or even "Hey! What an adventure! We're in this together, honey, and we'll cuddle up and make the most of it." It was like being in a siege together but feeling quite alone. Then I did something quite irrational, especially for me: I more or less demanded a diamond engagement ring. In those days, it was the first thing people asked to see when you said you were engaged. We couldn't even afford to go to the movies, but we were going to have a big wedding, which is what I wanted and what my mother and dad wanted, too, and were going to pay for, and by golly I felt I deserved it after scrubbing these floors. You couldn't exactly send out engraved invitations with five sheets of rice paper separating the cards and not have a ring on your finger! August was ten months away, and then all this crap would be behind me. By then we would be a beautiful bridal couple at an effervescent champagne luncheon at the Officers' Club, surrounded by one hundred laughing, dancing friends and relatives, but in these dark floor-scrubbing nights of November, I wanted a ring, dammit. I'd given a lot and asked for little in the relationship, and always paid my half, so Tom knew I was serious. He skulked home to Cleveland, bought the ring with money borrowed from his wealthy mother, and gave it to me without a kiss or a smile. That's not how it was for the fairy princess, but I put on a brave face and wore the ring with pride. We had the trappings of love at least, as well another monthly payment, this one to his mom to pay off the loan.

Other regular payments were coming due, among them something called "Pre-Cana" lessons. These were the premarital instructions required before you could be married in the Catholic Church. (The name is derived from John 2:1-12, the wedding feast at Cana in Galilee, where Jesus performed the miracle of turning water into wine.)

I was a Protestant; for me to marry a Catholic was not an easy thing to do, and the Pre-Cana lessons were just the beginning. Tom suddenly wanted me to convert to Catholicism, despite all of our liberal talk the previous summer about respecting differences in faith, all our hooting laughter about the stupidity of the rhythm method of birth control, and the jokes about girls not being allowed to wear patent leather shoes because you could see the reflection up their dresses. When it came to crunch time, Tom said it would be easiest if I converted, as if it didn't really matter.

I began serious exploration of this problem and found out that very recently the Catholic Church had become a bit more liberal. I did not actually have to convert to marry Tom, but the marriage ceremony had to be conducted by a Catholic priest, in a Catholic church. I still had to take the Pre-Cana lessons (even Catholics did), and I had to agree to allow any of our children to have Catholic religious instruction. All of this satisfied Tom, so I set about figuring how I could do it all without damaging my soul and compromising our future kids.

The Pre-Cana lessons were amazing. Tom and I felt like an old married couple among these dewy-eyed kids who sat there holding hands with their radiant faces turned toward the priest. One night, the instructing priest was talking about the sacred life of the unborn child and said that if a choice had to be made during childbirth to save the baby or save the mother, then the choice would be to save the baby. "W*hat?!*" I shouted out, and everyone turned. It was as if they all knew this and I didn't. Tom blushed and looked down.

"Yessss, my dear," said the priest, "the child's life must take precedence over the mother's."

"But if you save the mother, maybe she can have more children, and besides, you have no guarantee that a tiny baby could live without its mother anyway, and besides"—now I was kind of wailing—"the other children at home need their mother!"

You would have thought that I had called forth the devil right then and there. Tom was still looking down. I elbowed him. He continued to look down. When we got home, I was ashamed at Tom for not defending me. He got angry and explained that the priest was right. I felt my stomach drop.

"You mean if I were in childbirth and it was my life or the child's, you would let me *die?*" He said yes with no hesitation whatsoever, and I knew at that very moment I should have packed my bags and left. I knew it, I *knew* it. But I didn't.

• • •

Tom and I didn't own a TV, but at the reform school I often watched the evening news. It seemed there was a peace march once a week someplace, and I accepted what my army colonel dad had told me, that these marches were organized by professional anarchists and were not the true voice of the American people. I'd lived my life believing in the righteousness of the United States and was a very determined patriot. My dad and his dad and his great-granddad all the way back to the Civil War had fought in defense of the republic, and as my brother at that moment was in officer training school learning to fly helicopters, so he would too. Up to then, I'd never questioned the war in Vietnam, or any war America undertook, for that matter.

Then the next pictures on the tube would be of these guys in soggy fatigues and helmets, my age and even younger, looking scared shitless, wading through rice paddies with rifles at the ready. Then Pop! Pop! and a couple of our guys would go down in the swamp, and then get up—or not—and move forward. We could never see this enemy, which made it scarier. I don't know how many weeks or months I watched this before it occurred to me that it was real and that John Wayne was not going to step to the front of the screen with his revolver raised and vanquish the enemy as the music rose and the credits rolled. It went on and on and on. It looked like relentless, unmitigated hell. I didn't know what to think. I wanted badly for it to stop, and peace marches did not seem like a very bad thing; not *all* of the marchers could be anarchists. Mostly I turned it off, as I just couldn't watch, but sometimes Tom and I would watch the news together, and not once did Tom shake his head and say something like, "You poor suckers, God bless ya."

Tom was very critical of the military. He said they were a bunch of guys who couldn't get real jobs, so they joined the army. Of course, that pissed me off plenty, since my family all had university degrees and could do anything, and then Tom went on bragging about how he was "4-F, thank God!" and didn't have to "worry" about the war. 4-F was the official medical dispensation he'd received due to the fact that he'd had a knee operation to remove some cartilage from an old football injury. So now he was able to do huge amounts of power lifting, compete in a decathlon, be a nationally ranked hammer thrower, flip telephone poles from end to end in the Scottish Games, run the Boston Marathon, and be a black belt in judo, but he had a medical dispensation saying he was too incapacitated for warfare. I should have been happy for him and for us—why waste any human life?—but I was annoyed, as if he wasn't doing his part or something, and ashamed of him in front of my father and brother, who were conscientious warriors. No, that wasn't quite it. It's hard to relate exactly how I felt, but I think it was that Tom felt entitled to his dispensation, as if it were some kind of war wound he had *earned*, and he had no compassion for those who had to go instead of him. Really, I should have packed my bags and left, but I was getting ambivalent about the war myself and didn't feel entitled to make a judgment. After all, *women* didn't get drafted. Although I thought they should.

• • •

In late March, *Sports Illustrated* called me one morning at home. How the hell they got the number is amazing, but Time-Life had the resources to manage anything. The reporter told me that Boston officials had put "MEN ONLY" on the application form and he wanted to know if I was going to run the Boston Marathon on April 19 anyway. My heart sank. Tom was sitting at the kitchen table. All winter long he had asked me, begged me, not to go back to Boston, saying I would jeopardize his chances to make the Olympic team by antagonizing those officials all over again, and it would reflect on him. It sounds ridiculous now, but it was incredibly logical then. He said we got reinstated into the AAU once but we shouldn't push our luck; those AAU guys were tough bastards and the Boston guys are tougher. I had vowed both in the papers and in my heart to repeat at Boston, but here was Tom asking me not to, and anyway, I was in lousy shape. I could cover twenty-six miles, of that I was certain, but that is not the way I wanted to return to Boston. You had to go to Boston strong. Plus, I'll admit that I was scared of Jock Semple. I thought the guy was capable of anything, and I didn't want to face him if I felt weak. So I agreed not to go. But when the reporter called and Tom searched my eyes and I told the reporter no, that my boyfriend's Olympic chances were more important, I felt quite defeated. On the other hand, I was not going to make any Olympic team, and if Tom could, that would be fabulous. It had to be our number one goal.

The day after the Boston Marathon, I went to the journalism library and read every paper. Ambrose Burfoot—an American!—a student from Wesleyan College, had won the race, oh this was so great! There was not much coverage of the women, except that Roberta Gibb was back again, running unofficially in 3:30 this time. I wondered if I could run a 3:30. That was an awful lot faster than my 4:20. I wondered if I should give Boston up, give up trying to be somebody, and just jog around the woods. I was chewing nails.

Chapter | 10

The Tortoise and the Hare

The confident Hare took off at top speed . . . lollopped along, feeling pleased with its own brilliance . . . and stopped for a nap. . . . The determined Tortoise kept patiently padding and plodding along without any pause, until quietly it waddled past the sleeping Hare. . . .

—Aesop, 600 BCE, from an original translation
by Roger Robinson, *Running in Literature*, Breakaway Books, 2003

Tom didn't make the Olympic team. He didn't even qualify for the summer trials. We drove someplace—I can't remember if it was Dartmouth or Columbia—for him to get a qualifying distance in a meet. He was allowed three throws and fouled each one of them. The Olympic dream went POOF just like that. So we drove home in the dark and didn't say a word for the entire five-hour drive.

But we did have a tremendous wedding a few months later, after I'd graduated and landed a job. The wedding turned out to be the happiest day in my whole relationship with Tom. We had a priest, a minister, and the ceremony took place in a a nondenominational church, fulfilling all the obligations of both our religions. There were a dozen attendants, heaps of flowers, buckets of champagne, music, dancing, and all the guests and gifts that I had fantasized about. Everyone was happy.

It came very close to not happening at all. The night before, we were late to the rehearsal dinner because of a long confession Tom made to the priest. I asked what in the world he had to confess, and he said something like the last two years we'd been living in sin. This infuriated me. We'd sacrificed a lot of ourselves to live in the purity of love, and now Tom was confessing it as some kind of sin. It was as if it didn't count, and I wanted to scream. Once again, I should have packed my bags then and there, but I didn't.

We watched the Olympics on TV. When Bob Beamon long-jumped a massive world record in the thin Mexico City air, I thought he was going to fly right through the screen. I remember it quite distinctly because at the time Tom was accusing me of not taking a leap of faith when we discussed Catholicism. Every time anyone has said leap of faith since, I've pictured Bob Beamon jumping.

It was mid-October before I finished the thank-you notes for all the gifts. It seemed like there were hundreds, and because I wrote long and chatty letters, most of the people wrote back, which I thought was nice. Most of them felt compelled to write and say what a blast they had at the wedding, which made me smile. I had a great time, too. It gave me hope that Tom and I could relax and have a good time together after all. You know, start off on the right foot and all.

We'd bought an unfinished pine table and four captain's chairs, and every night after work I came home and worked on finishing them in a "distressed" style, which first consisted of bashing the nice wood with a chisel and chains before streaking the finish. The result looked the way it was supposed to—an antique set of furniture from an old ship somewhere. This was the kind of work that my dad and my brother did when I was growing up, but Tom said he wanted no part of that handyman stuff so if it was going to get done, guess who did it. I became good at painting and building. I had to; even though I had a job, we couldn't afford to buy nice furniture or hire any help.

Another thing I did was make a very stunning bookcase out of cinderblocks that I pilfered from a disused construction site and nice boards cheaply purchased from the lumberyard. I loaded the back of the Volks with the blocks and then hauled them up the three flights to our apartment. Tom would not help haul them as he said it would wrench his back, which really pissed me off since I'd already loaded the car by myself and this was hardly a big deal, even for a delicate "thoroughbred" athlete like he reminded me he was. Just to show him, I got huffy and carried blocks up two at a time; they were damp and exceedingly heavy even for me and the consequence was that I hurt my back and also sprang the shock absorbers on the car. But Tom loved the bookcase. He spent hours and hours arranging his trophies on it. It was the only household stuff he did, shining and dusting his trophies. Which was fine with me, I hated the darn things they were so ugly. In the end, I was really proud of all the stuff I could do.

I was also pretty happy with my life. I'd done it, pulled it off, and even got to sleep at night. But it felt so odd. I mean, here it was October, and for the first time in my memory, I didn't have to go to school! Sure, I had to go to work—I'd landed a pretty good job as a community relations liaison and the editor of the company newsletter for nearby Bristol Laboratories pharmaceutical company, where I was one of very few "professional" women—but the workday ended at five. I felt guilty, as if I were cutting class. I was just jogging a few times a week, but was closely following all the marathons and particularly watching for any developments in women's running. There were rumblings about women in some distance races.

Tom was back in the full swing of being the assistant coach for the cross-country team, so he was busy every afternoon from three till six. Then he took an evening class at the business school's downtown extension in something called Computers. He said it would really help him with his thesis, of which, as far as I could determine, not one word was written after a year and a half. But he came home all excited about the big machine that was the size of a room and which worked off punch cards. To use it, he had to learn languages that sounded right out of Eastern Europe: COBOL and FORTRAN. He was rarely excited about anything, so I wanted to be supportive, and the last thing I was going to do was needle him about writing his thesis. I'd endured so much of my mom asking me "How's that paper going?" that I vowed not to do it to him.

The plan was the one we had agreed on the previous year, and which had now been in effect for four months: Since Tom was the one with the athletic talent, I would work so he would have time to train and hopefully make the Olympic team. That didn't happen for 1968, but now there were four years to make the team for Munich. Tom would be thirty, a really good age for a hammer thrower, since so much time must be spent on technique. Tom's only obligation was to be the assistant coach from three to six in the afternoon, for which he had a fellowship that paid his fees as a graduate student, and the only student obligation was for him to finish his thesis.

Actually, this was pretty much the same as the year before, only then Tom also had to work in the reform school for rent money so he never actually did any writing on the thesis. I let him have that excuse, despite the fact that I managed to do the same and still carry eighteen hours and graduate, but I didn't want to be catty. So now he had every day until three to write and work out. I felt great about giving him this opportunity—if anybody has even a slight chance of making an Olympic team they should be given every possible break. I felt like part of the team that was making it happen.

I thought Tom would jump right into this, but he frittered away his time and stayed up late watching TV (we could afford a small black and white one), and then of course he had to sleep late the next morning. He could never manage to get to the library, and suddenly it was three P.M., he had to coach, and he hadn't even done his own workout. The longer this went on, the pudgier and grumpier he got, and our sex life was sporadic at best. I put on a smiling face, was peppy, said it would get better, and just started in again. Then the next day I would come home from work at noon with the car and find him still asleep.

Still, I was happy. One weekend in November we had a substantial early snowfall, and Tom was with the cross-country team at an away meet. It was Sunday. I made chili, just like my mom was doing at home in Virginia, and sat down to watch a football game. It was heaven, just me, snow, chili, and the New York Jets. As I watched the snow coming down, I got to thinking about how Arnie and I used to run in that stuff, even in the dark. It was only eighteen months but it seemed like a million years ago. I watched the game, ate my chili, and felt increasingly less satisfied. I thought about Roberta Gibb who I doubted very seriously was watching football on TV. I was sure she was training for Boston right now, she and God knows how many other women! Pretty soon I was so agitated I couldn't even concentrate on the football game.

Why can't I just have a moment's rest? I lamented out loud. Why does this damn race torment me so? Who cares if a whole bunch of women show up at Boston and I'm not there! And actually, that was the answer. Nobody did care. Well, maybe Arnie, and what was important for him was that I just loved running, not necessarily Boston, which he said he'd never run again after the way those jerks treated us in 1967. But Boston was important to me. It was a big-deal race; I'd made a vow to go back, and I would. But now my conscience was hissing, Okay, if not now, then when?

I knew it was like Tom's thesis. The longer you put off starting something hard, the more difficult it became. But starting training again seemed overwhelming: the cold, the snow, the relentless demand of a long run every single weekend. I wanted so badly to be free of *having* to do something and yet I couldn't kid myself. If I seriously wanted to do it, I had to make the commitment; you can't mess around with the marathon. I was going to have to actually get my shoes on every single day and do it, or Boston was going to get put off forever and then I'd wonder for the rest of my life what I could have done. I'd get to be fat and forty and be one of those who say, *Gee, I shoulda run Boston again.*

So I made a deal with myself to go for it, go hard, really train again, not for 1969 either, but for 1970, eighteen months away. Boston officials were seriously talking about a time restriction of four hours. If I couldn't break four hours at Boston, I would just relax and be a happy jogger for the rest of my life. If I broke four hours, maybe I'd try to be a real runner. Either path would make me happy, because it would answer the question and stop this nagging torment. Besides, I liked to run. Really I did, and I was missing it.

I started with an easy hour a day. Then I inched it up. I sometimes met Arnie and our old group on Sundays for long runs and soon we were up to regular twenty-milers. I also did plenty of long runs alone, taking the distance up to the full twenty-six and eventually twenty-seven miles, just to know I could do more than the marathon. I never told Arnie I was doing this; I needed to prove to myself that I could do the hard lonely stuff alone. These very long runs alone, particularly in the cold, bleak countryside, were some of the most creative, mind-expanding experiences I've ever had. Sometimes they were downright hallucinogenic! I got the most amazing ideas, particularly about race organization and book plots! I couldn't remember them after I'd had my shower so I began to write them down as soon as I came in the door. Soon these bits of paper were everywhere so I took an old shoe box, cut a slit in the top, and stuffed the scribbles inside. I called it my Idea Box, and it freed my mind of having to try to remember things.

All the training felt better because, surprise, surprise, I was getting enough sleep. I also could afford better shoes. I started reading Tom's copies of *Strength and Health,* and with Tom's advice—he was very good at this—added weight work. Tom convinced me that I could not build bulk no matter how hard I tried because I had low testosterone, but that I would build tautness and strength. I pumped iron at the new gym we had joined and I banished forever fears of turning into Tamara Press. I got back to my heavy routine of sit-ups and stretching and began taking Tom's vitamins. Amazingly, I grew an inch taller. The gym had a sit-ups contest and I won with 1,001. I did one more than a thousand to show I could go further, but the skin was rubbing off my tailbone. I still carry in my wallet the newspaper clipping about this feat because nobody believes I did it!

After a year, I happened upon an article in *Sports Illustrated* by Kenny Moore, an Olympic marathoner and *SI* staff writer. Kenny was a great hero of mine; he wrote lyrically about running, and in this article spoke about his own training and how he ran twice a day. Twice a day! What a concept! That's what will do it for me, I thought, so I got up to run at 5:30 each morning and again after work. I hated getting up in the morning, but my mileage shot up and my weight shot down. I was getting more sleep anyway because I stopped watching the late night news; my brother was now in Vietnam flying helicopters in and out of Da Nang and I couldn't bear to watch the reports of the war. Tom said the draft was bad enough but anybody who volunteered like my brother was a total idiot, so I took my grief and fears out on the road alone.

I began to miss school. What a glutton I am for punishment, I thought, but it felt very weird not having to keep on pushing mentally. My company had a tuition reimbursement program, and this was a gift too good to be true, so I enrolled in a three-hour evening course that semester. At first I told myself it was just for fun, but after two courses I was making sure it counted toward a master's degree. Tom was making no progress on his thesis. His MBA might never happen, and I thought if I had a master's I could earn a higher salary. Money was tight, and I could be supporting us forever.

Tom and I were now having regular talks about why he wasn't training methodically. We'd joined a gym at great expense. The refrigerator doors held brown glass jars of every vitamin imaginable. We bought expensive raw milk for Tom; I wouldn't drink it, saying there was a reason for pasteurization. We bought handmade kangaroo-skin hammer shoes. We bought a film projector and Super-8 training films of the great hammer throwers in action. Tom played them on the wall several nights a week. I could tell Anatoly Bonderchuk from Tom Gage in one blink. But it still wasn't working. You still have to put on your gear and go do it, and Tom was doing it far too infrequently.

Finally, Tom said, okay, this is it. The real reason was that he didn't have a tungsten hammer. He explained—but I knew anyway—that the ball of his hammer (lead encased in a brass shell) was bigger in diameter than a tungsten one. Tungsten, being a very dense metal, occupied less space. Therefore, when you threw it, it had less air resistance. Quite a lot, he said. I knew that Tom's throws were quite a few feet behind his competitors', and all things being equal, the percentage of difference he would gain would still not make him a contender. He needed more oomph! He needed the speed, strength, and technique that could only come from training. This was a hard thing to keep harping on to someone who categorically believed he was a naturally gifted athlete. And who was I to underestimate the psychological importance of having all the right gear? For some people, it was critically important.

Tom's eyes were like a puppy's. He said the new hammer would cost $230 and would have to be ordered from Kiev, then in the Soviet Union. I almost fainted; it was a month's rent, and after paying rent we only had $250 to live on and from that there were car payments, gas, the gym membership, food, vitamins, the sofa, and the ring. There was no way, but I took a deep gulp and said okay, we'd figure it out. Then I added, "But this is it."

In March, the wooden box arrived from Kiev. You'd have thought it was Christmas, and it was worth every penny to see Tom so happy. He got out his wires and handles and pliers, assembled the hammer, and dragged it around the living room rug for a while, and by golly, he started going out more or less regularly to train. I would even go out when I could and take pictures of him again, just like the old days.

Later that spring, we drove to Boston for a meet with Harvard that allowed invitational throwers. Sometimes, as in his trials qualifier, these meets were torture for me when Tom would foul all three of his throws. Give me a marathon! At least the four hours of running made the trip worthwhile. Tom was psyched about this meet because, of course, he was going to throw his tungsten hammer and show those cocky rich Harvard boys who was the real hot ticket at this meet.

The runners were out on a track somewhere; the throwers were separate, on one of the many beautiful playing fields that bordered the Charles River. It was a sparkling spring day and I positioned myself just outside the cage, flat on my belly and elbows so I could photograph Tom. Tom warmed up with his old clunker of a hammer, but when the competitive throwing began he walked into the ring with his tungsten one. There was an audible gasp from the other throwers; they instantly recognized this superb and exotic implement. Tom threw a beauty and strutted out of the circle like a champ.

The captain of the Harvard team ran over to Tom saying, oh wow, a tungsten hammer, ohmigod can I see it, ohmigod, could I take a throw with it, oh please? And Tom, now the hot ticket with expansive largesse, waved him over and said, "Of *course*."

The Harvard captain went into the cage, spun in the circle and released. I knew it was a foul the instant he let go of it, and like everyone else I followed the trajectory, which seemed to slow. Time itself seemed to stop for a moment as the hammer hung in the air and then went *ker-splash* into the river. Everyone screamed. Tom ran in circles, shouting and pumping his arms and hitting his head. The

Harvard boys raced to the river pulling off their shoes and socks as fast as they could go. In they went to try to find it, and immediately sank up to their thighs in the black mud. Tom was in the water, too, thrashing at it. Then they all had a hard time getting out, being stuck in the mud and all.

I was still lying on the ground. I had my head down on my arms and I was laughing so hard I was crying. Tom came over shouting now at me as well as everyone else. "Why aren't you helping? Do something!"

When he saw I was laughing, he screamed "It's not funny!" at the top of his lungs. I just said, "Yes, it is! Just imagine! That sucker is in *China* by now! It's the longest throw *ever!*"

That was the moment I knew my marriage was over. Oh, there were plenty of other things, really sad and bad things, that happened later that nailed the coffin shut, but the hammer in the river was the end of the era. I knew Tom was never going to really train and all my time and hopes for him were a waste. The hammer in the river was just going to be another excuse and it was. The captain from the Harvard team wrote Tom a check on the spot. (Can you imagine writing a check on the spot for $230? He had his checkbook in his gym bag, now that is what I call *wealthy*.) Tom ordered another tungsten hammer from Kiev and when it came, he said, "It's just not the same."

• • •

While hammer-throwing stayed esoteric, funny old running was going great guns—there was a boom starting! "MEN ONLY" or not, that spring of 1969, three women showed up at Boston. I was right; they were out there training like I was. Sara Mae Berman "won" in 3:22, Elaine Pederson from California was second in

3:43, and Nina Kuscsik from Long Island was third in 3:46. Roberta Gibb did not run. I was biding my time, getting ready for 1970, but I was pretty anxious as these ladies were moving very fast. Already there were seventy-three marathons in the United States, up from forty-four the year before, all for men only, of course, according to the AAU ruling. The guys we trained with were annoyed and wanted to help us. Our Syracuse Track Club reflected this growth as more and more people were joining the club and running in our events. Women were official in everything we staged, with special emphasis on the road races. I was trying to organize with amenities Boston didn't have, and to trumpet the opportunities to other women. Still, for years in all the local road races, I was the only woman.

We hosted our first national championship, a hot 20K in the summer, and then carried the program on with year-round events. At first, I was mostly in charge because I wrote the newsletter and got our meager sponsorships, but then it got so big everyone had a job. The other organizing guys were all my training buddies, and of course it was on the run that we decided to really go for it and stage our own Syracuse Marathon, with an aim to get the men's national championships eventually. There was a dual purpose to this, one of which was to allow women to run in these marathons officially. This meant I had to learn the intricacies of the governance of the sports, and began attending AAU committee meetings and then set up and chaired the first AAU women's long-distance running committee for the Niagara District (upstate New York).

But it was actually the Road Runners Club of America (RRCA) that was teaching me how to play this game. The RRCA was the organization championing the women's cause, particularly the vocal gang from the New York City area which included among others Nina Kuscsik, Ted Corbitt, Vince Chiappetta, Aldo Scandurra, and eventually a guy named Fred Lebow. Sara Mae and Larry Berman and the Cambridge Sports Union were doing the same thing in Boston. They were all way ahead of me but I was trying to learn from them as quickly as I could.

The RRCA was founded by a hero of Arnie's—and thus mine—named Browning Ross, an Olympian who thought there was a better way of organizing long-distance running. We loved the inclusive RRCA; they always said yes, while the AAU always said no. But the AAU was the official national governing body and they had the real power. So we had to work with them. Nina and her friends were particularly adept at this. It was harder for me since I distrusted them after they suspended me for running Boston in 1967.

I met Nina and Sara Mae at races; we conferred often and began developing strategy. Pat Tarnawsky (later Patricia Nell Warren, the novelist) joined in helping us with her writing and promotion skills. And I was at a *lot* of races! My buddies and I would take running road trips every weekend, sometimes hitting a race on Saturday in Buffalo and another in Toronto on Sunday before driving wearily, but happily, home. Every one made me fitter and gave me an idea for women's running.

My runs were going really well and I was in the best shape of my life when I heard that the Boston Marathon had confirmed a four-hour limit on all entries. Although we women were not official at the Boston Marathon—indeed, we were personae non gratae—we still considered ourselves competitors. If the men had to run sub-fours, so would we. Not that Sara, Nina, or Elaine had to worry; they were all well under four, but it was do or die for me.

There's an expression in running that you can run with the big dogs or you can lie on the porch, and that was my mind-set as I drove alone to Boston in the spring of 1970. I was just a pup compared to greyhounds Nina and Sara, but I was going to give it my all. I parked my little Volks on the first street off Main Street in Hopkinton, deciding I'd slip into the runners' stream near the Boston Common, which is where I presumed I'd bump into Roberta Gibb, whom I'd never met. Amazingly, I had no plans for getting back to my car from Boston. Like Arnie in 1967, I had the astonishing belief that something would work out.

A very cold rain was pelting down, not as bad as 1967, but miserable. I was trying to stretch against the car when a woman my age came out of one of the little houses and asked if I was running. Oh God, discovered by the Jock Semple police already, I thought. "Yes. Yes, I am," I said, slowly and strongly. She said, "That's great! Why don't you come inside and do your stretches where it's dry?" Carol turned out to be a PE teacher at Hopkinton High School, thought I was the cat's whiskers, and she said she'd meet me at the finish line and bring me back to my car. Arnie was right, there is a God.

And it was a very good thing, too, since as the runners swept past me on Main Street, I jumped in after what seemed like hundreds of guys went past, and got swept up in a quick pace. It felt good, but being downhill, it was deceiving. Well into the race, at about ten miles, Hal Higdon, whom I knew to be a very good runner and a writer for *Sports Illustrated*, went past me and said, "What are *you* doing here?" I was annoyed by the remark, realizing only later that Hal knew I'd gone out way too fast. I had no idea about pace and didn't understand the ramifications of what I'd done.

I was wearing a long-sleeved turtleneck leotard, tights, a very short velvet tunic, and my trusty gray cotton gardening gloves. Over the training months, I'd devised a running costume that both worked and looked nice—I got the idea from my old hockey tunics which were easy to run in as they allowed total leg movement and, with the ballet tights, no chafing. Shorts in those days were made only of canvaslike cotton, they were bad even for men and impossible for me, with fuller thighs. In the summer, Vaseline was my best friend, and I used it copiously wherever cloth touched skin—especially on seam edges and between the thighs. Today, though, like everyone else, I was soaked through and freezing, but I had on better clothes than many for the conditions.

It's just that I started nodding off on my feet at about eighteen miles. I would be running along and sort of realize that I was at the fire station, or over Heartbreak Hill, and then suddenly in the middle of the road would appear this nice bookish-looking lady in a tan raincoat who was pressing sugar cubes into my wet gloves. As soon as I sucked down the sugar, I would wake up and be in another neighborhood. I have no idea who this woman was, but she appeared several times with her magical sugar cubes along Commonwealth Avenue and again on Beacon Street. When I crossed the finish line, Carol was there, and as she wrapped me in a blanket, she very excitedly told me that not only had I broken four hours, but that I'd run a 3:34! I was beyond caring. I did a face plant in the backseat of her car and slept all the way back to Hopkinton, a trip which seemed to take hours and hours. God, twenty-six miles is a long way!

After a hot shower and some restorative hot soup, I got in the Volks and drove back to Syracuse, regaining my senses more every hour as the food kicked in. By golly, I did it! That is almost fifty minutes faster than my first Boston! When I drove up the driveway at midnight, Tom came running out of the house with a bottle of champagne fizzing. He'd heard the news on the radio and I'd never seen

Where the Girls Are – Lynchburg College Style

Two pretty coeds begin what may be the beginning of a new Hornet track era.

IN a sports year marked by Lynchburg College's first basketball All-America, the finest soccer record in history, a second Dixie Conference Tournament basketball championship in a row, an undefeated woman's basketball team, what received more publicity than any other single athletic occurance?

In the wording of a multiple choice exam, none of the above.

A pair of attractive young coeds, Kathy Switzer and Marty Newell, ran off with headlines (front page as well as sports page) from Bangkok to the Berlin wall.

Kathy, a sophomore from Vienna, Va., gained the bulk of the recognition because of an interesting combination of talent and interests. Not only did she run in three track meets with the Hornet men (as did Marty), but she was also a contestant in the Miss Lynchburg pageant, and serves as the sports editor of the campus newspaper, the Critograph. That unique set of circumstances served to put her across with newspaper, radio and television editors across the world.

They laughed when the girls stepped out on the track for the first time. Before long, though, it was obvious that the girls were sincere about running track and were working just as hard as the fellows. The chuckles stopped then. Some skeptics thought the girls' first appearance in competition, which was heralded by much ballyhoo, was a publicity gimmick. After they saw Kathy run the mile three times, taking a fifth, sixth and third, and Marty compete against three opponents in the 880-yard run, it was obvious that no amount of publicity could force undedicated girls run those grueling races.

By the end of the girls' brief running season, they had jointly scored one point—for Kathy's third place finish. That should not be used as a measuring stick of their importance to the team, however. They were able to compete in the first place because there just weren't enough men out for the track team, but with the determination they exhibited, the pretty duet inspired the men to work harder.

Hornet track coach Aubrey Moon is hopeful that a new program can come from the interest Kathy and Marty have shown in track. Moon would like to see other girls interested in running come out for a sort of girls' auxilary team. In meets with other coed colleges the girls would compete in a few special events against girls from the other school.

And how did Kathy do in the Miss Lynchburg pageant? Of the first five finishers, four were from Lynchburg College. She was not one of them.

Despite the disadvantage of facing many schools with highly subsidized athletic programs, Lynchburg College managed to have a very satisfying year athletically.

The soccer team started things off in fine fashion with a team that produced more than its share of stars and thrills and ended its regular season with a 13-1 record. After a round of post-season games the final tally was a 15-4 record. The general sports climate at the end of the fall was good since the woman's field hockey team ended up over the break-even mark and the cross country team had some high moments.

Basketball brought more bright days to Westover. The men wound up with a 12-16 record, a second straight Dixie Conference Tournament championship, and the college's first basketball All-America in history—Wayne Proffitt. The women's record was even more impressive, 16 wins and no losses. And, according to coach Jacqueline Asbury, the prospects for next year look just as rosey. Swimming turned out to be a sore subject as the team had to cancel the last part of its schedule for lack of participants. Lynchburg bowlers were among the top in the Dixie Conference.

In the spring the track team had a rocky season in dual meets, but snapped back to take its second straight Dixie Conference crown. The baseball team might just as well have played two seasons, because it turned out that way. After a terrible start, the team emerged as a real threat to the Mason-Dixon Conference title before ending the season with an 11-10 record. After a championship campaign in 1965, this year's golf team came down to earth, and the tennis team was once again quite weak. The woman's lacrosse team, in its second year, broke into the win column, while the women's golf and tennis teams had only mediocre results.

Kathy Switzer's last-place finish in the mile run against St. Andrews College didn't discourage photographers from NBC-TV and MGM movie news from recording her excellent form.

10 / THE LYNCHBURG COLLEGE MAGAZINE

April 23, 1966: None of us at Lynchburg College were quite prepared for the barrage of publicity that came from girls running on a men's team. Here are camera crews from NBC-TV and MGM movie news at the finish line. Photo credit: *Lynchburg College Magazine.*

All illustrations are from the author's collection unless otherwise noted.

WEDNESDAY, APRIL 19, 1967

SEVENTY-FIRST ANNUAL

American Marathon Race

UNDER THE AUSPICES OF

BOSTON ATHLETIC ASSOCIATION

Sanctioned by the Amateur Athletic Union and the New England
Association of the Amateur Athletic Union

OLYMPIC DISTANCE, Twenty-Six Miles, 385 Yards

Start at Hopkinton at 12 o'clock noon. The course is through Ashland, Framingham, Natick, Wellesley, Newton, to the PRUDENTIAL Center. The record for the present course is 2 hours, 16 minutes, 33 seconds, made in 1965 by Morio Shigematsu, Japan

OFFICIALS

MARATHON COMMITTEE	REFEREE	STARTER	PHYSICIANS
Will Cloney, Chairman	Robert S. Campbell	George V. Brown, Jr.	Dr. Thomas A. Kelley
Ellery Koch			Dr. M. A. Cohen
R. H. Kingsley Brown	JUDGES	CLERK OF COURSE	Dr. John Doherty
A. J. Notagiacomo	Ellery P. Koch,	Edward J. Powers	Dr. Warren R. Guild
George V. Brown, Jr.	Chief Judge		
John Semple	W. S. McFetridge	ASSISTANT CLERKS	REGISTRATION COMMITTEE
	William Gover	Carl Ciraface	Frank Rull
HONORARY REFEREES	Robert S. Campbell	Larry Mahan	John J. Sheehan
	William Sandler	Humbert Ciraface	William Downing
His Excellency,	Harold Goslin	John DiComandrea	Joseph M. Hines
John A. Volpe	Oscar Hedlund	Patrick J. Leonard	Alex Scioli
Gov. of Massachusetts	Clarence Dussault	George V. Brown, III	
	Joe Lewis	Thomas Hagerty	PODIATRISTS
His Honor,	Atty. Powers	Fred Brown	Dr. Edward R. Bloom
John F. Collins,	John J. Magee	William Smith	and Staff from Mass.
Mayor of Boston	A. T. Hart	Steve Nazro	Podiatry Society, Inc.
	Leonard F. Luchner		
	George Wilson		

WINNERS OF EACH YEAR

1897 J. J. McDermott, N.Y.	2 55 10	1929 John C. Miles, Olympic Club,
1898 R. J. McDonald, Cambridge	2 42	Hamilton, Ont. 2 33 8 4-5
1899 L. J. Brignolia, Cambridge	2 54 38	1930 Clarence H. DeMar, Melrose Post,
1900 J. J. Caffrey, Hamilton, Ont.	2 39 44 2-5	No. 90, The American Legion .. 2 34 48 1-5
1901 J. J. Caffrey, Hamilton, Ont.	2 29 23 3-5	1931 James P. Henigan, Medford, Mass. 2 46 45 4-5
1902 Samuel A. Mellor, Yonkers, N.Y.	2 43	1932 Paul DeBruyn, German American
1903 J. C. Lorden, Cambridge, Mass.	2 41 29 4-5	A.C. New York 2 33 36 2-5
1904 Michael Spring, New York	2 39 4 2-5	1933 Leslie Pawson, Pawtucket, R. I. .. 2 31 1 3-5
1905 Fred Lorz, New York A.C.	2 38 25 2-5	1934 Dave Komonen, Frood Mines A.A.
		Sudbury, Mont. 2 32 53 4-5

242. John W. Walsh, Arlington
243. Erich Segal, New Haven, Conn.
244. Jim McDonagh, Millrose A.A.
245. Anthony Farr, Vanderberg, Calif., AFB
246. Roy T. Vogel, Orlando AFB, Florida
247. Steve D. Gelver, Hunter AFB, Georgia
248. Virgil E. Yehnert, Cleveland
249. James Caplinger, Cleveland
250. Frank P. Scaletta, Sparta
251. David W. Whalen, Sparta
252. Ed Sienkiewicz, N.M.C.
253. Ira E. Locke, N.M.C.
254. Richard M. Welsh, Wachu
255. John Reeser, Toronto Stri
256. James Matthew Carroll, H
257. George R. Kinnear, Washi
258. Steven W. Jackson, Penin
259. Thomas W. Brown, Albany Track Club
260. Russell R. Holt, Mt. Park A.A.
261. K. Switzer, Syracuse Harriers.
262. Dr. Alex E. Ratelle, Minnesota Road Runners
263. Dave Tierney, USMC
264. Peter F. Kairo, North Medford Club
265. John Romasco, North Medford Club
266. James F. Dondeau, North Medford Club

258. Steven W. Jackson, Peninsula Track Club, Virginia
259. Thomas W. Brown, Albany Track Club
260. Russell R. Holt, Mt. Park A.A.
261. K. Switzer, Syracuse Harriers.
262. Dr. Alex E. Ratelle, Minnesota Road Runners
263. Dave Tierney, USMC
264. Peter F. Kairo, North Medford Club

The official program for the 1967 American Marathon Race, better known as the Boston Marathon. I got a little frisson when I saw number 261 beside my name, K. Switzer.

(BK27) HOPKINTON, MASS., APRIL 19 – WHO SAYS CHIVALRY IS DEAD? – A girl listed only as "K. Switzer of Syracuse" found herself about to be thrown out of normally all-male Boston Marathon today when a husky companion Thomas Miller of Syracuse threw block that tossed race official out of the running instead. Sequence shows Jock Semple, official, moving in to intercept Miss Switzer then being bounced himself by Miller. Photos by Harry Trask of Boston Traveler.

The spark that ignited the women's running revolution: Harry Trask's famous three-part photo flashed around world, along with the news that I had officially entered and finished the 1967 Boston Marathon. Above is the original caption that accompanied the photo. Photo credit: AP Images.

After the shoving incident, Jock Semple got back on his bus and came alongside us again, shouting. Here is my coach Arnie Briggs (#490) shouting back at him. Teammate John Leonard (in glasses) is upset, boyfriend Tom Miller (#390) is steaming, and I'm just keeping my head down. Behind us is Everett Rice (#225), not part of our team, but a friend from Syracuse. Photo credit: www.brearley.com.

At half-way, we left Tom behind. A few miles later, we were plenty wet and cold, and John is tired; here I'm giving him a hard time about missing too many long practice runs. We didn't know #690, Patrick Mahady, but he was very friendly and ran with us for a while. Photo credit: www.brearley.com.

Just past the Newton Fire Station at about mile 18, we head into the infamous Newton Hills. Heartbreak Hill is just after mile 20.

At the finish line in front of the Prudential Building, John and I pushed Arnie ahead of us so he could finish first, in about 4:20.

My feet were a bloody mess, but that was normal in those days. A friend lent me her coat, an official gave me a blanket, and once I got out of my wet clothes I was a very happy marathoner. We did it! Photo credit: www.brearley.com.

On the *Tonight Show* with Johnny Carson.

Making women official in marathon running was a big item on the agenda at a Road Runners Club of America meeting the day before the Boston Marathon in 1971. Here (left) I met up with the great women's advocate Sara Mae Berman, already a 3:05 marathoner. I also saw Fred Lebow again (bottom), who I'd met a month before in the Earth Day Marathon in New York City. Fred was a relative newcomer to running then.

The End of an Era: Jock Semple hugs me on the starting line of the 1973 Boston Marathon, saying, "C'mon lass, let's get a wee bit o' notoriety." Photo credit: UPI/Corbis.

Moscow, August 1973: The Ted Smits photo that almost got us arrested in Red Square.

We worked at getting publicity for the Olympic Airways sponsored New York City Marathon on September 20, 1973. Here am I on the *Today Show* before the race with Gene Shalit.

December 1973: Warming up for the Maryland Marathon with 1972 Olympic Gold Medalist Frank Shorter (middle) and European Champion Ron Hill.

him so excited about any of my accomplishments. I wish his excitement could have lasted, but it didn't.

Even though my job was growing professionally, and my master's courses ticking along, running now was really the big focus in my life. I was no longer an apologetic jogger but a determined new athlete. Increasingly, my spare time was filled with organizational work in the sport and with the other women marathoners. Sara Mae had run a stunning 3:05 and Nina a 3:12 at Boston; officials, press, and the public were noticing how good we were getting. We began putting pressure on the slow-moving AAU and the Boston Marathon in particular to accept us officially and, in September 1970, the RRCA staged the first men's and women's national marathon championship in Atlantic City. It was a bold statement to the AAU; Sara Mae won it in 3:07 and Nina, Pat, and I all ran it, too. We were gaining political strength.

On March 21, 1971, a carload of us went to New York to run in the new Earth Day Marathon in Central Park, which was the old Cherry Tree Marathon moved into the park from the Harlem River course. It was brutally cold, and whether it was the wind or the steak I ate the night before, I had terrible side stitches. The field was very thin and I was nearly last, as I had to walk a lot. I was rubbing my side when another sluggish runner came up behind me and kindly began massaging my side as we ran along. We looked quite funny, one in front of the other, jogging in lockstep. I know it sounds outrageous to let a stranger just jog along with his hands on you like this, but that's how it is in a marathon; we try to help each other out. I thought the guy must be Eastern European, as he spoke with an accent and wore a hat we never saw in America—it was the same kind of beanie that the European cyclists wore. We chatted and laughed, and pretty soon the stitch eased and I took off running again.

I waited for him at the finish to thank him. His name was Fred Lebow. He was fairly new to running but loved it and wanted to know everybody and everything that had to do with the sport. He was a native of Romania and marvelously engaging in a continental manner that American men don't quite have and we became instant friends. Fred started calling me regularly in Syracuse just to ask questions and find out what was going on, and reported on all the New York City news, too. I jokingly told Tom he was a one-man network, but I had no idea then how true that was. Among other things, Fred was very caught up in the women's marathon movement and kept rattling cages as well as kept us women even more in touch with each other.

Indeed, we women were becoming a strong voice in an increasingly pro-women era. It was an amazing time. I was one of the few salaried women in my office (there were as yet no "executive" women there) and was asked to be one of two first women admitted to the Syracuse Press Club. Some feminist organizations tried to appropriate me and in particular my first confrontation at Boston, and while this greatly annoyed me, there was no doubt that I was becoming a very outspoken defender of women's rights. I was on TV and in the newspapers a lot, and while I tried always to win people over rather than bash them over the head with pleas for equality, I found myself increasingly in positions of responsibility in this new area.

Tom was not wild about my new role. At all. He grew increasingly resentful of my work and of the attention I was getting. The harder I worked, the less he trained. The more courses I took, the less he worked on his thesis. He even got mad at me when the newspapers referred to me as Kathy (Switzer) Miller instead of just Kathy

Miller, as if that diminished him and as if I did that on purpose. Finally, he started accusing me of being less of a woman because I didn't want to get pregnant. This was actually more outrageous to me than it was hurtful, and when I reminded him that since I was the one who had a paying job, we couldn't possibly consider creating a child without having a support system. Tom disagreed violently, saying he would rise to the occasion if I got pregnant.

I have to hand it to Tom, because in this quite perverse way, he helped make me a pretty good runner. I was so anxious to get out of his bed that I never again minded runs in the snow at five thirty in the morning. By Boston 1971, I was ready to run hard.

PART III | SHARPENING

Sharpening is focusing your training to handle racing speed and technique.

CHAPTER 11

"HAVE YOU EVER RUN THE
MARATHON DISTANCE BEFORE?"

It was tremendous staying at Carol's in Hopkinton! I slept long and well and woke up gently on race morning without worrying about getting to the start. The day before, I was an active part of the RRCA meeting where runners gathered from around the country to discuss tactics to make women official in the marathon; it was a heady experience being around so many fellow believers, the vast majority of whom were men. Afterward, Sara Mae and Larry Berman asked me to join the group at their house for dinner. The place was jammed, and Sara Mae served spaghetti. Spaghetti! I was nervous about eating that the night before the race, but Sara Mae was chowing down and she was the champion so I ate it with delight and it has been my pre-race meal ever since. Carol made me a great breakfast. I couldn't thank her enough. I pinned a ten-dollar bill inside the hem of my top. If disaster struck, I could get a taxi to the finish. If disaster did not strike, I would buy myself a beer at the Lenox bar, which was just near the finish line. It would be my first beer in a month, and well deserved, too.

I felt absolutely great as I walked in the pale spring sunshine to the new meeting place that Sara Mae had organized for the BAA at the First Congregational Church; we had our own "locker room" at last. I was only worried about whether my foot would hold up from getting run over by a grocery cart five days before, and nervous that I hadn't run at all in that time. I'd never not run at all the week before a race. Well, it couldn't be helped, here I was, and I just forced myself to think of something else, like my shoes. I was wearing a brand-new pair, normally a totally stupid thing to do, but I judged it a better choice. In those days, running shoe stores didn't exist. You had to order shoes from a distributor. I'd ordered mine weeks before and since they were one of the smallest men's sizes (women's running shoes certainly did not exist for many years) it took a long time for them to arrive. For six weeks I suffered in my old shoes, which had gone flat dead. My new pair, called Tiger Onitsukas, had soft puffy nylon uppers and were light as a feather. To wear them was definitely worth the risk.

Sara Mae and Nina Kuscsik were upstairs in the church getting their gear packed up, and Gloria Ratti, the only woman on the BAA committee, was bustling around carrying a transistor radio for the weather reports, and a supply kit of tape, towels, and tampons. Gloria was our self-appointed godmother and was a godsend, too. It was wonderful to be among these women and for us to be the most official unofficial athletes in the race and not to have to skulk around in the bushes to get into the event. It was a convivial occasion. Nobody was there to race. The idea was to run the best we could and get personal records, but most of all to hold up the female side. It was a little like going into battle—we were all comrades, and we wanted each other to survive and win the greater war of showing the world we deserved to be official entrants in the marathon. The tacit understanding was that no matter what, we would each finish the race, and if one of us collapsed, we wouldn't do it in front of a camera.

So many people who didn't understand our personal goals expected us—wanted us!—to wimp out and we could simply not let that happen. It was unfair pressure, of course; the marathon can (and does, with diabolical frequency) throw the most unexpected disasters in the way of the runners. Instead of letting the pressure get us down, we used it to inspire us. The press were especially quixotic on this point: we were now six years into women's running Boston, and press coverage had become increasingly athletic and supportive of us. They knew, for instance, that Sara Mae's 3:05 in 1970 had been close to a world record, and that she and Nina could perhaps better that time here at Boston. Indeed, the women's race was commanding most of the attention because of the possibility of new records and also about who would be the first woman in history to break three hours in the distance. It could happen in this race. At the same time, however, the media were there with their cameras, vulturelike, to catch any falter or distress and overly dramatize it. A male runner in distress is a heroic figure; a woman runner in distress is further proof that we are fragile creatures who are physiologically unsuited to marathon running.

We hugged each other as we left the church to begin our warm-ups; these were our good-byes until the finish line. Warm-up was the time when I wanted to be left alone, and I suspect it was the same for Nina and Sara Mae. There was a battery of photographers at the start on Hayden Rowe so any last-minute concentrating and focusing had to be done on the side streets. I jogged slowly up and around the little back streets, quietly shouting down the last of the what-ifs that kept popping into my head with positive rational thoughts about how good I felt, how much I loved the course, and of how all the training time had led at last to this joyful release. Well, it would be joyful for a while anyway, and then, I promised myself, a cold beer at the finish no matter what.

Even though I was now very used to being part of the start at big races—all of which except for Boston I registered for and wore numbers in—Boston made me nervous also because it was the biggest race in the country. The four-hour qualifying from 1970 did little to discourage runners, so the BAA decided to make the qualifying time 3:30. That may have intimidated some people—there were only three women this year—but it didn't solve the problem, since there were still over a thousand starters. It was monstrous! A thousand people who can run a marathon in less than three and a half hours! Everybody in the world who can do that must be here, I thought. It was pretty funny. By trying to reduce the field, officials just made Boston more appealing, and everyone trained harder and got faster.

The media contingent was huge as usual, and I knew there would be a surge of excitement and picture-taking if any of us women were sighted by the press up front. I didn't want that hassle right before the start, and setting the cameras into a rushing, clicking flurry would be unfair to the elite men who were nervously pacing there. Jock Semple would undoubtedly be prowling the start line, and I definitely wanted to avoid him.

Jock's legendary irascibility on race morning now had become a part of his everyday life as the marathon grew and grew. Stories spread quickly about how he was increasingly fed up with the numbers wanting to run and how he had to deal also with women's pleas for admission to the race. His phone rang constantly, and he had to try to continue his practice as a massage therapist. We runners loved and were outraged both with the stories of how Jock simply hung up on people the minute the phone rang, or how he demanded the entry fees for the marathon in cash, or how he and Will Cloney said they had more important things to worry about than the women in the race. Well, we women would take care of ourselves, and we could laugh later at the stories. Today, race day, Jock would be a man on the rampage and I was still a red flag to him. To tell the truth, he scared the hell out of me.

So, I came up from the back and entered the race from the side, unnoticed by the press, and said hi to all the guys around me. As usual, this created an excited buzz. They were very happy to see me and some were quite surprised, as if they hadn't known that women running marathons had become a possibility, much less an issue. When one of them asked what I planned to do, I was pleased that I could answer confidently that I planned to break 3:30. Another innocently asked if I'd ever done the distance before, and I just smiled and quietly said, oh yes, yes I have. I wanted to shout "I've done seven consecutive weeks of twenty-seven-mile runs every Sunday for this, and that's not even the half of it!" But I didn't want to jinx it, not with my injured foot and new shoes.

Right before the gun, I saw hot orange gardening gloves among the runners; it was the nice guy I'd run with in the New Bedford Half-Marathon the month before who had an easy stride and the exact pace as I did. We greeted each other like soul mates and instantly agreed to run together; it was good for both of us, as we'd each have a reliable companion for the journey. Thank God he wore those gloves, or I would not have recognized him. It was a good omen; you don't get to see people's faces very often in a road race. And then we were off.

Everything seemed so familiar, so easy. Nina and Sara Mae started in front of me this year; I never saw them in the race and didn't give them another thought. They were twenty to twenty-five minutes faster than I was, which was a different league from me, and it seemed an unachievable one. They had started running marathons at paces I had since bettered, but for some reason I still could not believe that I could ever improve the way they did. I settled into my own race, setting the dial on cruise control.

Even though there was a companionability between them, Nina and Sara Mae had each thrown down a gauntlet of sorts with their Boston performance of the previous year. This year both of them were in great shape, and were hoping for personal records and course records at Boston; with luck, one of them just might break three hours, too.

Still, it wasn't supposed to be a race until Sara Mae, who had been in the lead and running comfortably at her own pace, was passed by Nina on Heartbreak Hill. Sara Mae watched Nina continue on, getting a lead of half a football field. Sara Mae later recounted her slow realization that Boston was, after all, a race. So she started pushing her pace, caught and passed Nina on Beacon Street, and held that lead for the two miles into the finish, winning by less than a minute, in 3:08:30. Something new and exciting was developing: women marathoners were becoming competitive!

Meanwhile, Orange Gloves and I ran stride for stride pretty much surrounded by runners. It was like surfing a nice wave, I'd caught the pace exactly as I wanted it and we just sailed. The women at Wellesley at last were all I had hoped for, and more. In 1967 they were nonexistent, and in 1970, also a cold and miserable rain, they were scarce. Today they were out in force and went absolutely crazy when they saw me. For the first time, I felt the noise of their screaming bounce off my chest; the only time I'd felt that before was when I was a kid at a parade and felt the concussion of the big drums in the marching band. I was always proud of being a woman and I was proud enough of my running to need little outside affirmation, but the cheers of the Wellesley women made up for a lot of dark training nights. I felt my eyes sting with tears; I knew the cheers would sustain me for months. The guys around me apparently felt the same, for when we swept away from the college and out of town, the cheering stopped for a while and all was quiet on the road except for the pat pat of our feet. "Wow," said one guy, "I'm going to stick close to *you*!" and suddenly total strangers all began to talk about how remarkable it was.

The cool day got warmish, especially for me in the leotard outfit with the velvet top. But over the last year I'd come to train in the black tights and loved their ability to eliminate friction entirely. Plus I had my period; there was no way, even if it were 100 degrees, that I'd not wear those tights in case I had a leak and something showed. Wouldn't that have been a great photo! I couldn't imagine anything worse. I knew from experience that the black tights meant I didn't have to worry about it.

The miracle was my feet and my condition. I'd never felt so good in a race, so rested. My foot didn't hurt a bit, and I didn't get one blister from the new shoes. That had never, ever happened. Orange Gloves and I finished in 3:28, a six-minute personal record at Boston for me, and perfect eight-minute miles. Throughout the race I felt as close to Orange Gloves as a brother, and when we finished together in 3:28, we were so bonded we would have risked our lives for each other. We hugged in relief and gratitude, and then he went off to the men's locker room and beef stew, I headed back to my hotel, and forty years later I cannot even remember his name.

The Lenox Hotel was in a perfect location, about a hundred yards from the finish line, with an entrance to the bar right on Boylston Street. The ten-dollar bill was a bit soggy but still pinned to my top, and I was determined to fulfill my fantasy. I walked straight in and ordered a cold one at the bar. There were only two people in the joint, a fat customer who looked like he lived there, and a surly bartender. After the warmth and sunshine outside, the place seemed dark and rancid, and I knew it wasn't what I'd had in mind. I guess I thought the place would be jammed with jovial marathon people, but everyone was still outside watching the finish. Once there, I didn't want to be a ninny and back out. The customer eyed me and said, "Whaddya do? Run the marathon or something, ha ha ha!" "As a matter of fact, I did," I said chirpily, feeling pretty good about having a six-minute personal record. The bartender slid the beer over, and took my ten dollars, and brought back my change, saying, "You women just have to have it all, don't you?" He tried to stare me down. I said absolutely nothing but drank my beer calmly and then slowly gathered up my change, taking it all as he watched me. Then I looked up to make sure he was looking, put a nickel on the counter, and left. When I got to my room and into the shower, I just laughed it off, thinking how completely emasculated that poor slob of a bartender who thought he was so tough would be if faced with a thousand of the fittest and most virile men in the world, men with whom I'd just labored and been encouraged by, men who were so confident in their masculinity they could welcome a woman like me into their world. God, this was a wonderful sport!

The New York Road Runners Club had a hospitality suite, and everyone congregated there. That's when I heard that Álvaro Mejia, from Colombia, had won the race by only five seconds over Pat McMahon, an Irish American who lived in the Boston area. Then I heard about the women's race. Everyone was excited and talking about what Sara Mae and Nina had done.

As we sat there that afternoon in the suite, I think we all sensed a sea change in women's marathoning. By anyone's estimation, Sara Mae (3:08:30) and Nina (3:09) had run great times, had a great competition, and even started a great sporting rivalry. It was the beginning of the competitive age of women's running, and it was mostly created in Boston in 1971. The media loved it, the public was following it, and we knew that the increasing pressure on officials to let women run marathons legally would have to amount to something soon. It was reaching a breaking point—the officials and their rules looked pretty silly once the myth of women's fragility could no longer be used as an excuse. More than ever before, we women runners bonded in 1971 and worked to agitate against those who blocked us, particularly those in the AAU who refused to think there was a place for women in marathon running. A lot of the AAU officials were in the New York area, and Nina especially was applying pressure on them and submitting legislation to support the argument. It was bewildering to try to reason with officials who worked harder at excluding us than undertaking the simple task of inclusion. After the 1971 race, even Will Cloney and Jock Semple were softening; they could see the performances and were impressed even before they read the papers.

Early in the evening, Hal Higdon was launching his book *On the Run from Dogs and People* in another suite at the Lenox, so we just moved the party over there. I was excited to be invited to this book launch; like being invited to the Bermans', it meant I was welcome in elite running company. Hal had often contested Boston to win, and on top of that he was a famous writer; I'd read his stuff in *Sports Illustrated.* Here he was with a book—about running, no less—and if you bought it, he would autograph it and give you a free T-shirt. Authors were like gods to me, and to have a signed book was a treasure. The blue T-shirt bore the title of his book. Since all my T-shirts were plain white, this was very special, and it would also answer all the idiots who stopped me in training to ask me why I was running.

Like many good writers, Hal was slightly intimidating with his acerbic and clever conversational retorts; I did not want to say something stupid at this party. The room was packed with skinny beer-drinking guys, all of whom seemed to have run under 2:40, and about five women, who of course were very conspicuous. Everyone was high on their races and reliving them; ten runners after a race will have a hundred stories. The guys were impressed with the women's times; we discussed the race and women's running in general, and then one guy asked me what I thought the ultimate female performance in a marathon was. It took me a minute to figure out what I thought was reasonable based on Olympic times at shorter distances, and then I decided to err on the side of conservatism, answering about a 2:32, but that it would take about ten years, and then that time would gradually decrease. The room went silent, and people just stared at me as if I'd said a really bad word. How Hal Higdon heard this from across the room I could not imagine, but he shouted out in the silence, "That's *ridiculous!*" as if I were from outer space. I just shrugged my shoulders. Perhaps I'd put a foot wrong at this party, but I didn't think so. A lot of important guys got to thinking about it, and just seven years later Grete Waitz ran a 2:32—but I'm getting ahead of myself.

A really nice group of guys were there from California and they invited me to join them for dinner; again, I was very flattered to be included in such an important occasion. At least it was to me; the night after running the Boston Marathon was nearly as special as Christmas Eve. We went to a warm and noisy seafood place and had a ball. I had never laughed so hard and had never felt so significant in male company. It was the first time in my recent adult memory that I didn't feel I had to be defensive or explain myself; I was a runner, they were runners. One in particular was very attractive to me, an alarming thought that I pushed out of my head. When dinner was over and we all got ready to go, the one I was attracted to said, "You guys go on, I'll walk Kathrine back to her hotel." It was late, the streets were dark, and nobody had been chivalrous to me in a long time. It was kind, and that's all I thought until he asked me to bed.

I thought people were supposed to feel guilty about having an affair, but I didn't at all. I felt saved, as if I had been hooked on something underwater for a long time and at the very moment I was about to drown, whoosh! I shot to the surface and gulped air and felt sunshine on my face. He was an interesting and substantial person and even though he lived twenty-five hundred miles away, the relationship gave me something to feel happy about—not just positive, which I always felt about my running and work, but *happy*. I also had an outlet to express myself, since we wrote to each other at least once a week. I felt attractive and desirable and was thrilled to see the letters in the post office box I'd rented.

It put joy back into the training, and made the hard work I was doing on running fun again. I loved organizing events and promoting them, seeing them grow and getting good attention for runners, who seldom got the slightest notice in the newspapers. It really became fun when I could share the significance of them with someone, particularly my dreams about women's races—even the Olympics— and I did that in the letters.

How I had time to write those letters is one of life's wonders— I started my first run at 5:30 A.M., then worked from 8:15 to 5:00, ran again from 5:30 to 6:30, and went to night school, a committee meeting, or to the gym from 7:00 to 9:00. After 9:00, I studied or worked on some kind of running legislation. Most weekends there was a race somewhere, often a marathon, and when there wasn't, I worked part time at a local modeling school on Saturdays, teaching exercise for extra money. Then I did a twenty-seven-mile run on Sundays, and finished up on Sunday night at the university library working on a term project of some sort. Laundry was a real problem, as we couldn't afford a washing machine, so I usually hit the Laundromat on Sunday night, too, or sometimes when I went to the gym to lift weights. Writing the letters was the most pleasurable thing in my task-oriented life, but it also proved the old adage that no matter how busy you are, you will find time to do the things you really like to do.

The affair also shocked me. Somewhere on the road to getting a master's degree in communications so I could get a better job, writing press releases to help women's running, and organizing races in Syracuse because our club needed them was the realization that I also crammed my life full of these things because they were more significant to me than my husband. Being a nice wife who said yes to buying more hammer shoes and then expressed her anger over it by becoming an essentially absentee spouse wasn't facing up to the fact that we had a lousy marriage and that I was very lonely. I couldn't live like this for the rest of my life without losing my mind, so I screwed up my courage and told Tom several times that we needed to talk. His answer was always the same: we have nothing to talk about. A few weeks later, I said that I wanted us to get marriage counseling, and he said that was idiotic, everyone has problems and he certainly wasn't airing his dirty laundry in front of anyone. Tom was taciturn when he got angry, so for days on end the only conversation in the house was me on the phone or whatever was coming from the TV or radio.

So I went to marriage counseling by myself, and it was great. I had thought running worked out anxieties, and it does, but professional counseling helped me articulate feelings and hear other suggestions. I didn't have to have all the answers. Then we reached the stage where we really needed Tom to progress. Telling him was going to be dicey.

I came home from work one evening and found the TV, the radio, and the stereo all going at once and Tom reading the newspaper. I said "Hi, honey, did you have a good day?" and he didn't answer. So I said it again, louder. Still no answer. I turned down the radio and before I could ask again, Tom snapped, "I was listening to that."

"Which? The radio, the TV, or the stereo?"

No answer.

"Hey, Tom, I need to talk to you."

No answer.

I went over to the newspaper, turned back the corner, and peeked over it. "Helll-ooo there. This is me. Wanna talk about it?"

No answer.

I turned off the stereo and then the radio, and I walked over to the TV.

"I am *watching* that!" Tom said as I reached for the knob.

Before any real thought came to me, I had already reacted. I had on high leather boots, and with a sideways kick spin, I put my foot through the TV screen. In case you want to know, it makes a kind of small explosion.

"Not any more," I said.

"Jesus Christ! What the hell are you doing? Are you crazy?" he screamed.

I'd never felt less crazy in my life. It was wonderful!

"Oh good, Tom, I've got your attention. So now you *will*, you goddamn *will* listen to me."

We did talk a little, aided by the fact that we no longer had a TV. Actions speak louder than words, though. Later that summer I was briefly hospitalized for some minor surgery and Tom would not visit me, saying he hated hospitals. (Like, who doesn't?) The door closed then and I made plans to leave Tom as soon as he got his MBA which—glory be!—was going to happen in six months. He had a job offer in New York contingent on his completing the degree; when he left, I intended to finish my master's and instead of going to New York to join him, I made plans of my own to go to Munich alone instead. There was no way Tom would make the team; he didn't even have a qualifying distance for the USA Trials. But by this time, the 1972 Munich Olympics had become a part of my life and I wanted to see firsthand how they worked, and how the women's marathon could become a part of them. I was also running away from home with my broken heart.

The surgery kept me out of the year-old New York City Marathon, which in 1971 already featured drama: Nina Kuscsik, Beth Bonner, and Sara Mae Berman were all going to make a serious assault on the three-hour marathon barrier. All had come close and it was sort of the women's marathon equivalent of breaking the four-minute mile. Pat Tarnawsky was also running and I longed to be there with them in solidarity, as the race also was as much a political statement as a physical one. Fred Lebow and Pat had pulled out all the stops on publicity.

Just two weeks before the race, however, we were shocked to hear that Australian Adrienne Beames had run a 2:46:30 marathon in Werribee. At first we thought it was a hoax; that was a fifteen-minute improvement on the world record, come on! An investigation was launched.

Slightly deflated, Bonner and Kuscsik went head to head anyway, with Bonner winning in 2:55:22, edging Kuscsik by only forty-four seconds! It was a stunning race and the times were fabulous. For a long time Beth Bonner and Nina Kuscsik were declared the first women to officially break three hours until it was revealed that Adrienne Beames was for real, and fighting acceptance battles of her own in conservative Australia.

The women's marathon races of 1971 were as dramatic as many of the most thrilling in the three decades that followed. More than ever, women's performances screamed for acceptance. Meetings and legislation continued, and pressure mounted.

Chapter | 12

Official at Last

And so, uh . . . you ladies are welcome at Boston. But you have to meet the men's qualifying time!

—Jock Semple (somewhat grudgingly), April 16, 1972

Finally, after another year of wrangling, the AAU gave the BAA a convoluted permission for women to run if the women had a separate starting line and didn't run against the men. So the women were to be scored separately, which of course is what we'd always done, and put on a corner of the starting line, which we'd never done and never wanted to do—we knew our place was not among the elite men, but midpack. Oh, and we had to meet the men's time restriction of 3:30. It has never been so hard since for women to qualify to run Boston. Seven of us could do it, and we were all there; it was a historic and triumphant moment we wouldn't have missed. For my life, I also wouldn't have missed Jock Semple's "welcome" to us the day before the race when he sputtered out "And so, uh . . . you ladies are welcome at Boston. But you have to meet the men's qualifying time!" That sure was Jock; he just couldn't welcome us without a warning and I was still wary of him.

We were official! We did it! It was an exhilarating victory and the end of a six-year campaign that was by turns controversial, exasperating, and exhausting. We were free to be *athletes* and no longer had to run carrying the banner of the whole female sex. It was very important: this acceptance marked the first time in history that women were given permission (and thus, endorsement) to participate in what had previously been a men-only sports event. We knew we were breaking down a political and social barrier just as surely as our suffragist foremothers did when they won the right to vote, or forced universities to become coeducational.

The only limitations now were self-imposed. Today, in the age of extreme sports and the triathlon, it is important to remember that in 1972, the marathon was considered the most arduous of all sports events. Giving women permission (endorsement) to participate alongside men threw thousands of years of preconceptions about female weakness out the window. It also implied that women could hold their own against male competition, even though the rules clearly stated that we women would not be competing against the men, but participating alongside them. Fifty years earlier, people had been afraid to let women exercise their brains. Until 1972, people were afraid to let women exercise their bodies. Inclusion in the Boston Marathon was the turning point in that thinking.

We were the women who made it happen, we were here together, and when we stepped over the starting line we knew we were stepping into a new era. We were still nervous, though! There naturally was a burden of expectation, but the pressure and defensiveness of previous years was over. We'd already won the big race.

It is interesting that two months later, on June 23, President Nixon signed into law Title IX, the equality of education amendment that prohibits sex discrimination in any education program or activity within an institution receiving any type of federal financial assistance.

This wasn't directly related to our work in getting the Boston Marathon to open its door to women, but the timing was significant. Clearly, if women can run a marathon, they can do anything. Our success in Boston, along with the strong images and performances coming from women there and in other races in ensuing years, helped greatly in starting running programs and teams in schools and was a powerful voice by the time the equality-of-sports-opportunity component of Title IX took effect in 1978.

I knew the media were going to be in a frenzy at the start line in Hopkinton over the women, and people then and forever after were going to look at the photos of us, the First Official Women. I wanted to both run well and look especially good for this race. I was ready for a 3:15 and had devised the perfect running outfit—leotard and tights, covered with a sort of Grecian white wrap. It looked beautiful, but best of all, it was light, friction free, and would not impinge on my competitiveness. As usual, I'd tied my hair in a tight bun with a ribbon. The look was a combination of my two heroines, Atalanta and Margot Fonteyn.

There was only one problem. It was designed for nothing warmer than a 60-degree day, and since I'd only run Boston in cold weather, and since I was coming from Syracuse, where snow was still on the ground, I hadn't brought an alternative outfit. I know you must be thinking what I feel as I write this: how many thousands of miles had I trained by then not to consider this possibility? As noon approached, the temperature began to rise.

Since Nina was the fastest, she took the one designated place on the far left of the front line. I thought this was doubly deserving, as Nina had legislated so mightily to get us official. I stood behind her, and the other women lined up behind me. It was our separate starting line from the men. Right from the gun, we knew how it was going to go: Nina was going to win in about three hours, I was going to be second in 3:15, and Elaine Pederson from California would be third in about 3:30. Sara Mae Berman was there in support and only to finish this year, having been unable to train over the winter.

The outfit was fine for the starting line photos, and it was fine for the first several miles of the race. At about three miles, the press truck came by clicking cameras, and as I began to give it a big wave, my hair pin came loose and I reached up to push it firmly back in place to secure my bun. Then I waved and said hello since by then I knew most of the press guys. They drifted up to the start.

At about four miles, the sun burst out. My black outfit absorbed it and I felt like I was in a steam box. I couldn't shed anything; everything was layered. Even if I could, I was faced with a serious dilemma: under the tights I was wearing the skimpiest of pink lace bikini panties, which the Grecian wrap was not long enough to cover. I came up with a solution and dodged into a gas station asking for scissors. They had none, only a serrated knife. I ran into the dank ladies' room, which had no light. I undressed completely, even having to unpin my numbers, hacked the legs off the tights, rolled the raw edges into shorts, threw away the leotard, and hoped that the single safety pin I had was enough to hold the top of the wrap closed. Then I ran back onto the course, and started to run too quickly, hoping stupidly to make up time. I have no idea how much time I lost. It seemed like hours but was probably seven or eight minutes. I passed Sara Mae, who clucked sympathetically when I told her what had happened.

From then on, I didn't see another woman and only hoped I'd regained my second place. For a while, I was angry with myself. I'd blown my chance for a 3:15 and possibly a chance to place not so much by vanity as by stupidity. Because of my faster pace early on, I had some tough patches later, but I finished strongly, in 3:29:51, just nipping under the qualifying time which had been so easy only the day before. I looked like a wrung-out scarecrow, the exact image for women I was trying to avoid.

We had our own locker room, and when I arrived, it was bustling with people, including Bud Collins, a reporter who was covering the women. I had to laugh; now that we were so important, we got one of the top reporters! Elaine Pederson was beaming; she'd run a personal record of 3:20, and being from California, the heat had not bothered her. We had a big hug; I was delighted for her, and all things considered, I was happy to be third. Nina was lying on the floor wrapped in a blanket with the laurel wreath on her head. She had won in 3:10 but she was exhausted. She had bad diarrhea throughout the second half of the race and since there were no toilets along the race route in those days, she had to make the awful choice of quitting or letting it go and keep running. She did let it go but worried the whole rest of the race about what kind of negative image this might create for women. As it turned out, none of us had to worry about negative images. Official status brings wonders: everyone thought the women at Boston were nothing short of courageous.

We went upstairs to the cafeteria of the Prudential Building to eat our first bowls of official beef stew. Arnie was right—it wasn't so great, and it was the last thing you wanted to eat after a hot marathon. Then Jock Semple presented the trophies. There was no fanfare with this, as I recall the trophies were still in boxes and not even on a display table. When he presented me with my third-place, the running figurine on the top was broken. I could tell he was embarrassed about it and explained that if I sent it back, they would replace it. Then he sputtered, "I've been mad at you for five years and you deserve a broken trophy!"

When I got back home to Syracuse, I wrote an effusive thank-you letter to Will Cloney and Jock Semple, saying, "If someone had told me five years ago that I would one day write this letter, I would never have believed it." In addition to thanking them for the race, and their efforts in accepting us, the letter all these years later is interesting in that it also expresses how hard we women tried to perform well, and how willing we were to help with any aspect of the organization in the future.

Finally, I added, "I personally would like to apologize for being your pesky little nemesis for these past five years. I never for a moment believed I was wrong in the 1967 race nor since, but I honestly never tried to personally antagonize anyone. Anyway, full steam ahead now!"

Will Cloney answered, "I am sure that now we have broken the ice, women long-distance runners will find many more doors open to them. As for the 1967 race, that is past history. Like you I am much more interested in future history and hope that you and the other girls will play a major role in writing some of it."

The news was full of the women at Boston, and our spirit captured the imagination of the world. Suddenly, everyone was talking about our breakthrough, and how wonderful it was. Personally, I was stunned to see a picture of me pinning up my hair shown in so many places, as it was such an accidental moment. It created grumbling from some people who thought I purposely had set up a cheesecake shot. What a hilarious accusation, given the complexity and timing of the situation! Others loved it so much that they framed it, made paintings of it, or wrote poems about it. One poem was even published in the *New York Times*:

Bouquet to Kathy Miller
(America's Atalanta)

Kathy Miller, pretty miler
Running in The Marathon
Taking pains—just like a woman
—To fix thy hair in a bun!

Patron goddess, fair Diana,
On this day is proud of you,
Taking part in distance running
'Gainst a hardy, manly crew!

In the steps of Atalanta,
Thou dost follow admirably;
Thou wilt not let "golden apples"
Catch thine eyes and tarry thee!

Thou dost run as in flotation
—Dancing 'pon New England air!
Shapely silhouette you fashion
As you tidy up your hair.

You have caught the public's fancy
With your gesture to your hair;
And I find myself a victim
Helpless ever in your snare!

Harry Dee
Poughkeepsie, N.Y.

One of the most exciting developments from the publicity was a call to Fred Lebow from Carl Byoir Associates, a public relations agency. They were assigned to launch a new product called "Crazylegs," a ladies-only shaving gel from Johnson's Wax, and they thought a first-ever all-women's marathon would be just the vehicle to kick it off. They wanted Fred and the New York Road Runners to organize it. Fred was one of the most vocal men supporting women in the marathon, but even he knew there were not yet enough women to sustain a respectable-looking women-only marathon. It was a hell of a good idea though, and the suggestion spun our heads around.

Fred did some fast talking, as he didn't want to lose this opportunity. Fred loved making history, and even more so if someone else was paying for it. He told Byoir Associates that a far better idea would be to have a women-only six-mile race, one lap around Central Park, and call it a Mini-Marathon. Fred was in the garment trade, where you had to be quick. The miniskirt was in high fashion and this was a fun double-meaning of the word. As for history, it would still be the first-ever women-only road race.

Then Fred began calling everyone for their opinions, which is the way he did business and finally made a decision. When he called me in Syracuse, I had left my job and was deep into writing the final paper for my master's degree and trying to figure out how I was going to get the money for Munich in just three months. I was so poor that I recall being grateful he was paying for the call. His idea of the race was brilliant. Fred then said the agency wanted Nina and me for spokespeople and he needed us to help him. Johnson's Wax was covering expenses, which was too good to be true for us who would do anything to help women's running anyway. We said yes in a flash and never imagined asking for a fee.

Heaven help us, this was going to take place in June, and here it was the last week in April. Fred was panicked because he wasn't sure he could get a decent-sized field together. The press conference for the event was in mid-May and he didn't have a lot to show for it, despite printing ten thousand flyers and mailing them everywhere. Nina and I ran all over New York with Fred distributing these flyers, and Fred and I even went down to Max's Kansas City, the "in" singles bar at the time to pass them out to women, who thought we were nutcases. Desperate for some diversionary publicity, Fred went to the Playboy Club and enlisted some "bunnies" for a photo op and to line up at the start of the race. That was Fred; he was a male chauvinist who totally supported the women's movement.

The press conference was at Tavern on the Green, which was a tired old restaurant at the time but which was already the traditional start/finish line for so many races in Central Park, including the New York City Marathon. Fred came over to my hotel ahead of time with some dresses from his factory that he wanted me to try on. They were all very nice but not as good as the svelte burgundy sheath I'd brought. Actually, I think Fred wanted to see me climbing in and out of clothes; this was the '70s, we weren't shy, we were runners, and most of us had changed clothes together in cars before our races without giving it a thought.

The press conference was a great success; after the formalities, there was a receiving line where Nina and I had to shake hands with and listen to every male guest tell us he had run the 440 in high school. As I looked down the line, I locked eyes with a man who was devastatingly handsome. He had black eyes, and I'd never met anyone with black eyes before. When it was time to shake his hand, I said, "Okay, so why are you crashing this party?" He was heartily amused that I'd figured him out so quickly and said, "I looked at the press list for the evening. I was looking for a free drink and dinner, I thought this sounded a bit more exotic than attending the do at the Honolulu Chamber of Commerce."

He stepped out of the line to get me a drink and surreptitiously passed it to me behind the line so it wouldn't be in any photographs; I had told him I had to uphold my jock reputation. He told me his name was Philip, waved, and said, "See you at the race."

On a hot and humid June day, 78 women runners appeared for the Crazylegs Mini-Marathon, including a few bunnies in rabbit ears. It was considered a huge field; we were surprised that so many women could run six miles! We all wore the same shirts—our bib numbers were actually stenciled on them, a clever ploy of the sponsors, which annoyed many of the more experienced runners, who didn't want to be obligated to wear a commercial. They harped on Fred as he protested his innocence. Still, for all the high jinks and the publicity that the bunnies got before the race, it was great to see that once the field assembled, the whole focus changed from silliness to seriousness.

Jackie Dixon, an eighteen-year-old from San Francisco, won the race. She'd won the Bay to Breakers and was flown to New York by the *San Francisco Examiner* for her race prize. Nina was second and I was sixth. I was delighted that an unknown won; it trumpeted to the world that there was tremendous talent out there that only needed an opportunity like this to blossom. The women were ecstatic; I was imagining how seventy-eight of them just got their own Secret Weapons. We were ebullient with our success; Fred was already thinking how he could make it better the following year.

My thinking took a different tack: it occurred to me that this could be the way to get the women's distance races, the marathon especially, in the Olympics. Women-only events would show the International Olympic Committee that our request wasn't just about a few feisty women barging in on men's races. A single-sex race would also show that we could do it on our own. I was hopeful I'd get an inside scoop on this at the Olympics themselves in a few weeks.

I was also thinking about dark-eyed Philip sitting on the grass watching everything. When it was all over, he asked me out to dinner and I said yes, feeling a bit daring since he was fifteen years my senior. He was disappointed when I told him he would not see me again for months, but he understood when he saw the schedule ahead for me. Before I checked out of my hotel the next day, a small package arrived from him. Inside was a set of keys to his apartment with a note, "If you run into any trouble and need a place, here are the keys and the address." A clever come-on? No, to me it was one of the kindest things anyone ever did for me. For six months all over Europe, I carried those keys in the bottom of my purse like a security blanket.

While wrapping up some other city business, I walked by the offices of the *New York Daily News*. On impulse, I just walked in— you could do that in those days—and introduced myself to the sports editor. I knew that the *New York Times* was sending reporters to Munich for the 1972 summer Olympics, but I had heard that the *Daily News* was only using wire services, so I told the editor he should hire me as a stringer. I was going to Munich anyway, all he'd have to pay for was stuff of mine they published. Having just earned my master's degree in communications, I was feeling pretty cocky. He agreed, and gave me a formal letter of introduction, since actual press accreditation for the Olympics had closed months before. It wasn't a real job, but it was more than just being a spectator.

Based on having a "sort of" job in Munich, I got a $3,000 loan from the First Trust Key Bank; I guess they couldn't refuse after I'd organized their sponsorship of two marathons—one of which was the national championship—at no cost. I used some of the money to buy matching chronographs for Arnie and me; they were the first running watches either of us had ever had. Then I packed up my apartment and after a wrenching good-bye to Arnie, I left Syracuse, presumably forever, and headed to New York to run the Puerto Rican Day Marathon, my last item of business. I didn't really want to run my fifth marathon of the year in the scorching July heat, but the first two women finishers would win an all-expense-paid trip to the first-ever international women's 10K race in Guayanilla, Puerto Rico, the following February. Nina, Fred, and I felt it was very important to support it. Nina was first and I was second. I showered, packed my suitcase, and flew that night to Oslo, where the American Olympic track and field team was training for Munich. I began my new sports journalism career the next morning.

Chapter | 13

"I'm leaving on a jet plane; don't know when I'll be back again."

I made two important European stops before I went to Munich. I wanted to get a story on the Americans in their training camp in Oslo before they left for Munich, and then I wanted to do a story on the first World Masters running tour that was starting in London. Also, I had agreed to meet Laraine Epstein, a marathon-running friend of mine from New York, who was staying in London.

Steve Prefontaine was *the* American running personality before the Olympics. All the newspaper stories about him showed him as an arrogant and outspoken man. Since most Americans thought he was a sure bet for gold in the 5,000 meters, he was a perfect first story for the limited amount of time I had in Oslo. I wanted to report on his training and get an aggressive quote about how he was going to smash the opposition. Instead, I wound up going for a warm-up run with him, timing some of his amazing 400s, and hearing him say how, when the pressure was off, he was looking forward to becoming a jogger one day. He was laid-back and philosophical, a nice young man, unlike any stories I'd read about him. From this experience, I could see why he hated journalists. An expanded version of the story I wrote would have been good for a magazine piece but it didn't have the punch that would appeal to *Daily News* readers. I sent it in anyway.

Before checking out the Masters runners in London, I met up with my friend Laraine. She had astonishing news. While out running on Clapham Common a few weeks before, she had run into David Holt, who was running the 10,000 in Munich for Britain. They'd been dating since; in fact, they had just become engaged. It's always been a fantasy of mine to meet a Heathcliff kind of runner on a sweaty twenty-miler, so this news was too good to be true. When she told me she couldn't afford to come to Munich to see David run, though, I harangued her with no mercy, telling her to sell her fur coat if necessary. "You cannot miss the biggest day in your future husband's life!" I added that we could split our costs by sharing my apartment and food, so she agreed.

David was a member of the Hercules-Wimbledon running club, a name Laraine and I found wonderfully hilarious, and after training with them one evening, we had a great time socializing over tepid shandies (equal parts beer and lemonade). These guys accepted Laraine and me immediately as runners, but we were curiosities in the extreme as marathoners. They wanted to learn more and I wanted them to give me the inside story on women's running in the UK. I told them about how we'd become official in Boston and were hoping to bring British women into the movement, but outside of Dale Greig's 3:27 run in 1964, I didn't know of any British women who ran the marathon. The guys were already supportive from the point of view of equality, because British women had been running for a long time with no discrimination, including no overt discrimination in the marathon. It was just a question of why run a marathon at all when there were so many other wonderful club races and cross-country events. There was also a theory at the time (since disproved) that unless you were someone like their world-beating champion Ron Hill, the marathon was something you did at the end of your career, when you couldn't go fast anymore. When we complained that we saw no one out on the roads, they just laughed. With thousands of miles of beautiful public-access dirt tracks across properties, who needed the hard and dangerous roads?

America actually still had a lot to learn from Britain about setting up convivial, developmental clubs, which is something the Philadelphian Browning Ross was inspired by well over a decade before, when he founded the Road Runners Club of America based on the British system. We also needed to be better about utilizing our massive land space for recreation. I had come to take Posted: No Trespassing as an American standard, and it didn't have to be that way. As for British women in the marathon, it was a great relief to know it was just a matter of opportunity, not politics.

The Masters runners were important because their developmental arc was not dissimilar to the women's, and we were very supportive of one another. We were pioneers in breaking down gender restriction in running, and they were pioneers in breaking down barriers of aging. Just as people told women that we'd never be able to have children if we ran, people said that once you were over forty, you were risking premature death or serious injury if you trained hard, and implied that it was somehow undignified for older people to run. Even those heroic older runners like the sixty-five-year-old John Kelley the Elder in the Boston Marathon had as many critics as fans. This tour was an attempt to make the Masters running movement global.

The other reason the Masters runners were important is that they were the age group I trained with at home and with whom I organized events. I had a lot of good friends on the tour and I wanted to see them. In addition to writing about their venture, I ran a local race with them in Epping Forest (once again being the only woman among three hundred men). I heard their hilarious descriptions of the communal bathtub in the changing room, and at one of the receptions got to meet Sir Roger Bannister, probably our sport's most famous athlete. In 1954, Bannister was the first person to break four minutes in the mile, a feat once considered impossible; ever since I had first heard about him, he'd been one of my heroes. I also thought I'd have a terrific story about him to submit to the *Daily News*.

Meeting the tall, slightly stooped Bannister was a bit of an anti-climax, as it often is when you meet someone you've admired all your life. I actually felt a little sorry for him, as on this particular evening he seemed tired and beleaguered. He was, after all, a busy neurosurgeon with a family at home, and here were all these runners his age who vividly remembered his big moment and wanted to remind him of it, as if Bannister hadn't told his version and heard *their* version a million times.

I decided not to interview Bannister, just listen, and only asked if he still ran. He said rarely, only for fitness, he just didn't have time. I felt sorriest that he couldn't jog a little every day, but he came from a generation and tradition that once you embark on your career, other activities fall away, and he categorically seemed to have no regrets about that decision.

I dutifully wrote up stories about the Masters and about Bannister, hardly scintillating stuff on the eve of the Olympic Games, but in the fullness of time, both very significant for me. I wanted to run into old age with no restriction, and so far I and thousands of others have been able to do that, thanks to the Masters movement and these early movers and shakers. Bannister has continued to inspire me, something he might be surprised to hear. I've always felt very sympathetic toward him—a man who was famous for one thing but actually had to earn his living at another and was expected to be in top form for both. I was not nearly in his league, but I understood this pressure of expectation.

Not surprisingly, just before the Olympic Games, there were no student airfares to Munich, so I had to fly to Paris and take the overnight train across Europe, schlepping baggage the whole way and fending off the midnight perverts who always appear in your second-class train compartment once the lights are dimmed.

Once I arrived, though, the apartment I was renting was too good to be true; it wasn't even a mile from the Olympic Stadium and the athletes' village. Expecting a ramshackle student flat, I couldn't believe my luck at landing a place that tourists, many of whom were commuting hours outside of Munich, would pay a fortune for. There was plenty of room for Laraine. I thanked my mother heartily, as she had arranged this; the generosity that she had shown people in Germany thirty years before seemed to have worked its way down the gratitude pipeline to me.

As I headed over to the press center through the Olympic complex, I was awed by the curved structures, the stunning Plexiglas-and-steel spider web stadium, the color scheme of pale green and baby blue, and the flowers that had been planted everywhere. Every corner in the walkway had either an enticing café with beer and coffee or an oompah-pah band. It was a beautiful, happy place. I had read that the Munich Olympic Organizing Committee was determined to erase every vestige of the 1936 "Nazi" Olympics in Berlin, and to my eye they certainly were making a good job of it.

The press center knocked me out with its soaring ceilings, chrome, modern machines, and most of all, color television sets from every sports venue suspended from the ceilings. You could watch sprinters on the track, swimmers in a pool, horses on the equestrian course all at once. I know it doesn't sound out of the ordinary today, but try to remember that at that time, many people had not even seen color TV. It was clear that price was no object for this enterprise, which was also a way of showing that West Germany was an economic power once again after WWII. This was a huge effort since, even in 1972, there was still war rubble in plenty of towns.

With my testimonial letters from the *Daily News,* I got into the press center, which was not going to be easy once the Games actually started, as by then every legitimate person would have a press pass. If German rules said press accreditation closed in May, there was no way they would be flexible about it in August. Now I had to figure out a way to get into the events and also how to cover them.

The AP office was right there, and some of the guys knew me from Boston. They generously said I could use their equipment and they would transmit for me; in a pinch, I could watch the events on TV. The trick was going to be getting in and out of the press center, so I came up with the ingenious plan of running over to the center in my sweats and telling the guard I was an athlete showing up for an interview. I certainly looked the part, and it worked. Pretty soon the guards would just smile and wave me in, and I transmitted a story nearly every day.

I didn't miss any live events, either, again thanks to the running network. Jim O'Neil, one of the masters from the tour, came to Munich and had a stack of track and field tickets. I offered to buy everything he had. It would take most of my money, but in a flash of inspiration, I felt certain I could scalp the tickets I didn't need for double the value and make enough money to pay for most of my stay in Munich. This was before Olympic organizers made scalping illegal; indeed, it was a time-honored custom, especially if you were from New York.

Jim and his traveling friends were holed up far outside Munich, and when they saw my apartment, they asked to use it as their running base and to take showers between watching events. Laraine arrived from London; immediately David, too, was there, staying as often as he could be away from his team and also bringing along Chris Stewart and a few teammates who needed a place to relax in and an audience for their funny jokes. It relieved a lot of tension; David in particular was getting quieter as the days went on and his race approached. Laraine, too, had a very down day soon after her arrival, as she went to visit Dachau, the remains of the infamous concentration camp, needing to pay respects to her Jewish relatives who had perished in the Holocaust. That seemed a million years ago to us then; we honestly thought the worst thing that could happen here in 1972 was David tripping in his race. In the meantime, the apartment became Running Central, piled high with enough running shoes for an entire cross-country team, a hubbub of happy people, and me clacking busily on the typewriter between the lines of drip-drying shorts and T-shirts.

One evening, I was running back from the press center lost in thought yet again about the women's marathon. That day I'd just transmitted a story about Francie Larrieu, the United States' top prospect for the women's 1,500-meter run, a new addition to the Games and an important event since it was the longest ever distance event for women in the Olympics. I wanted to be more excited about it, but all I could think of was how long it would take for the women's marathon to also be on the program. This trip was supposed to help me figure out how that could happen, and I wasn't getting any closer to a solution. Looking across at the futuristic skyline of the Olympic complex, which glittered at night like an ice palace, I could see above it the powerful neon logos of Mercedes, Coca-Cola, Kodak, and Adidas. I'd never seen this kind of sponsorship wealth and power at a sports event; even the Super Bowl looked like amateur rodeo compared to this. I thought, oh, how insignificant we athletes and our dreams are! We are mere trimmings to these corporate giants who actually run the show.

Then, I swear to God, the penny dropped. It was another pivotal moment in my life, and this time it hit me right between the eyes. This is what makes sports happen! Not ten-dollar wristwatch prizes at the Mini-Marathon or going around to used car dealers and hounding them to sponsor a race trophy. The drivers here are these commercial forces. If we are going to make women's running really happen, at least in my lifetime, it is going to take major commercial sponsorship. With big money we can *create* the events, develop stars, put the events in the public eye—even put the events on TV! Then the Olympic Committee would not only notice, they would want a piece of the action.

It was simplistic, of course, but my thoughts were falling in the right slots. Who's getting the most publicity in marathoning right now?—the women! Why did Johnson's Wax want to sponsor a women's race?—because of the publicity! Johnson's Wax told Fred Lebow they had put $30,000 into the Crazylegs Mini-Marathon, which meant they put in at least $60,000 and they were thrilled to bits with the exposure because $60,000 was nothing compared to what similar advertising would have cost. What I saw on the skyline represented millions. I focused on one logo—IBM—imagining the enormity of the possibility of such a sponsor.

As the time got closer to the semifinals of the 10,000 and David's race, we all tried to stay nonchalant but naturally found ourselves getting drawn deeper into the drama. We were like a little family and wanted to do the right thing. Eventually, we just turned down the noise and didn't say anything about the event at all. We were all runners; the last thing you want to do is talk about it.

By the day of Dave's semifinal, Laraine was in an agitated state herself. We went to the stadium together and watched as David ran very well but he didn't make the final. We left the stadium together feeling morose.

"Boy, no joy in Mudville tonight," I said. That's what my dad always said when everyone was gloomy.

"All that training, all those hopes, poof! His Olympics are over," Laraine said as we shuffled along.

"Maybe in another four years?" I said, hopefully.

"I don't know. Four years is a long time, but I'd hate for him to quit if he had a chance at an Olympics."

"Hey, you know, let's look at it this way. The guy already made an Olympic team—for Great Britain, no less—and that is a really big deal. Then he ran a personal record in an Olympic semifinal, and you can't do better than your best effort."

"Yeah, but will *he* feel like that?"

We prepared ourselves, expecting black clouds of depression, anger, silences—who knows, maybe some tears. By the time the doorbell rang that evening, we were very jumpy.

Instead, David was ebullient. Full of smiles and laughter, he kept hugging Laraine and then flopped on the sofa, arms outstretched, eyes closed, with a big smile on his face and a beer in his hand. He looked ten years younger. Laraine and I were stunned to see how much tension had been tied up in him and now it was over at last. A lifetime of training, fatigue, pressure, and expectation had passed and a new life could begin. Now I could understand what Steve Prefontaine meant when he told me in Oslo, "I can easily see myself becoming a jogger"; at this level of elite performance, these guys know when they've proved themselves, and they don't have to do it anymore. I was really happy for Dave and Laraine, but a bit envious, as I could not foresee a time when I didn't have to keep proving myself.

A couple of days later, at about 6:30 in the morning, we were all awakened by the repeated buzzing of our downstairs door. We'd had a fun late night and were fast asleep; the buzzing went on and on and finally I got up to curse at whoever was ringing the wrong apartment. It was Chris Stewart, out for his morning run, could he please come up. Everyone in the apartment groaned and put pillows on their heads and Chris came in, all sweaty, saying he'd had his run but he couldn't get back into the athletes' village so could he have a shower and stay with us? I'd gone back to bed and mumbled, did you forget your ID card or something, and Chris said, very matter-of-factly, no the army is there and they have blocked all the entrances because terrorists are in the village holding athletes hostage. He made it sound like a minor inconvenience, like a fire drill.

I shot out of bed and began pulling on clothes as fast as I could, grabbing notebook, pen, and shoulder bag, and licking my contact lenses and sticking them in my eyes as I told everyone I'd see them whenever I saw them. I ran down the stairs and out onto the street toward the athletes' village. Halfway there, both sides of the street were lined with olive-colored military trucks with tarpaulin covers, and every few yards were soldiers with automatic rifles slung over their shoulders. When I got to the village entrance, there was a crowd of about seventy people—bewildered volunteers in their now silly-looking pastel outfits, some bored-looking athletes in warm-up suits, and journalists. I was used to seeing rather paunchy affable sports journalists or trim glib TV guys in blue blazers, so these hard-core guys were like none I'd ever seen before—rugged, with deeply lined war-weary faces, cynical eyes, wearing the real-item, well-worn safari jackets. How did these guys get here so quickly from whatever war or famine they were covering?

I walked up to three of them who were talking as if they knew each other—not as friends, exactly, but the way tough professional runners do, who never meet at home, only at an event in another country. They looked to be of three different nationalities and I was right—they were French, American, and English—and none looked like the type that would even have a real home; they looked like they just moved from bunker to bunker. Trying not to sound stupid, I introduced myself and asked what the news was so far.

They explained that some members of al Fatah climbed the village fence during the night and were holding some Israeli team members hostage. Perhaps one has been killed already, they were not sure.

"Why did they bother climbing the fence? Anybody with a warm-up suit could walk right in," I offered. This information seemed of interest to them. I explained how I had circumvented my lack of credentials. Then I asked them to repeat the name of the terrorist organization, which of course confirmed my political and journalistic ignorance.

"They are Palestinian terrorists, who also go by the name Black September," the British journalist said kindly. I'd heard of Black

September but knew I was seriously out of my depth with this kind of reporting.

"So what is the status now?" I asked, trying to be cool.

They all shrugged. "There is no news—we have no access to the scene, and there are no updates."

"It's just like 'Nam," said the American. "Never get any news from the front until it's all over or comes watered down in the general's press release." They all nodded. "So we'll do what we did then, I guess, which is to interview each other." They all chuckled quietly. I was feeling awful; my God, the guts it took just to be Jewish in Germany, and now this. I was feeling awful for the Germans, too, who had tried mightily with these Olympics to overcome their wartime anti-Semitic reputation.

We hung around talking for an hour and then all sensed this was going to be a very long process. The American and the Frenchman drifted away, and the Englishman said, "What are you doing for dinner tonight?" It was weird, out of the blue. My mind was focused on my sadness and inadequacy to help with—or even get information about—a life-and-death drama that was happening just a building away. This skilled journalist could not only stay impersonal in the crisis and wait for the information to break, he covered his bases for food and presumably sex all at the same time. I didn't know if he was being tasteless or just acting like a survivor, but either option left me feeling hollow and wondering if I was really cut out to be a journalist. I left then, too, and headed over to the press center, knowing full well that my friendly guard, should he even be there, would never let me in now. He was on duty, looking pale and terrified, along with some prowling soldiers. I showed him all my papers, but he waved me away.

So now I was quite isolated from information, as any news on radio and TV (neither of which we had in the apartment anyway) was in German. It was disorienting to know I was physically close to the news situation but knew much less about it than the average American watching Jim McKay on ABC-TV back in the States. I finally resorted to watching German TV in hotel lobbies, trying to make sense of the pictures. Finally, pictures of a bombed-out helicopter appeared and the people who had gathered around the set in the lobby slunk away.

"What did they say?" I kept asking anyone who looked like they spoke some English.

Finally someone said, "Zay are deed."

"Who, who are dead?" I said.

"Allis deed," The German shrugged and walked off. Twelve members of the Israeli team had been murdered.

I was gutted. It was all incomprehensible, and worse, it was done on what I believed was a holy altar. During the ancient Olympics, wars were stopped for the Games; in thousands of years there had never been a violation like this. So when it was declared that the Games would continue after a day of mourning, I was very ambivalent. It seemed barbaric to continue, but it seemed equally bad to stop. Cancellation would not bring the Israeli athletes back, and it would be a signal for future terrorists that the Games were a tasty mark. There were also other innocent athletes whose dreams depended on the events continuing. No solution was going to be satisfactory.

When I got back to the apartment, Laraine was packing furiously, saying "I'm getting out of here *now*." There was a telegram from the *Daily News* wanting three hundred first-person words on the scene in Munich. Since I actually knew so little, I could only write about the scene. It seemed so feeble as I phoned it in to my friends at the AP for transmission. It got published, though, and as it turned out, it was the only thing of mine on the whole trip that the *Daily News* did publish.

I wanted to leave, too, but I'd come for the marathon, and it was the last event. I sat in the stadium watching the other finals and followed the progression of the marathon on the big screen. I had no expectation. Not only was I too sad to speculate, but these Games had been wacky. For instance, Steve Prefontaine ran a very gutsy 5,000 and didn't even place. He was beaten by Lasse Virén, a Finn I'd never heard of, who also won the 10,000 in a world-record time, and this after he fell midway, an almost impossible achievement. Jim Ryun, the American hope for the 1500, fell, too, and his Olympic dream was over. Two of our American sprinters missed their finals race because they got the starting time wrong.

Since the marathon is the most unpredictable event of all, I was quietly stunned when Frank Shorter broke from the field and set out on his own. "C'mon, Frank," I whispered, and only when the stadium was in his sight and victory was sure did I stand and shout it. Then a final indignity: A prankster with a fake bib number lurked outside the stadium tunnel and dashed in ahead of Shorter, waving to a tumultuous ovation. I was alarmed; where is the security here?! When the officials finally reached the imposter, the crowd was booing and hissing loudly, which unfortunately was what greeted Shorter as he came into the stadium, and tarnished another dream and another beautiful event.

I stayed until the last finisher dragged himself, injured, into the now empty stadium, and I turned off my watch. Paper cups and old programs were blowing around in a cold wind. Several women would have had respectable finishes even among the men in this race, but that was beside the point. The point was being here and seeing how it could happen. The other point was hurrying to catch the evening train out of here.

For the next four months, I tried to put it all in perspective. I kept moving, traveling all over Europe, criss-crossing from Lausanne to Istanbul, from Athens to Paris, from Dubrovnik to Córdoba to Basel. I stayed with runners and their families and ran in each country, and was invited to many races, almost always being the first woman to run in them. Without fail, the men and the organizers welcomed me into the races; they had been wanting to open their races to women and were happy for me to be the first. In only one race did I cause a problem, which had a happy ending for all, and that was when my hosts in Switzerland, wishing to push for women's inclusion, gave me what turned out to be a fake number for the famous men-only road race from Morot to Fribourg. My duplicate number messed up the scoring system, but when it was sorted out, athletic authorities declared that this was a good lesson for everyone and that it was time to let women run officially. This part was clear.

What was also clear was the wonderful international perspective I was gaining of my sport. With minor cultural differerences, we runners were all the same and liked each other, had the same sore Achilles tendons and the same ambitions. Ours was an astonishing network whose only admittance requirement was that you ran. As a woman, I was totally welcomed, and the sense of equality that I found in even remote running communities had no parallel in any other section of society, even in the United States. Every place I visited, I talked to women who wanted to run and men who were proud to help them.

Whatever I did to inspire them, I am grateful, because by the time I moved on, they were already making their own action plans. I was determined not to forget these people who helped me and our sport so much. I wasn't sure how yet, but I knew I'd find a way.

What was not easy was coming to terms with my personal life. Near the end of my trip, in Athens, I made a private pilgrimage to the small coastal village of Marathon, which would be about as close to a spiritual center for me as anyplace on earth. It is the site of the turning point of civilization, in 490 B.C.E., when 1,500 Athenians supposedly defeated 10,000 invading Persians, and thus saved the concept of democracy. When a messenger ran from Marathon to Athens to bring the news of this victory, the distance was about 25 miles and his heroic run was commemorated 2,400 years later with an historic event in the Olympic Games called the marathon, which is now 26.2 miles long.

The village of Marathon is also a shrine, it is the resting place of the bones of these Greek heroes, and as I sat on the gray beach at Marathon one afternoon looking at the sea, I felt insignificant in their mighty presence. It was late November 1972; in fact, it was Thanksgiving Day in America, and my thoughts drifted to my mother busy in the warm kitchen at home, and I was so homesick I wept. I wept also because my road home was going to be a long one. And I wept for the Israeli athletes.

Nothing, not even sports, seemed simple and pure anymore. The Olympics, despite amateur trappings, were above all a commercial and political event. The only people who were amateurs at the '72 Olympics were the athletes, even those who were getting illegal cash. Women were marginalized the most, both by the lack of events and by cultural restriction. We women had the 1,500-meter run for the first time in the Games—a big breakthrough!—but at this rate, it could be forty years before a women's marathon was added. Yet all over Europe I was meeting women who were running and wanted to run more. Was I just ahead of my time or was I crazy? I could also see how to organize it, to make it happen with money, but what sponsor was going to buy into a nonexistent event?

What about my own running? Was I just going to be a 3:20 marathoner all my life? No, I wanted to be a sub-three-hour one, or to try anyway, or else I'd find myself on a beach at forty wondering what kind of runner I could have been. What about a career? I wasn't going to make enough money as a journalist. I didn't want to settle for a job that had nothing to do with sports, but maybe I'd have to. And what about Tom? The marriage was over, but I still had to end it.

It was indeed a long road. But from this very spot, that messenger, so named Pheidippides, ran to proclaim a victory over enormous odds. I took heart from the old legend as I flagged down a school bus and bounced along with the children back to Athens, and eventually toward home.

CHAPTER | 14

NEW YORK CITY OMO

As the plane took off and climbed above Reykjavik, we could see a huge volcano in Iceland spewing lava against the midnight sky, an occurrence once in a thousand years. This seemed to me a very good omen, confirming that the greatest redeeming thing about being away so long, even with the risk of loneliness and insecurity in distant places, is that you are a live witness to incredible events. You are living it, not getting told about it. Some things, like Munich, were horrifying; some stunning, like this volcano. There is just no substitute for being there.

I needed a good omen, because my post-Olympic European wanderings were over, and I was on my way to New York for an interview at Carl Byoir Associates, the public relations firm whom I worked with at the Crazylegs race. Their slightly battered letter proposing the interview had finally caught up with me as I shivered in the early winter at a runner friend's borrowed and unheated cabin in Switzerland. I was on a cheap flight home on Icelandic Airlines, and in Reykjavik airport's duty-free wool store, I'd bought a beautiful skirt and belt—in 1973, a woman did not show up for a job interview in slacks. I had just enough money to get the bus to my friend Jane's apartment, and with a blouse and boots borrowed from her, I looked great. But the interview never took place. The female executive who was to see me had perished a few days earlier in a small-plane crash during an African safari, exactly the kind of accident that could so easily have happened to me on my low-budget European journeys. Their office was numb, and I was unneeded, out of work, out of prospects, and out of money. The loneliness and insecurity were not over.

I temped as a secretary, interviewed search firms, and called every newspaper contact I knew for freelance assignments. That meant I desperately needed my little Smith-Corona typewriter, which meant an encounter with Tom. When we met at his midtown commuter bus stop, he had a request before he handed over the typewriter. He wanted my signature on a tax form, to certify that I had been his "dependent" for the last year. I felt disgusted with him. I'd half-starved for years trying to support him, and here he was gloatingly saving a few tax dollars on the fiction that he had supported me. But I needed the typewriter, so I signed.

"So when are you coming back?" he said.

Oh boy, here it comes, right on Lexington Avenue.

"Tom, I wrote to you. I'm not coming back. I want a divorce."

"I'm never ever giving you a divorce. The Church does not recognize divorce, you know that."

"Well, an annulment then. The Church sure recognizes *that*. Honestly, I'd help work toward that for you."

The bus to Riverdale drove up and people started to get in.

"That just shows, once again, what *you* know about the Catholic Church!" he said. "Thanks a *lot*. You've just condemned me to *hell*." He got on the bus, the door closed, and it pulled away. Wow, what a curtain-closer.

In case you are interested, getting married is a lot easier than getting unmarried, and if you have no money, getting a divorce is very difficult.

My father, meaning the best for me, made things even more difficult, by pressing me to come home and find a job in Washington. When I told him the jobs I wanted were in New York, he exploded into a tirade against the city and its dirt and degradation. I'd never defied my father before, never suffering the years of angst and resentment toward parents that many of my friends had. But now I said no and hung up the phone. I was shaking. Now I was really on my own. But I was on my own in every marathon I ran and I had been alone all over Europe, and for years I was the sole supporter of Tom and myself, so I could do it.

One of the first calls I made was to Philip. He was so happy to hear from me that he canceled a lunch date with Neil Armstrong, the first astronaut to step on the moon. At that time, Philip was director of public relations for the American Institute of Aeronautics and Astronautics, and had had similar jobs with airline companies. We began seeing each other—quite tentatively at first, since the last thing I was interested in was a committed relationship—and he didn't mind meeting me late for a burger and a beer after training. We had lively and creative conversations. Philip had been a very good club tennis player and a near-success as an opera singer. I was flattered that an older, accomplished guy was so interested in me. He knew nothing about running, but he understood the level of commitment it takes to be good at something really difficult. He respected my running, admired it, and was curious about it. And his urbane manner and saturnine good looks were compelling. So while he encouraged my running, I overlooked his smoking, his copious drinking, and his tendency (especially after drinking) to express a lacerating and unkind wit. Philip was new and, even in his dark moods, exotic.

The New York Road Runners and Fred, now the president, were, however, reassuringly familiar. The trip that Nina and I had won six months before to Guayanilla, Puerto Rico, was only a month away, and the invitation had been extended to four other women, so we now had a team of six. Fred asked me to organize the trip. This was another Fred business specialty; he asked whoever was most immediate to do the job for him. Don't get me wrong, he always asked in a flattering way that made you feel invaluable to the success of the project. So I dived in, wondering what would have happened if I had stayed in Europe. Even unpaid and time-consuming, working on anything to do with running was a lot more fun than the boring temporary secretary work anyway.

Besides, Fred had a full-time job himself, and the Road Runners Club was growing wildly. Most evenings, after work and training, Fred would hold court in the Brasserie, a restaurant on East Fifty-third Street. It was *his* place, and because it was a block from his rent-controlled apartment, it was like an extension of his dining room. Every night, or at least the nights I was there, he would look over the menu and then always order the same thing—scrambled eggs, which were not on the menu—because he was a vegetarian. "Fred! For God's sake, you can cook scrambled eggs yourself for five cents!" I'd say.

"Yes," he answered, "but I like being waited on." Fred would always carry a sloppy manila folder with papers jammed into it, and every night he'd have a new report on the rapidly increasing membership of the New York Road Runners Club. It was growing by the hundreds!

It is no exaggeration to say that almost everyone who ran in New York in those days was actively involved in the club. Fred stumped for volunteers like a politician and pressed them into service by making them feel what they contributed was not just important but essential for the growth of the organization. Honest to God, he made you feel downright guilty if you were not part of the effort. Fred had the ability to find out quickly what people were good at and to pull something unique out of them, and this was a great gift, considering that the people involved were the oddest assortment of characters you could imagine. Everyone had a role and no one was left out at the Road Runners. One of the best things Fred did was to enlist old-time runners whose fame had long since faded into regulars—as coaches, organizers, and registrars. Wonderful people like Kurt Steiner and Joe Kleinerman became the revered stalwarts of the club, teaching us newbies our running history and giving us the benefit of decades of their own experience. I had an automatic in with Steiner and Kleinerman since they had raced with Arnie, and Arnie loved to have me call him in Syracuse from time to time and tell him the latest about the club and his old pals.

Like everyone else, I threw myself into the exciting activities of the organization. It's hard to imagine now how we made the time, with jobs, kids, and all the training we were doing. Most of us were pushing more than sixty miles a week; an incredible amount of mileage when you consider that today, runners think thirty-five is a big week. We had a sense of mission and self-discovery as we pushed ourselves faster and farther, and we had a sense of sharing and zeal as we built an organization that was a hub for a shared passion. We loved to run, and the world thought we were nuts, but at last we had an organization that understood and encouraged us. In reality, this club only existed in spirit and on Fred's messy kitchen table. It was amazing.

We also were becoming very cool. Among the sleek go-getters, running was the new "it." You wanted to be a part of every new event created, as you knew for sure that each of these races was making some kind of history. There were not a lot of runners on the Central Park roads or the path around the reservoir those nights, but every time you passed one, there was a clear understanding as you made all-knowing eye contact: I don't even know you but I know that I can trust you with my life.

During the several weeks that I crashed at Jane's on East Eighty-fourth Street, I would run in Central Park every evening. Everyone said Central Park was a dangerous place then, especially at night, and thirty years later they still say that. But when else could you run? In the winter, it was dark by four thirty, and a few of us figured that the more people there were running, the less dangerous it would be. That's what I told myself, anyway. Some people ran indoors at the McBurney or Vanderbilt Y, but indoor laps on a small dusty track was my vision of hell. Besides, muggers in the 1970s were knocking people over right in the streets; they didn't have to hang around in Central Park for penni-less joggers they'd have to chase.

Every weekend, I ran a different road race. New York was like having a built-in family and cornucopia of events just a few blocks away. If I couldn't jog or take the subway to the start of a race, then someone always had car space they'd share—usually it was Fred and his little green Fiat, which doubled as the pace vehicle for almost every race anyway.

The thing I have always liked best about runners is the cama-raderie. There are no secrets among people who run together. Call it endorphins freeing inhibition or the simple need to share a new idea, but we told each other everything and kept every secret. Post-race was always a good time for vigorous discussion, and one cold Sunday, Nina, Fred, and I all ran the Earth Day Marathon on Long Island (it had moved from Central Park in 1973), and followed it with a convivial post-race gathering. The talk went on to how the marathon in particular gives you strength and determination in all areas of your life, not just running.

Our male friends concurred. They were happy that running gave women this independence. I think they were among the first men who not only sensed that women deserved freedom, but they wanted to take it home to their wives. Threatened? Heck, no, *relieved*. Anyway, they all knew that Nina and I had both recently separated from our husbands and they agreed with us that after doing a marathon, you feel you have the courage to do anything difficult, even get a divorce.

We even came up with a married couple's theory: If a man starts running and the woman doesn't, the marriage can survive. If both the man and the woman start running the marriage will probably be a lot better. But if the woman starts running and the man doesn't, it will never last. We all laughed. Gerald Eskenazi, a reporter for the *New York Times*, was there covering the race, and he found the mind of the marathoner a more curious and marvelous subject than the competition. The subject of running as an empowering awakening for women was a fascinating subject for the *Times*.

The next day, the *Times* ran Eskenazi's story with the unprecedented and eye-catching sports headline, "2 Women Marathoners Abandon Marital Route." The article stirred Tom to decisive action. His boss saw it and recommended that he cut me off at the pass by suing me for abandonment. I tried not to sound too delighted, happily gave up all claims to property except my clothes and the car (all of which I had paid for), and one morning at six, the apartment door-bell rang and divorce papers were thrust in under the chain. Big Tom was out of my life. He was to reappear briefly in 1982 when he requested an annulment that would free him in the eyes of the church to (re)marry. I did not hear of him again until the news of his sudden death from a heart attack in 1992 at the age of forty-nine. By then, he was a successful and very wealthy businessman, a husband and father, he was in shape (he died while bicycling), and he was apparently happy, all things he had failed to find while he was with me. It seemed very much for the best that I was out of Tom's life and he out of mine. But he will always be part of my story.

CHAPTER | 15

"WHY WOULD ANYONE WANT TO
PAY US MONEY TO SPONSOR OUR
MARATHON?"

Guayanilla was an unlikely place for the first international women's 10K road race in history, more about macho than the kind of sensitive New Age guys we were used to in the American running community. The women's event was a sort of precursor to Puerto Rico's really big annual running event held the next weekend, the San Blas Half-Marathon, which hosted the best runners in the world as well as thousands of local men and boys. I really wanted to run the longer event, too, but hesitated pushing the local culture too far.

It was New Jersey's 160-mile-a-week, tree-trunk-legs Tom Fleming who convinced me to do it when he secured a room for me with the American family who were hosting him and the other American guys—Jeff Galloway and Jon Anderson—in San Blas. Tom was like a big enthusiastic kid, and I regarded him as a kind of little brother; thanks to him, I now felt set for both races.

The U.S. team for Guayanilla was Katy Schilly, eighteen, from Syracuse; the phenom Kathy Schrader, fourteen, from Schenectady; Nina Kuscsik, thirty; Anita Scandurra, twenty; Diane Andrade, twenty-one; and me, twenty-six, all from New York. Nina and I stressed that Puerto Rico was not a progressive place for women and we would all have to behave ourselves. We wore suitably conservative but spiffy red, white, and blue tunic uniforms, made by Katy's seamstress mother. It seemed to us that all the unmarried women in Puerto Rico were slim and flagrantly sexy, while all the married women were overweight and wore pink hair curlers. They were our biggest critics, convinced that racing would prevent us from having babies. Nina laughed and said she had three already and that was enough.

Let me tell you it was hot, and the race didn't start until some insane time like three in the afternoon, just when the heat and humidity were at their worst. Not that it would have made much difference; all of us had come from a cold winter, and this steam bath was pretty overwhelming. But we were confident of a team title and knew time was not terribly important. It was an out-and-back course, and at the turnaround it was Kathy, Diane, Katy, Nina, Anita, then a Puerto Rican woman, and then me. Try as I might, I was not going to catch the Puerto Rican. I felt bad that it was me who was going to screw up a mainland sweep, but I thought how great she was feeling being the one who broke up the mainland team! About 300 meters from the finish, as we were all going just as hard as we could go, I numbly realized I had passed Nina, who was kind of running sideways. I looked back in time to see her legs buckle under her as she fell into the crowd. I figured the best thing I could do was cross the finish line where there would be help and dash back to Nina, which I did, grabbing an official as I crossed and circling back outside of the crowd. When I got there, she already was being loaded into the back of an ambulance. I jumped in the back with her and we had one of those siren rides to the hospital. Heat exhaustion had knocked her out like a light. The doctors kept her in the hospital for a couple of days just to be sure she was okay, and she was, but it was an eye-opening experience for me. I'd seen plenty of heat exhaustion and it always seemed there was a warning, but this was so sudden.

I suppose there was an awards ceremony, but I can't remember, because I was at the hospital. What I do recall the next day as most of the others left to go back to New York, was that a very polite and very well-groomed delegation of men from the race committees of Guayanilla and San Blas came to ask if I was planning to run San Blas, as they'd heard.

I explained that I wanted to do it, was capable and that as women on the mainland were already official in all distances, I didn't see that there was a problem.

But they did. Politely, they asked me to change my mind. They were not opposed to women's running; it was just that there was an old chap who ran the race every year, "kind of like your Johnny Kelley in the Boston Marathon," and they were afraid that I would beat him in the race.

"I think I will beat a lot of men," I said. "I really can't apologize for that. We need to explain somehow that I'm not doing this to beat the men, but to run this great race and hopefully encourage other women to run. Besides, sooner or later, another woman will run it, and I'm here now!" I suggested a photo op, with the old guy and me shaking hands. Since it was clear I was doing it, officially or not, the committee to their enormous credit issued me a number. The radio and newspapers went into full swing: A woman will run San Blas for the first time!

While I was never one of the guys there, I was welcomed at all the meals and functions and was stunned to see the dining hall filled with legendary international athletes. They were mildly surprised to see a woman there, but none of them made a big deal about it. Our hosts provided touristy things for our entertainment, and one day they took us to a cockfight. I knew it would be unpleasant to watch, but I had an anthropological curiosity about seeing something that was banned on the mainland; it is not often you have permission to witness something that is illegal elsewhere. It was also interesting to see the reaction of the other athletes. Lasse Virén and Olavi Suomalainen, from Finland, were completely impassive. Fleming caught my look and made a face that said, "This is really weird." But the best was Ben Jipcho from Kenya; his eyes were huge and terrified, popping right out of his face. Poor guy, he had no idea we were going to a cockfight.

Come race day, I wasn't nervous in the slightest; my only anxiety as usual was the unexpected, like getting diarrhea in such a public place, but that was not a problem. The problem was the crowd. Thousands of spectators had begun arriving days ahead of time, setting up tents and barbecues all along the grassy slopes beside the race route, which went from Cuomo to San Blas, and I knew that they had all heard about the woman in the race. They had been drinking all day—some of them for three days—in the hot sunshine. Wild with excitement and participatory zeal, by the time I came along in the race, at least two minutes a mile after the leaders, they had nearly filled the road. I was surrounded by male runners, but we had to run packed shoulder to shoulder to negotiate the chute left open in the road for us.

"*Gringa, gringa, gringa!*" the crowd screamed when they saw me. Told to water down the runners in the heat, spectators would run alongside shouting "*Agua, agua, agua!*" and hand me a paper cup. I would drink—inevitably it was a piña colada or a daiquiri. "This is going to be a great race!" I thought. Sometimes they got so excited they simply threw whatever drink they had in their hands all over me; soon I reeked of beer, was sticky with coconut syrup, and had specks of lime pulp all over me. As I came around a curve, a man saw me and got so overwhelmed that he heaved a whole bucket of water right in my face; he staggered and almost knocked me over. The heat, sweat, and booze dripping in my eyes blurred the colors of this packed crowd; it was like running inside a Monet painting, a long linear Impressionist vision.

I became aware of a runner alongside; he'd been there a while, a young Puerto Rican man, I could tell by his thin tan forearms and as yet unlined hands. (You often come to know runners in a long race only by their fingertips.) He'd be there, and then he'd drift back, and then he'd be there again, our shoulders and elbows brushing occasionally. We passed a few miles like this, ascended a particularly steep hill, and suddenly, at the top, he veered to the side of the road and collapsed on the grass. As I ran on, I realized he'd been struggling to keep up with me because I was a girl, and I felt sorry from the bottom of my heart that he'd taken it all so seriously.

The last mile of the race was total madness. I'd somehow taken on a motorcycle police escort, which was supposed to part the sea of spectators and clear the way for the finish. Instead, it came to a dead stop in the crush. I had to climb over the back of the bike and kind of hop off the front, straight-arming the crowd in front of me. There was no danger, just a kind of Mardi Gras silliness. It wasn't just me; the elite men had the same problem!

Colombia's Victor Mora was the repeat winner, which thrilled the locals, who claimed as one of their own anyone who spoke Spanish. Mora deserved to win—he not only ran tactically well, he ran ferociously, attacking the hills and incautious of the heat. He also savored the drama of the race, and the crowd loved it. It was the first time I'd seen a runner "do a Hollywood," since most of us, particularly we Nordic types, were raised to be modest, giving at most a little wave to the crowd. Mora worked them like an opera diva.

While the women's 10K in Guayanilla was a nice festival, even Puerto Rican officials could see that it was San Blas's welcome and invitations to women in the ensuing years that made the biggest change for women's running there. Over the years, the San Blas field of invited women was never as deep as the men, but that's okay. Organizers are allowed their emphases, and besides, there is now a race in Puerto Rico called the World's Best 10K, where as many top women are invited as men, and the prize money is massive. In fact, Paula Radcliffe set a 10K world record of 30:21 there in 2003.

It was fulfilling to be an innovator, but it didn't pay. Back in New York, I was still just temping and not earning enough money to live on. Then, I got a lucky assignment: *Argosy* magazine wanted me to go fishing in Florida with the great baseball player Ted Williams. Williams was notoriously irascible and had sent two previous reporters packing. *Argosy* was desperate for the story and I was desperate for the money so I told them, sure, I could fish, I mean, how difficult could it be?

I got doubly lucky when my novice first cast landed right in front of a humdinger bonefish lying still and long and silvery in the aqua glare. It sprang onto my line.

"She's got a hit! She's got a hit! Get the net," shouted Williams to the boat driver; I had netted the biggest fish I had ever seen alive. I stayed outwardly calm, but inwardly I was saying, "Thank you, God, thank you, God." It established me with Williams as a real athlete, so for three days we fished and bantered and sparred over many subjects. On baseball, Williams talked as if it were poetry.

Once again, I had been able to relate to another athlete on equal terms, without being intimidated, even though he was one of the greatest baseball players of all time, and a skilled fisherman. Athletes are all alike—we work hard, we sweat, and we try our best. Ted Williams saw that and trusted me. I wrote a terrific story and earned $500.

At last I could afford the down payment on a sublet rental on East Twenty-ninth Street next to a fire station, which gave me some sense of security in an insalubrious neighborhood. The firemen cheered and wolf-whistled me every night after work when I set out on my run, and cheered me home again. I was glad they kept an eye out for me, because now I was running in a different part of the city.

I would run down to Twenty-third Street, cross the FDR Drive, and run along the path bordering the East River, going under the Williamsburg, Manhattan, and Brooklyn bridges, sometimes all the way down to the Battery and the Staten Island Ferry. This area was adjacent to what was then some of the worst crime areas of Manhattan and since my runs inevitably ended in the dark, I always clipped a can of pepper-spray dog repellent to my waistband. But there was usually nobody there. Sometimes a man would be walking a very large, mean-looking dog ("Please hold him back, mister!" I'd shout as some foamy-mouthed Hound of the Baskervilles tried to lunge at me) and once a very fat flasher on a park bench waved his tiny limp member at me and called, "Hey, I'd bet you'd like this." I laughed so hard I got a side cramp.

Mostly those nights were quite magical; they had a beauty at night that masked what was a very ugly area during the day. Half of the lamps on the promenade were broken, but there was a mass of twinkling lights from the Brooklyn side of the river, from the Rheingold Beer sign and from the strings of fairylike lights draping the bridges. My way was illuminated as if I were surrounded by the moon and stars. They even made all the broken glass along the promenade sparkle like frost, a nice fantasy on the hottest summer night. The river has a ferocious current, and at night you could see it rushing, black and menacing, very close to the promenade. Then it would swirl into eddies around the massive bridge abutments, which would loom above as high and dark as skyscrapers. It made me a little dizzy. The cold rush of air under the bridges had a scary, wet dungeon smell, and the noise of the traffic overhead was magnified by clanging echoes; I never liked it under the bridges and sprinted through those parts. Sometimes I'd run through the old Fulton Fish Market, nearly getting knocked over by the stench, and at other times not minding the smell of honest work. Farther along there would be a cozy glow and raucous laughter coming out of a dive called Sloppy Louie's, which I suppose was a pretty rough joint but where I imagined they had good oysters and cold beer. On those nights, I knew I'd run long enough when I moved further and further away from the river railing as I thought somehow the whirlpools might suck me in.

I don't know if any of these old places still exist, which I guess is a good thing since the whole area has been renovated with the shops and restaurants of the South Street Seaport. And of course now there are runners everywhere, day and night. But those nights, it was only me, the river and the twinkling lights.

Argosy gave me more freelance assignments. I even began to get personal letters from readers, especially notable were some in penitentiaries who would write to me about their maps for hidden treasure and offer to split the take with me in the far future—like sixty years—when they were eligible for parole.

I had a more practical glimpse of part of my future when I interviewed Curt Gowdy Sr., the veteran radio and then TV broadcaster. I learned from him that no good athlete, and no good broadcaster, however famous, just shows up and performs. They all do their homework and preparation. Five years later I'd be using this lesson as I began my first foray into TV broadcasting. Amazingly, ten years later, when I was commentating for ABC-TV, my boss was Gowdy's son, Curt Gowdy Jr.

I also did some unpaid writing for the early running magazines. The editors of these publications were both friends and heroes to me, especially Browning Ross at *Long Distance Long*, Joe Henderson at *Runner's World*, and Europeans Noel Tamini at *Spiridon* and Manfred Steffny at *Condition*. They were like gold to us, those magazines. They were our news, our network, and our sense of history. *Athletics Weekly* was the sport's bible in the UK, and in this era they were all growing as fast and enthusiastically as the number of runners.

One evening I was animatedly telling Philip about the fishing trip and the race in San Blas and how different the attitude was between Ted Williams, who was a well-paid athlete for many years, and those at San Blas who were all poor and had a short competitive life. It just wasn't right; the amateur system really was poison to runners. It was very difficult for anyone to get to a race like San Blas and make their name known in the first place; they had to get known before they got an invitation. I must have been on some kind of post-run high, because I told him what had dawned on me in Munich, how I wanted to remedy that with creative sponsorship.

I wasn't even thinking of women at that point, I was just thinking of the sport as a whole. I kept going—maybe it was the wine we were drinking—and told him about an idea I had while I was in Greece. Since the original marathon, as it were, was Greek, wouldn't it be a great publicity idea for Olympic Airways, the national carrier of Greece, to sponsor the fledgling New York City Marathon and then fly the winner to Athens to run in the Marathon-to-Athens race? That way, a runner would get an international trip and get noticed, Olympic Airways would get promotion on both sides of the Atlantic, and the New York Road Runners Club would get a real budget for the marathon.

I expected Philip to smile at my naïveté, but he thought it was a fabulous idea. Having worked with foreign airlines himself, he knew how difficult it was to get good New York visibility. It's such a winner, he said, that he would set up a meeting for me with the director of public relations for Olympic, whom he knew. Okay, I said, great, just give me a couple of days first to talk to Fred Lebow about it.

The next night, I met Fred at the Brasserie and excitedly told him about my idea. Fred furrowed his brow.

"I don't get it," he said. "Why would anyone want to pay us money to sponsor our marathon?"

"Fred! For heaven's sake, for the publicity! You remember Crazylegs last year. Look at all the publicity they got."

"Yeah, but that was their race. This is the New York City Marathon. What kind of publicity will they get from that?"

"Plenty, Fred. You'll see, they'll be delighted. But first we have to work up a budget, then convince them to sponsor it."

Fred said he needed at least $3,000. I said we should double that, since we'd need new banners, special bib numbers, and trophies with the name Olympic on them. I also wanted a finish line tape with the sponsor's name on it so it would be sure to make it into the newspaper photos. This was a particularly ingenious idea at the time, when the news media did everything possible to cut out a sponsor's name. Eventually, we couldn't make this last item. We thought the tape had to be broken, plastic was too tough, and to print a roll of paper with repeat Olympic Airways as a one-time print job cost too much money. Too bad, since this proved to be the best of all the media ideas. It only occurred to us later that the tape could be made of anything and one of the two people holding it could just drop it and achieve the same effect. In any case, we knew we were onto something hot: if we gave the sponsor more value in visibility than the cost of the sponsorship, we were both ahead.

At that time, Olympic Airways was owned by Aristotle Onassis, who had married Jacqueline Kennedy a few years earlier. Jackie's best friend and college roommate, Nancy Tuckerman, who also had been Jackie's social secretary at the White House, was now director of public relations for Olympic. I was very uncomfortable with glitterati and people whom I suspected had gotten their jobs through favoritism, so it was a delight to find Nancy Tuckerman a thoroughly nice and effective person. She and Olympic's general manager loved the marathon idea, agreed to sponsor it, and asked if I'd help with PR on a consultant basis. This was what I always wanted to do, and for the first time I was going to get paid something for it.

Unfortunately, it wasn't enough money for me to quit being a temporary secretary a few days a week, and being a temp meant you didn't have time during the day to work the phones calling journalists or write press releases. Plus, Boston was coming up! I thought that maybe out of respect for the race I shouldn't run it since I wasn't in such great shape. On the other hand, we'd worked so hard to get women official status that I didn't want to show disrespect by not being there on this second official occasion. I had the base, the distance was not a problem; I just wasn't going to be as sharp as I would have liked. No matter what, Boston was a part of what I was, and I didn't want to miss it.

Both Jock and Will had exchanged increasingly friendly letters with me over the past year. They'd come to realize that we women runners were not using Boston as a feminist platform, that we trained hard because we liked to run and were athletes who believed with all our hearts in the beauty of the marathon event. In hindsight, I can imagine that they were denigrated for a number of years by the media and by feminist organizations who branded them old curmudgeons. This was a bad rap for two dedicated and sincere guys who had pulled together for years to keep the Boston Marathon afloat. When they realized we women runners were for real and respected them, they were really grateful.

So I showed up at the starting line in Hopkinton as usual. As defending champion, Nina was to take the one women's spot on the start line and I was next in line behind her, due to my third place the previous year. (Elaine Pederson, who was second in '72, wasn't running.) There were more cameras and helicopters than ever. A big cherry picker holding a TV cameraman hung high above the start line. It was hot, and there was Jock, going ballistic as usual, shouting at the runners and pushing those who had a higher number back off the start line. I was feeling a little less kindly to him right then, as he was indeed formidable when he was out of control.

Then he spotted me and grabbed me around the shoulders and I let out a little cry, thinking for a moment that he was going to hit me. But instead he flashed a big grin and turned me toward the cameras with his arm around me and said, "C'mon lass, let's get a wee bit o' notoriety." And then he planted a big kiss on my cheek. It happened in a split second and I was stunned. The cameras whirred and clicked. Jock's eyes twinkled. People have all kinds of ways of asking for forgiveness. I smiled back, and then it was time to run.

We'd had a warning about the heat—temperatures had been rising for the last two weeks. I'd learned from my stupid getup the year before to wear the minimum, so before I left for Boston I bought a lightweight red nylon dance tunic that was friction free and opaque even when wet. It was one of the best running outfits I've ever had, and I'm amused to see that similar apparel is now fashionable in women's running. At the time though, I took plenty of chiding about my outfits from people who thought I was just being too cute, which always infuriated me. Here we women were inventing a sport for ourselves and why we should adopt the male uniform of shorts and singlet, which was not functional for us and was highly unflattering anyway was beyond me.

With the heat slowing everyone, and with no expectation for once of a personal record, I had absolutely no pressure. It was my first and last fun-filled Boston. Nina, however, was favored. We'd all heard that a young speedster named Jacqueline Hansen who trained out in California with the famous coach Laszlo Tabori was in the race, and to us, she might be the next evolutionary step in the women's marathon. We'd always said someone was going to come along who was track trained and would put her speed talent together with endurance training, and presumably here she was. (We didn't know it until later, but she had won the 1972 collegiate title by running the mile in 4:54.) She zipped by me going down Main Street in

Hopkinton wearing gingham terry-cloth shorts; her legs were utterly fantastic, and I knew I was witnessing the next generation of women's running.

All along the route, the spectators were out in force with hoses and buckets. It would be years yet before Boston would organize water stations, so the spectators set up all kinds of sprinklers and tables of their own. At the top of Heartbreak Hill, I met Fred Lebow walking; he was drinking a cup of water and looked annoyed. He said his feet were blistering; with six miles to go and no ride to the finish, it's a desperate feeling. I insisted on pouring cold water over his feet. At first he screamed in protest—everyone said then and still do now that this will make your socks wet and cause blisters, but in my experience it is the buildup of heat that causes blisters, and cold water stops the heat. Besides, your socks are wet with sweat anyway—if you even wore socks. In those days, socks were so ropey and useless that I taped my feet and went barefoot in my shoes. Fred felt better immediately; and started running again and eventually finished the race. Everyone was dumping cold water over our feet, our heads, our bodies. It was like going from a hot beach into a cool lake, and every time we watered down we got a rush of coolness and felt better.

Up ahead of us, I wasn't to know it, but Tom Fleming was battling it out with our old teammates from San Blas, Jeff Galloway, Jon Anderson, and last year's winner, Olavi Suomalainen. Tom's incredible mileage made him confident coming into Boston, a race he desperately wanted to win, but he naively didn't cover Jon Anderson's move at seventeen miles. He couldn't catch up and lost. Oh, was Tom annoyed with himself!

I was astonished that I finished in 3:20:30, in fourth place. It was my fastest time so far at Boston! Even with the heat and my overweight body, I had not lost as much fitness as I'd thought, and it sparked again my desire to train to run a sub-three-hour marathon. Jacqueline Hansen did indeed win the race, in 3:05:59, which set an official course record time and was only 52 seconds slower than Sara Mae Berman's unofficial course record of 1970. What was especially remarkable was that Jacqueline did it in the heat and in only her second attempt at the distance. Nina Kuscsik was not far behind, in 3:06:29, which was also her fastest time so far in Boston, but not indicative of her talent and fast times from New York. After her experience in Puerto Rico, she was very careful with the heat, too. As always in a marathon, we wondered what we could do if we had enough training, sleep, no pressure, and perfect weather. It was every marathoner's dream.

The next day, the *New York Times* ran the photo of Jock Semple hugging me at the start line, with the caption explaining how he was the man who had been against women competing. I was sorry they printed this picture and not one of Jacqueline or Jon winning the race, but that's what the *Times* specializes in—a big story told in one memorable image. It was the end of an era and the photo has since been included in many books about Boston and women's history in general.

I had no time for my usual postpartum Boston slump. There were a lot more races that spring—not just those in New York, but full marathons in France, Syracuse, Terre Haute—and I felt obligated to honor the invitations. One, in Hluboká, in what was then Czechoslovakia, was particularly important because it would be my first actual race in a communist country and I had promised both the race director and Noel Tamini, the editor of *Spiridon*, that I would attend. Tamini had been generous in finding me hospitality all over Europe, and I returned the favor as much as possible by writing for him and by getting publicity for his friends' races by running in them. Thus, at the same time, we all helped build a base of women's running in Europe.

Hluboká was a small village that knocked itself out for their annual road race. They had no resources, and we all wanted to help. For weeks they had been building the hype about the American woman who would grace their event. I had to scramble for airfare sponsorship and the appropriate visa, despite discouragement from the Immigration and Naturalization Service.

I'd spent enough time in Eastern Europe on my trip to know that parts of it were sad and gloomy, but that was all the more reason to help these people who were doing their best to promote running. In many ways, the women there needed an inspiring role model more than anywhere else. I confess that I did not tell my parents about this trip, and Arnie was very nervous about it, as it was behind the Iron Curtain, and therefore considered a dangerous destination. But I knew there was no need to be afraid. These small-town people, so very poor, welcomed me like a queen and seemed to give me every-thing they had. If running gave me so much pride and made me feel so free, I knew it would do wonders for those who were otherwise trapped, and I was very glad to make the effort.

But I was sure tired. I was the busiest person I knew and didn't even have a real job. I was offered several, but I was still holding out for one that was sports-related. Finally, all my interviews and chasing down leads paid off. I got an offer from AMF, a big sports equipment conglomerate that was looking for a generalist who could write press releases and stories as well as organize events as part of their trans-formation into a glamorous leisure company with products that included Hatteras Yachts and Head Skis.

On the opposite side of the country, another obscure company that was also looking for recognition had just adopted the brand name Nike. This, too, was the beginning of a new era, as well as the end of an old one.

Chapter | 16

And this was just the beginning.

Well, it was mostly the end of an old era, anyway. My boss at AMF confessed a year or so later that he had been able to hire me at a much lower salary than a man with the same skills, a left-handed compliment that nowadays someone could be sued for. Since AMF was located in suburban White Plains, and everything cool was happening in Manhattan, I was glad I'd insisted on a salary of $13,000, $2,000 above his offer. It meant I could continue to live in Manhattan, and for the first time in a while I wouldn't feel that I was just scraping by.

I could hardly believe it—a full-time sports-based job with a Fortune 500 company, my own sleek office, secretarial help, and a health plan. It was bliss, even though after taxes my sublet was more than half of my salary. Luckily, I also had the freelance work, and at the office I had my own IBM self-correcting typewriter and access to a copy machine. This was very hot stuff in those days, and it allowed me to do freelance work during lunch or after my boss had left for the day.

I didn't want to admit it, but the job was much better for my running, too, since I ran in White Plains right after work and went home in my running clothes. I felt a lot safer. There were miles of long, beautiful, traffic-free streets in White Plains, with street lamps, gorgeous homes, and golf courses.

The running was so good I was actually beginning to think about leaving the city altogether when a fire at my apartment house prompted a different move. I came home to find everything, including my new clothes, covered in black greasy smoke and the apartment unlivable for a few days. Philip, who had already started to say he loved me, jumped at the opportunity for me to stay with him. I knew it was a risk, but I needed a place to stay, and I convinced myself that it would be for only a few days.

Of course, what happened is that we had a lot of fun living together, became a romantic item, and soon it didn't seem to make sense to live apart even though I really didn't want the obligations of living with someone. It's a nice trade-off to have someone expecting you, and sharing a Manhattan rent has lured many couples into living together. The danger is that you can't afford to be single again! That was just one of the problems ahead, but I was happy enough and Philip was ecstatic; frankly, it felt awfully good to be adored and fussed over for just about the first time in my adult life.

I also loved the routine of going to work again; especially that morning moment when, coffee in hand, you sit at your own desk, in your own office, settle into work and are launched and cranking. One of the best things about my job was my counterpart, Ted Smits, the retired sports editor of the AP. AMF had snagged Ted at age seventy-five, and by then he'd been to every Olympics since 1948, knew every newspaper and magazine editor in New York, and loved gourmet food. "Uncle Ted" mentored me; I got to know his many wonderful and powerful contacts, how to order food and wine, and how to jump on a story and write quickly to deadline. Ted loved my running—indeed, he'd covered my 1967 Boston for the AP—and his contacts all began to follow my career, and hence marathon running, with great interest. This, along with initiatives of my own, was a huge boost with the Olympic Airways sponsorship of the NYC Marathon coming up.

One of my boldest moves came one morning when I just happened to see Gene Shalit on the *Today* show as I was getting ready for work. He struck me as someone who would love the romantic and somewhat wacky idea of a New York City Marathon, so I impetuously wrote to him before I lost my nerve, suggesting myself as a guest for the show, since my purpose was to get the Olympic Airways mention on the air. Much to my surprise, I was immediately invited to appear. It was such a hit! Shalit and I shared a passion for the history of the marathon and that enabled me to explain why Olympic Airways from Greece was sponsoring the event, and how we were sending the winner to the "original" Marathon-to-Athens race. The segue was so natural it didn't even sound like a commercial reference, and Olympic was thrilled. It threw open the floodgates, as other media became interested. We had a ton of publicity and Fred Lebow was beside himself with excitement. Now Fred wanted to find sponsors for everything. Another new era was dawning.

But first we had to get a good field together. The top women like Nina and me were a given, so the challenge was the men's field, especially because it was a man who would win the air ticket prize to Athens. Nina and I accepted this. There were not enough women to make it a real race, and besides, the marathon in Athens wouldn't welcome women yet anyway; I knew because I'd applied the year before when I was in Europe and I was politely declined. But we were making headway, even if it seemed slow.

One evening, Fred, Philip, and I met late at a bar to discuss the progress of the race. Philip had drunk plenty of Scotch, and after we'd discussed the marathon field, Fred began talking about my running and harped on Philip to give me more encouragement to improve, saying I could and should be a better runner. Philip had heard me refer to the magical three-hour barrier several times, so he started asking what it would take for me to run that well. Finally, I said doubles, which I think he first understood as in shots of whiskey, but then I explained that it would take two workouts a day to build my endurance. I'd also need the dreaded speed work, at repeated intervals.

We dropped the subject because yet another trip came up. Amazingly, just when I was enjoying a less peripatetic life, AMF announced their sponsorship of the American team to the World University Games in Moscow, and Ted and I were to go for eleven days in August to do PR. Ted had never been in a communist country; I knew he had no idea what a grind this would be, starting with the fact that once again we had no press credentials, despite being in the top tier of VIPs. Accreditation had long been closed; this seemed to be a recurring nightmare to me, and the security a year after the Munich disaster meant no flexibility on anything. After a few days in Moscow, where we waited in line for everything like all the other sad souls in the country, we knew we were not going to get any visibility for AMF out of this. We had no access and no publicity hook.

Then Ted hit upon the rather nutty idea of getting AMF exposure by having me run across Red Square with the colorful onion domes of St. Basil's Cathedral in the background. Ted would take the picture, write the caption, and get his friends at AP to move it on the global wire.

Ted had a good Rolleiflex camera, but he also had a bit of an old-age tremor, and since you had to hold the camera very still and look down into the viewfinder at the action, I was going to have to run across the square several times to make sure we got the shot. As the epicenter of Moscow and the symbol of all things Russian, Red Square was especially patrolled by Soviet guards whom we knew would forbid us from doing this. Probably even photos were prohibited; we didn't know and we sure weren't going to ask, so we rehearsed how we'd walk nonchalantly across the square like tourists and how we'd wait until a guard was at the furthest point from us and then I'd start jogging toward the clicking Ted. Of course, how nonchalant could a long-haired, long-legged woman in bumhuggers be in Red Square? Every other woman there was four foot ten and wearing a babushka. On my first step, I could see a guard look up.

"C'mon, Ted, just keep clicking, I'll turn around and run toward you, don't try to get the perfect shot, just keep taking them as fast as you can." The guard started running toward us.

"C'mon, Ted, shoot, shoot, shoot! At least one of them will turn out okay!" When the guard was upon us, I was beside Ted with my arm looped through his. Smiling broadly at the guard, I whispered to Ted, "Okay, just start walking and don't stop. Smile at the nice man." Ted smiled and nodded at the guard who held out his hand for the camera.

"Keep smiling, Ted, keep walking, act calm, don't give him the camera."

"Film, film!" shouted the guard. Ted looked startled.

"Pretend you don't understand, Ted, keep calm, keep walking. *Smile*, Ted."

Ted put on his best idiot's face. It was priceless; the young guard obviously thought he was dealing with my dotty old grandfather. I smiled one of those understanding "Gee, thanks for indulging this old simpleton" smiles, as if the guard were in on the escapade. He was bewildered, and hesitated just long enough so we were actually off the square, and since that was his assigned turf he hesitated again at the thought of stepping off it, and then we drifted into the crowd on the sidewalk.

"Don't say anything yet, Ted. Keep walking innocently."

Then we were back in our hotel lobby and both said, "SHEEE-IIIIT!" at the same time.

"He was gonna take my camera!"

"Well, he was at least gonna take your film!" I said. It was about the closest we ordinary folk would come to being in a spy thriller, and nutty or not, it was the most publicity AMF got out of Moscow. When we got back to work there was a big pile of press clippings from it and our boss didn't know whether to be happy or not.

When I got back to New York, I hardly recognized Philip, who'd become taut, lean, and very tan. He was also very irritable. It turned out that while I was gone, Philip had taken Fred's admonition to heart and was going to help me break three hours in the marathon. He'd spend all his evenings working out training schedules for me, an irritating process, since he had to do a lot of research first. And then, to get a sense of how it felt, he started running himself, which meant he quit smoking, and that of course was really why he was irritable. I was amazed at the transformation in just eleven days, and even more surprised that he was already up to three miles.

Unfortunately, he didn't happily suggest this program but was dictatorial about it, telling me what I had to do from now on. I had not even unpacked my bags, so this was not the reunion I wanted after such a hard trip and a twelve-hour flight. We argued. Philip said I had to start prioritizing my life, that I was all over the map and needed to focus. I said that it was important to keep women's running visible in as many places as possible. He answered that I'd long since proved that women could do it and that I'd have a lot more credibility if I were a better runner. When he poured himself a drink I knew it would be pointless to continue the argument. I looked at the training charts, which were extremely difficult. That discussion could come later.

"When am I supposed to start?" I asked.

"Tomorrow," he answered.

I didn't know if this was the greatest expression of love or the greatest attempt at control. A lot of what Philip said was right; I just didn't like how he said it, nor his demanding nature. On the other hand, he was stepping up to take responsibility, and if it was going to work, I'd need to follow instructions. I'd prided myself on not knuckling under to anyone, but I did want to be a better runner, I did want to break three hours, but I was certain I was a basic no-talent and would never become a world-class athlete, even with all the training in the world. Philip probably sensed my insecurity; for all his tempestuousness, he read me pretty well. What finally convinced me to try was my nagging sense of knowing I'd never find out how good I could be unless I gave it my all. I'd long said I didn't want to look back when I was forty and wonder what might have been. I was already twenty-six; if not now, when? Jet lag and all, I started the next day.

Philip's schedules mostly were based on the principles of the famous New Zealand coach Arthur Lydiard: three months of heavy base work, two months of repeated tempo and interval work, and a final month of sharpening and peaking. There would be double workouts six days a week, and at least two of those would be faster work. Saturday would include a time trial or controlled race, and Sunday was the easy day, with only one run of twenty miles. I would run only two serious marathons a year.

All this work for two major races a year? You've got to be kidding. Some years I had run ten or more marathons. We argued over how many good marathons a person has in them. Philip's philosophy was that I could go on running 3:20 marathons forever but it was more important to run a few well, and you could not run all out, at the top of your game very often. Since I didn't even have a top game, it was a difficult concept for me to grasp. The concentration was going to be only on New York and Boston. Occasionally, there would be a race like the Maryland Marathon, but we'd incorporate that as part of the training. Since New York '73 was only a few weeks away, the first one wouldn't really count.

People always admire runners for their ability to withstand pain; that is not the issue. What people should admire us for is the ability to have the courage to face it. These workouts, especially the high-volume, fast intervals, were going to hurt. I didn't want to do them, but I also didn't want to be a coward.

Doing double workouts again at first felt like I was running and showering all the time. My legs felt leaden—they were not used to the extra impact, especially since I still weighed close to 140 pounds, up from my pre-Europe 128. I decided I had enough to worry about without trying to think about dieting; I needed good fuel for the workload and knew that if I ran like this I'd lose the weight. This was one of the smartest things I ever did. Losing weight is pretty simple—you can eat less or burn more. The best way to burn more is to eat enough to keep the energy high so you can work out hard day after day. The more you work, the hotter the burn anyway, and it is this consistently higher burn—metabolism—that keeps the weight off. Within two weeks, my rings began to feel loose on my fingers.

I kept up the schedule but decided to taper down the week before the marathon. Even Philip knew that there was no point in trying to run a hard marathon if you'd already done a hard training week. I did my usual twenty miles on Sunday the week before the race and then tapered down, staying with two workouts a day, but with a much-reduced afternoon run. On Thursday, I started running just one easy workout a day, and on Friday, I did a couple of light miles and took the day off from work to do interviews all day in the city to help promote the race.

On Saturday, I did a few light strides, laid out all my stuff, and took what seemed like a hundred phone calls from Fred. Ever since the sponsorship thing had happened, Fred had been calling me at work several times a day with ideas. Some of them were off the wall and some downright brilliant. At first, I was flattered by the calls but later I found out that Fred called everybody with the same ideas. Then he compiled all the opinions and made his decisions. Fred would have hated e-mail. He needed the voice and the sound of the reaction. As race day got closer, his calls were more frantic, and the day before the race, it seemed as if he went to every pay phone in Manhattan with a pocketful of dimes and called everyone he knew.

The men's field was strong, though mostly local, and very colorful. Tom Fleming, who was tired of being a second-place guy, was the favorite, and he won with a 2:21. Dr. Norbert Sander, age thirty-two, finished second. He was one of my personal heroes; he inspired me by continuing top-flight running in tandem with the relentless sleep-deprived obligations of a medical career and family life. In fourth place was Art Hall from Staten Island, one of the most familiar and popular runners in the area and, along with Ted Corbitt, one of the few African Americans running the roads. Fred Lebow and I could never figure why there was so little ethnic diversity in a sport so egalitarian, friendly, and inexpensive. Gary Muhrcke, winner of the inaugural New York City Marathon in 1970, wasn't running but years later it was revealed that at the time of some of his running victories he was on paid disability from the New York City Fire Department for a bad back. Personally I always thought the wryly humorous firefighter looked far too emaciated to schlep one hundred pounds of equipment up a ladder anyway. The news interest was a bonus. I joked that he was New York's first professional runner!

I was delighted with my second place among the women, with a 3:16. On a course that went four times through the cruel hills at the northern end of Central Park, it meant that my three weeks of increased training were already paying off. Nina Kuscsik won in 2:57—an incredible feat on a warm day. My sights were on that twenty-minute gap; I tried mightily not to think how huge it was.

Even more important for my developing other career in public relations and race promotion, was the front-page coverage the next day, with Tom Fleming breaking a tape held by the general manager of Olympic Airways. They thought we were geniuses. Even Jackie Onassis let it be known that she thought the coverage was great. Fred and I were jumping up and down with delight, and I knew this was just the beginning. It couldn't have been at a better time for us women, either. We didn't get the air ticket in the New York City Marathon, but we got plenty of publicity and we'd be getting a lot more, thanks to a little tennis match that took place in Houston that Monday night. Billie Jean King thumped Bobby Riggs in the "Battle

of the Sexes," a made-for-TV spectacular that went beyond entertainment and galvanized a nation. Interest in women's sports and
women's capability began to soar.

CHAPTER 17

VERY HARD WORK. IT'S *ALL* HARD WORK!

In running, as in life, there is always another race to train for. My schedule became similar to being a yachtsman in the Southern Ocean, where you have to keep your eyes on the task right in front of you, because if you saw the size of the waves hanging above your head you'd take such fright you'd never sail a boat again. Once I did look ahead at what I'd be doing and my stomach churned as it did just before a big race. It was never the pain of the running that bothered me, it was the prospect of not being brave enough to face it that always gave me the terrors.

Hard week followed hard week, and the Maryland Marathon in Baltimore in December gave me another encouraging progress report, a 3:10 on a tough course. I didn't trust the course measurement, but I knew that meant that the 3:16 at New York was for real. I was chipping away at three hours; Philip and I felt we had a shot at breaking it in nine months in New York, 1974. Everything else, including Boston in April 1974, would be a step toward getting there. Another important step was meeting Frank Shorter and Ron Hill in Maryland. Frank was the big star, of course, with his recent gold medal from Munich, but Ron Hill was an icon with his years-long world standing and his current 2:10 course record at Boston. We were all there to help the Maryland people build the publicity for their event, and I was happy to meet these two superstars on equal terms as an invited athlete, as their support of women in the marathon would be very important globally. For years I assumed that Frank and Ron had received some money under the table to be there, but Ron tells me now that they were as nervous about losing their amateur status as I was and came only for expenses.

The pattern of work, training, and domesticity left little room for play. Every morning I'd get up at six, run six miles along the East River, shower, change for work, pack my gear for the afternoon workout, and drive to White Plains while listening to the news on the radio. I'd work hard all day at my job and by 5:15 be in the ladies' room changing and stretching, then head out to run on the streets of White Plains.

Twice a week I'd run on the White Plains high school track, which had a fabulous new 3M surface—springy, absolutely state of the art then—and was always deserted by that time. After nearly two hours of running, I'd come back and, to the great amusement of the security guard, do one hundred sit-ups, twenty push-ups, and fifteen minutes of stretches on the carpeted hallway outside my office. Then I'd gather up my business clothes, toss them in the car, and drive back to Manhattan with rock music blaring to give me a treat, getting into the apartment about nine. I'd take another shower, make dinner, have a glass of wine, and Philip and I would eat at around ten. Dinner would be nicely presented, not just slopped down, and I'd always redo my makeup and wear something attractive. As amazing as that is to me today, it was important for me to look nice for the man in my life, who mostly saw me in sweaty running gear.

Even more amazing is that with the added burdens of the commute and training, I was the one who did all the shopping, cooked dinner, and cleaned up afterward. It's odd how long it took me to change some of those old roles. The schedule suited Philip perfectly. He slept until I got back from my morning run, went to his office, enjoyed a long martini lunch, and after work went to his favorite bar and drank Scotch with friends, arriving home about the same time I did. He was mellow from the Scotch and I was zonked from the workout. After a couple of glasses of wine with dinner, he was out like a light. It took some time before I saw anything peculiar about this behavior.

At times during the training, I felt that I was on a personal mission: I knew I was exploring depths of myself I didn't know I had. I'd had an exciting sense of pushing the limits when I first ran with Arnie, but I never felt doubt then. Now the awareness of how much work there was to do was often overwhelming. My God, I'd think, just when you get to a level you have worked so hard to achieve, there is another and another and it will never end. More than occasionally, I felt proud of testing myself, but there were also plenty of bleak winter nights when it was dark even before I started my run, and sometimes when the run was very long and I was tired I'd find myself flat-out afraid of the dark. "Grow up, get tough, or get over it, you wimp," I'd scold myself.

People always ask what you think about when you run, and to runners, it's a weird question because our heads are full of so many thoughts. Running is not a boring activity to us, it is a creative one. Doing intervals—say, twenty fast laps of the track with a slow lap between each one—interrupted my normal stream of thinking, but my thoughts still began with the mundane tasks of the day, such as shopping lists, or how annoying my boss had been that day. Then my mind would drift into the great imponderables of life and love, spiced with long-forgotten flashbacks from childhood.

Mostly though, I'd think about women's running and try to come up with another idea that would get us into the Olympics. Sometimes that seemed impossible, until I thought about our victory in Boston. We needed more numbers. We needed more events. If we had the events, we'd have the numbers. We needed the Dream Race, the one that did it all. But first, women needed to learn how to run. Before they could run, they needed to get over being intimidated about starting. They needed to believe that they were capable. They need to believe that it was appropriate. If the marathon were in the Olympics, then the whole world would know it was appropriate. These women needed to feel the way I did: powerful, strong, and not (always, anyway) afraid of the dark. They needed instruction, groups, clinics, events. How would this happen? Who would do it? I could, and so could Nina or Sara Mae, but we all had jobs and/or kids, and we were too busy doing our own training. Plus, how were we supposed to live while we created this miracle? I could create the Dream Race, and I wanted to do it. Badly. But I had to prove myself as a marathoner first. And so it would tumble, around and around and around.

As with my running, there were some signs of progress: more meetings, seminars, and TV shows in New York to discuss the advancement of women's sports. While these were time-consuming, they were important, as you never knew who you'd meet or who you could pitch on sponsorship. One of the most important was meeting Billie Jean King as she announced the founding of *womenSports* magazine, the first issue of which was to appear in June 1974.

If Billie Jean didn't like something, she changed it. Since there was no publication uniquely for women's sports, she created it, made herself the publisher, and hired Rosalee Wright as the first editor. How she did this while still playing at a top level—indeed, only six months after the big Bobby Riggs match!—amazed me. The press conference room at the Plaza Hotel that day bustled with the usual group of us women athletes, some male journalists who bristled at the assumption that women needed their own sports publication, and one sharp-eyed observer who happened to be my journalistic idol—Nora Ephron. Billie Jean was right: *womenSports* magazine was critical, as we had no collective voice or method of communicating with each other across our sports boundaries. There were issues such as Title IX, scholarships, prize money, and running's push for Olympic admission that were important to share across the board. This magazine was the first unified vehicle. It lasted for twenty years but sadly does not exist now.

These meetings were good for me, too, as they always made me feel significant again after the mind-numbing training. Inevitably, attending every meeting was Donna de Varona, who was a two-time gold medalist in swimming and was now a TV commentator. She was totally adamant about advancement of women's sports, and we became good friends as we shared thoughts and commiserations. Even if a meeting was inconclusive, time spent with Donna never was and I always felt enlivened and hopeful talking to her. Donna not only was a great resource but she had a great sense of humor and, like me, loved men and food and wine and laughed with her whole body at a bawdy joke. What we shared most however, was our ambition for women's sports advancement, and our willingness to work tirelessly to make equality happen. Together with Billie Jean and sports innovator Eva Auchincloss, Donna was key in forming the Women's Sports Foundation (WSF), which created a unified organization for women's sports which even now continues to be very important in the women's sports movement. The WSF was also crucial in my eventual career.

Best of all were the press conferences and fancy launch lunches to announce new women's sports programs and sponsorships, particularly those held by David Foster, the chairman of Colgate-Palmolive. Foster always did it well; his lunches were at places like 21, where he'd announce a new women's golf tournament or TV sponsorship. After these events, I'd tackle my runs with renewed energy and optimism, convinced that I, too, could come up with sponsorship for women's distance running.

Each press conference gave me ideas and personalities to think about over the miles. One of them was David Foster himself, who in my view was one of the greatest women's sports visionaries, right alongside women's professional tennis founders Gladys Heldman and Billie Jean King. Sometimes charming, sometimes irascible, and always brilliant, Foster's customers were women who bought soap, laundry powder, and toothpaste to the tune of billions of dollars. So unlike plenty of other chief executives who sponsored men's events so they could snuggle up to superstar jocks, Foster threw his sponsorship dollars into women's sports, especially golf. Women golfers were highly criticized in the early days, the way women runners or tennis players were, for being poor imitations of male players. Unlike women runners, however, the women golfers were not supported and encouraged by the male golfers, so Foster changed that by changing public perception. He made the sport glamorous and gave women the visibility they needed in several innovative ways. First, he created the Colgate Dinah Shore Golf Tournament, using one of the most popular entertainment celebrities of the time to front the tournament and be a television presence. Second, he paid to put the event on TV and bought the advertising around it, and third, he used the stars of the tournament in ads for his products. So the athletes got double and triple benefits. Women who watched daytime TV—called soap operas because they were originally sponsored by the makers of laundry detergent—saw women golf stars doing their own laundry. "Hey, Carol Mann has to wash her sweaty clothes but she's a golf pro, too; I think I'll watch her in her next tournament!"

Foster loved all women's sports, and he also championed the underdog. One of his most brilliant decisions was to sponsor the efforts of Fred Thompson, a young African-American lawyer who had been a runner in the army. Thompson wanted to pass the benefits of running on to the young black kids he saw, aimless and out of control, on the streets of Brooklyn. His Brooklyn Atoms Track Club, an after-school developmental running program for girls, was a spectacular success. Not only did the girls quickly begin winning in almost all of the AAU meets, those in the Atoms experienced almost no school drop-outs, drug use, or pregnancies. Parents all over Brooklyn begged Freddie to let their girls into the program. Some of the older girls went on to be Olympic athletes; those and the others, all beautifully groomed and well spoken, became superstar role models for the younger ones.

David Foster sponsored Freddie's idea of a whole new series of track meets, hired Madison Square Garden for what became the Colgate Games, and put it on television. Twenty years later, I was doing some stadium announcing in New Zealand, and there it was again—the Colgate Games! I hadn't realized the program was so global. New Zealand kept Fred Thompson's egalitarian ideal by requiring all the competitors to run barefoot, so that no child had an economic advantage. Thirty-four years later, this program is still going, but back in 1974, Freddie, the Atoms, and Colgate all inspired me greatly.

Meanwhile, workouts did not get easier, which was the whole point. In hindsight, I know that being on a team or having a training partner would have made all the difference in the world. It helps to have someone to talk to and to share the workload. You still have to run it yourself, but not having to take responsibility for the pace every single interval gives a physical as well as mental rest. A group also jokes with you and never lets you take yourself too seriously. At the same time, you can share ideas and rise more easily to their competitive level.

Of course, at the time there wasn't a training partner or a team nearby and on my schedule, and being both stubborn and naive, I felt I had to do it alone. Nowadays, I'd even consider moving to a more climate-friendly place like California, but I felt my job was paramount, and even though I treated running as a job, too, it was unpaid, always would be unpaid, and therefore a hobby, so not worth moving for. I never considered looking for a job in California anyway, because most New Yorkers honestly believe that New York is the epicenter of the world, and if you wanted a significant career path, New York was the only way to go.

In the cold days of December of 1973 and January 1974, though, California was on my mind, as all kinds of women were running well there. They included Cheryl Bridges, Jacqueline Hansen, and all of a sudden a new name, Michiko (Miki) Gorman, who popped a 2:46.36 in the December Culver City, California, Marathon, a new American record.

In early February, the first AAU American Women's Marathon Championship was held in San Mateo, California. This race was a tremendous step forward in creating championship status for women in the marathon, and it was a triumph of legislation, particularly for Nina Kuscsik, who put her heart and soul into making it happen. I wanted to run in solidarity, but Philip said no, our focus was Boston in April and it would interrupt training. On a snowy training day, I read that Judy Ikenberry won in 2:58; ye gods, I'd never even heard of Judy Ikenberry, and there were plenty of other new names there, too.

In fact, a lot of women were beginning to run very well. One big bunch in Germany was working under the visionary Dr. Ernst van Aaken, who was enacting his theories that women were superior to men in endurance because of their childbearing capacity and additional fat as a fuel source. It was van Aaken's protégée Anni Pede-Erdkamp who had set a world record of 3:07 when I did my first marathon in 1967 and, in October 1973, van Aaken staged the first all-women's marathon in his hometown of Waldniel to prove his point. He was planning an international edition of the race in September 1974, but in the meantime two new athletes of his, Christa Kofferschalager and Manuela Preuss, were coming to Boston. Both were sub-three-hour marathoners. So many good times, exotic names and scientific coaches—it made me feel slightly faint.

Pretty soon the high school track in White Plains got covered with snow and ice and was unrunnable. Nowadays people would get on a treadmill, but in 1973, nobody I knew had even heard of them. So Philip had me come back to Manhattan, where he'd measured off the distance around Peter Cooper Village, a housing complex a few blocks from our apartment, where the sidewalks had been shoveled.

Philip stood there with the watch in that brutal winter's cold, jumping up and down and occasionally running the recovery lap with me to keep warm. I counted these evenings as one of the greatest acts of love in our relationship.

One snowy Sunday in February I jogged up to Central Park to do my long run. There must have been six inches of snow on the ground and it was still coming down, but I didn't have a choice, it wasn't going to improve. As far as I could determine, I was the only person in the park. I ran the five-mile loop of the roadway, cutting my own path and when I came around the second time, it was still just my track there. For a while, I felt like I owned the entire sleeping island of Manhattan. Then I ran up the east side; I'd done ten miles but still had ten to go, and it began to seem a long way in the slow-going snow. I looked up at all the expensive apartments along Fifth Avenue, imagining the number of people having coffee or Bloody Marys, reading their thick Sunday editions of the *New York Times*, or looking out the window and watching this solitary figure running through the snow. I wondered if they admired me or if they thought I was a nutcase. At times like this I usually laughed it off and thought how envious they must be of me with my youth and vigor, and that all their money wouldn't buy the health and accomplishment I had. I also thought that soon running and even women's running would be recognized as the significant sport it is. The fact was I wanted just for once to curl up on a Sunday with coffee and the *Times*. That's when I knew I was tired. So I stopped for a moment and shouted up to the buildings, "There will be a time in my life when I don't have to prove myself anymore!"

By the third lap, other people were out, kids playing and sledding, a few other nutty runners like me were plodding along, and I knew I could muscle through the last lap. After this twenty-miler, though, I was just too beat to run the thirty blocks home. I felt insulted to run another step. I had five bucks in my pocket so I took a taxi to the apartment and peeled off my sodden gear. Philip was watching a tennis match on TV. I got there just in time to see Chris Evert win her final point and then receive a check and a full-length lynx coat. "I don't know where I'll wear this *in Florida!*" she joked. I went into the shower and let the hot water pour over me as I held myself up against the wall. It wasn't the money that got me, nor Chris, who deserved every dollar. It was the coat. There has to be a better way for us women runners, too, I thought. I was insanely envious of that coat, which turned out to be a good thing, as it was a turning point in my thinking. From then on, for years, every day would include some time spent on specifically how to make it better. Deep down, this now interested me much more than being a better runner myself. I dug out the old Idea Box with the slit in the top, and before taking a shower every night I would scribble the Idea of the Evening and slip it in. Some ideas were just vague conjectures and others seemed like Eureka! moments, but they all went into the box.

My workdays flew by. I loved my job. Learning about motorcycle culture or a new graphite tennis racket or how to assist with the quarterly earnings report was never dull, but in training I was literally counting down the time, second by second, for almost three hours every day. I was hoping to break 3:06 at Boston. That would be a four-minute personal record, maybe more if that Baltimore course was short. I couldn't ask for more.

There were many bonuses; the waists on my slacks and skirts were loose, and I became expert on the weather: I could feel rain or sun coming a half day in advance. I could smell a snowstorm's arrival faster than the weatherman could predict it, a particular pride of mine from my Syracuse days, and then later could both feel and smell the early snowmelt and the earth softening and then hardening again, and then at last softening into a mud smell that meant spring was really coming. March, at last. Six weeks to the Boston Marathon. Just the word "April" made my buttocks tingle with nervousness.

It's the last six weeks that can shake you. If you are uncertain about your preparation, that is when you realize it is too late to make it up. If it has gone well, you worry that something might derail you. As you approach the limits of your fitness, paradoxically this is the time you are also at your most fragile and susceptible to a cold or an injury—we call it "going over the edge." One evening during this time, I mentioned to Philip that I was worried that I wouldn't be placing as well as I had in past years. I guess I was looking for a little confidence boost.

"No kidding," he said sarcastically. "You're gonna get hosed in Boston."

"Hosed? I thought you said I was running on target for 3:06!"

"Miki Gorman is coming. Nina is coming. All kinds of birds are coming from California and Germany. A 3:06 means you're gonna get beat by twenty minutes. *Twenty minutes.* Now that should put it in perspective. So yes, your placing will not be very good this year."

Philip was a tough-ass guy. But I learned never to whine again.

And then it was just one week to go. Happily, there was no doubt in my mind that I could not have done another step of training. I was as ready as humanly possible. Seeing my naked self in the mirror was a revelation—I was down to 123 pounds, the lowest in my adult life, and most of it had come off in just six months, a thrilling accomplishment for most of us women. That doesn't sound so low, but weight isn't as much an indicator of fitness as is size, and mine was dramatically smaller. I'd gone from a size 12 dress to a size 8, because muscle mass weighs a lot more than fat but takes up less space.

With less fat, it was especially difficult to go through the carbohydrate-depletion prep stage before the race. This was a new system all the runners were talking about. I did my last twenty-miler on Sunday a week before the Boston Marathon, and the next day I switched to a high-protein, carbohydrate-free diet for the next three days, getting extraordinarily hungry and cranky. I stayed with two much-reduced workouts a day, fighting the urge to cry as I knew it was just chemical, and on Thursday, I started running just one easy workout a day and went to an all-carbohydrate diet and within an hour felt ebullient and strong again. On Friday, I did a couple of light miles before work and we drove north that evening, and stayed with friends of Philip's who lived in a town between Boston and Hopkinton.

That weekend, Philip was like the commander of an army. He made a huge scroll of the course from maps he got from the U.S. Geological Survey, and exactly marked the five-mile points along the route, as Boston still had no water stations, mileage markers, nor meaningful "split times"—elapsed time at specific miles along the route. It was insane; the BAA insisted on giving out times at anti-quated locations such at the Framingham Train Station, 6.6 miles, as they had for the past seventy-five years, which helped nobody, as you figure out your per-mile time in exact mile segments. Accurately measured and marked courses are critical for the serious runner, and here was Boston, supposedly the most prestigious race in the world, without so much as the miles painted on the road.

Philip arranged for local friends to move from point to point to call out my times and give me water; he supplied them with a watch, a car with a radio (so they could hear when to start the watch), and buckets. You had to do these things yourself at Boston if you wanted them. I was flattered that these men wanted to be part of my crew, and they loved the challenge of getting through the traffic around the twisting, narrow Boston route. I'd never heard of anybody getting to more than two vantage points to see the runners. Our friends learned how to wind up the watches and call out the elapsed time; the fancy Ironman watches we have today didn't exist then, of course; even the Ironman Triathlon wasn't yet invented as a sport!

On Sunday night, I laid out all my stuff. As a tribute to AMF's product line, I wore again the white Head tennis dress I had worn in New York and Maryland. I decided I would continue wearing a skirt until decent shorts were created. The Vaseline was making it a bit gray in the armpits, but it was fine for another race. Then I went to bed. Philip said he needed to stay up to work out my pace for the race. I woke up about midnight to see the lamp on the desk still on, with Philip going over the map, and calculating figures.

"Still at it?" I said.

"Yep. I'm trying to calculate how much you will slow on the hills."

"Why don't you just go to bed? When the gun goes off I'll just run the best I can anyway."

"No. We need to keep you to pace. But I don't want you discouraged when you slow for the hills, so I have to add a bit of time there."

"It will be okay. Why don't you just come to bed?"

"I don't know how you can sleep! Aren't you nervous?" He obviously was.

"Hell, no. I could sleep for a hundred years. There is nothing more to do; I can't do any more training tonight."

"Well, that's true. Go back to sleep. I'll be there shortly."

I feel back to sleep and dreamed golden dreams. Philip loved me so much that he stayed up to work out my pace chart while I slept.

I woke feeling like gangbusters, as I usually did before Boston because it was the one morning in the year I could sleep in! What irony. After a breakfast of toast, oatmeal, and tea, I dressed, taking special time and care to grease and tape my feet, and spin little cocoons of lamb's wool around my toes. The tape had to be perfect; one wrinkle could mean a big blister and ruin the whole race.

Hopkinton was its usual marathon morning madhouse, but we easily found a place to park and I went into the First Congregational Church, where Gloria Ratti had the bib numbers for the women. There were forty-two of us; so many! There were women I had never seen or heard of before in my life—imagine that, in a marathon, where all of us always knew everyone else. Good, I thought, the movement is growing. That's what having an opportunity and being official is all about; make it count and they'll run. We can be athletes now, not pressured iconoclasts. For once, I was relatively anonymous, and it felt so good just to be free of that obligation.

I went outside and Philip helped me pin on my number, and then I ran my warm-up, finding again that the little backstreets were a quiet place where I could gather my thoughts. Thirty minutes later, when I got back, and was taking off my sweats, Philip said, "There was a big photo session with all the women, they were looking for you. Fred Lebow thought you'd be upset at missing it, but I didn't think you would," Philip said.

"I'm *happy* to miss it!" I said. It was true; I felt my story had been told a million times and now it was time for the media to move to someone else and the next level of coverage. We walked to the start. Philip handed me his business card; on the back was a little grid with the splits written on it. I knew this was what he'd been up all night working on. The duplicate was on his clipboard.

"For what it's worth," he said.

"Thank you for all that effort," I said. "I'll give it my best shot."

I put the card in the little pocket in the front of the tennis dress. The final number on the card was 3:06. I got a shiver of fear. Could I possibly improve this much?

I stood in the pack about thirty rows back, at the edge of the road, and at last the gun went off and we were flying down Hayden Rowe and out onto Main Street and straight downhill. At last. Boston. Spring. Mecca. Heaven. At last.

Above the sound of the thundering feet, the snorting and spitting, I could hear a commanding voice ahead shouting, "Five forty-two, forty-three, forty-four, FIVE FORTY-FIVE, FORTY-SIX loudly, in my ear. A 5:45 opening mile? I couldn't run one mile in 5:45! Doesn't matter, it's downhill. Nice of that guy to give us the split, must be injured or he'd be running. Then a group of guys, with Miki Gorman in the middle, swept past. She had absolutely perfect form and was such an interesting mix: being Japanese, she was small and delicate looking from her head to the tops of her thighs, then her legs told another story. They were powerful pistons with a stride that seemed as long as she was tall, and a whopping foot plant. No little pitter-patter here. As she sped away from me, I noticed that her shorts were actually bumhuggers, but they were so loose they flapped like bloomers. Talk about fit! She was wonderful! I had a new heroine. I'd never catch her, never run as fast, but by golly, she was marvelous.

As it turned out, there were also at least four van Aaken athletes who had come from Germany, Christa Kofferschlager and Manuela Preuss among them, but I never saw them, nor Nina Kuscsik. I started further back than usual, so most of the women were in front of me. After Miki, I didn't see any other women at all. Guys were all around me as usual, but it was a different scene. There were nods of admiration and acknowledgment, and quick shouts of "Go for it!" but there were none of the effusive monologues that I'd gotten in past years. It dawned on me that we were all going too fast to talk much.

Suddenly, there was our friend Bob at the five-mile mark shouting, "Thirty-four fifty-five, thirty-four fifty-five, got it?" And our friend Joe was running alongside with a cup of water, trying not to spill it, and carrying the plastic jug; he was struggling with the jug. I could tell I was going much faster than he imagined. To people on the sidelines, we probably looked like we were jogging and that it would be easy to run along. I gulped some water and threw the rest on my head. "Thanks, guys!" I shouted and I was gone. A dozen men around me were shouting at once, "Was that five miles? Was that accurate? What was it?" I was slightly breathless. "Yes, yes, yes! 34:55!" They had inked their own split times on their forearms and the backs of their hands, and were looking at them, and I felt pleased; I had done a service for my fellow runners. I had a *crew*!!

It occurred to me to look at the card in my pocket, which was not easy, the lines blurred with the bounce, it said something like 35:45. I was under the pace, but there were too many numbers. I couldn't do the subtraction. We were going downhill, so I just kept it going.

The downhills seemed a lot steeper than I remembered, and I felt like I was flying at ten miles when suddenly, there was Philip. I didn't even have to look for him, he was alongside giving me the time in a perfectly conversational tone and handing me water. I still didn't feel like I needed it but took it and dumped the other half.

"You're going fine. How do you feel?"

"Great," I said, "but we're still going down. Real work is ahead."

"Okay, see you at Heartbreak."

I didn't even look at the card. If he said I was going fine, that was enough.

As we went through Wellesley, the sound was unreal—it hit my chest so hard it hurt. I could tell that feminism had arrived at last at Wellesley, for when the women saw me, the cheers became screams and wails and even some aggressive shouts of "C'mon sister, do it, do it, *do it.*"

Bob and Joe were at fifteen, and then it was sixteen already, it had gone fast, and here was my Monster. I attacked it and it slapped me back hard. I'd just run the fastest fifteen miles of my life and Mile 16, over Route 128, gave me a reality check. I was slightly puffed. My legs felt a bit heavy, and coming down the other side there was a little sting in the quads. Gonna be sore tomorrow, baby, very very sore.

Then it was past the nice houses and the country club, a little balm there, and around the corner onto Commonwealth Avenue at the Newton Fire Station, a marvelous place, jammed with cheering people, every one of whom felt their individual voice was the one that would carry you up the three big hills ahead. For an in-shape runner, it is a course highlight, because when you round the corner it is like entering a wide tunnel of people, all of whom have been looking just for you to pull you up. The adrenaline surged again, I took the first hill in a scoot, and the second one felt like an easy swell. Save something for Heartbreak, I was thinking, but also remembering Arnie then, and our first run in '67, and how I didn't even know I'd gone over Heartbreak.

Then it was Mile 20. And there was Philip. I couldn't believe he'd made it here. He ran along beside me, with another cup of water, saying, "You're doing fine, just hold the pace." He stayed with me a while, and we topped Heartbreak together. "You just ran up Heartbreak Hill!" I said. The crowds at the top of Heartbreak are the Holy Rollers of the Boston Marathon, the zealots who believed that topping Heartbreak was like touching the hand of God. They were wild with joy to see another woman, leaning into the roadway and screaming until the veins popped out on their necks. I looked over at Philip and saw something I'd never seen before, which was him striding very pridefully alongside, with an expression of open awe. I was very pleased to have shared the appreciation with him. Then he peeled off, saying he'd see me at the finish.

Five to go. Just keep it going. Don't think. I began running through runners who were slowing, stopping, bent over, grabbing the backs of their legs. It was as if the other side of Heartbreak was the dark side of the moon. My quads were pinging like a bad engine. Four to go. A little up, and then another down. Not sure I like downhills now. Three to go. Flattening out. Townhouses flying past this year, people in street. Zoom. Quads feel like there are little razor blades inside of them. Coolidge Corner coming up, cross the trolley tracks, careful, careful! Watch it, cross the tracks, okay. Two to go. Knees are glass, put them down gently, gently, don't break, please don't break now . . . the Citgo sign, one to go. In a mirage, someone running alongside, orange *Spiridon* shirt, old friend Gilbert Roland from

France, both too tired to be surprised or happy or anything . . . eyes meet in exhausted recognition.

"Gilbert." A whisper.

"Katty." A returned whisper.

Hereford Street coming, a turn, another hill, another turn, an insult as always this close to the finish. Thousands of people are cheering but I can only see mouths working, arms waving, I can't really hear them. Why are they *smiling*? We are dying and they are smiling. Someone is whimpering, someone is dying like me. I don't care if I die. I am perfectly willing to die. Gilbert is whimpering.

"Courage, Katty," whispers Gilbert.

God, it's me who is whimpering.

There is the finish . . . don't slow up, run through it . . . get every second, it's okay to die, just die with *everything you've got*.

I saw Philip hit the stopwatch as I crossed the line, marveled confusedly over how he could manage to be there, right on the finish line, and as I stood bent over with my hands on my knees, swaying, I thought, it's over. Thank God it's over, I'm alive, I *think*, and it's over. Philip put his hand on my back, I stood, we embraced and walked through hundreds of shuffling runners. He was smiling broadly.

"Did I do it? Did I run the 3:06?"

"Lady, you ran a 3:01! A 3:01!"

I shrieked. "Are you kidding me?! Are you sure?!"

"Two watches—take a look!" There it was, 3:01:39.

Oh God, I thought. Oh dear God, I can break three hours.

Miki Gorman had won the race in 2:47, lowering the course record by over *eighteen* minutes. It was not only a phenomenal personal accomplishment, it made a highly visible breakthrough statement about the place of women in marathon running. You can't deny the stopwatch. Her time was a respectable man's time. Four women in one race broke three hours! I was fifth. The press noticed the women, and applauded loudly. Miki's time was just the kind of ammunition we needed to convince the IOC that women deserved a marathon event in the Olympic Games. Driving back to our friends' place, I thought of how wonderful and amazing her performance was for all of us, and I felt pleased with myself, too.

Back at the house, the party was in full swing and I was welcomed as if I'd won the whole race. "Beaten by fourteen minutes," I tried to say, but they all shouted, "You beat *yourself* by nine minutes!" People understand the concept of achieving a personal best, and they wouldn't let me do anything but be thrilled. The best part, though, and the most revealing, was that all of them felt that they had contributed to the performance, were fueled by it, and they slapped each other on the back as much as they slapped me on the back. We *did* it! Clink! went the beer bottles. As soon as I took a shower and did the last unpleasant task of the day, which was cutting the tape off my feet and piercing my blisters, I joined them. It was the first beer I'd had in a month and it wasn't going to be the last.

Somehow Fred Lebow found my phone number and called, screaming his joy at my performance. Then, as usual, because Fred always asked for more even when he got the moon, he said, "Gee, if you had gone just a minute and a half faster, you would have broken three hours!" I could only laugh. "Fred, there was not another second left to trim in there, that was *it!*" Because 3:01 sounds a lot slower than 2:59, runners sometimes joke, "*Hey,* I ran a 2:61!" People who say they don't care about their time are lying; no matter how much they consider themselves a jogger, just as soon as they run a personal best they're ecstatic.

In the ensuing days and weeks, there was a lot of chatter. Suddenly, Kathy Switzer was no longer just the marathon rabble-rouser, the pinup girl, or the also-ran. Now she was knocking at the door. There were a few people who had disliked me for a variety of reasons since 1967, and now they had to contend with the fact that I'd done my homework, I'd come to Boston with no fanfare, and I'd run my guts out. In any previous year, my time would have won Boston. Maybe that doesn't count when five women ran better than I did, but it did to me.

I felt as good about my running as anyone could feel, and on Tuesday, I took Philip and my friends to Anthony's Pier 4 for lobsters and champagne as a way of saying thank you for all their support. I'd saved up especially for the occasion, and I'd been looking forward to it for months regardless of my performance. That's the good thing— and the bad thing—about the marathon. When it's over, it is over for quite a while. So no matter what, you should celebrate. That's my philosophy, anyway.

CHAPTER | 18

THE MAGIC THREE-HOUR BARRIER

I had five months to knock two minutes off my marathon time. You think, who would ever work that hard for five months just for the sake of two minutes?! But two minutes, even stretched over 26.2 miles, is huge. For a man today who runs a 2:10 marathon compared to one who runs a 2:08, it is the difference between being extremely good yet unnoticed and being one of the best in the world and invited everywhere. For both men and women, two minutes often means qualifying for the Games, the dream of a lifetime, or not. For me, it meant breaking the three-hour barrier. We always said three hours separates the men from the boys, and we didn't care in those days that there was no equivalent feminine expression.

Breaking three hours would give me total legitimacy as a runner. I would no longer be accused of being an oddity or an attention-seeker, a media event, a photo of a scuffle, or a kiss. When I first ran Boston, it was because I wanted to be a real runner. Sub-three would do it.

My attitude had changed. I was a believer in Philip's methods; draconian as they were, he got results. So the spring and summer loomed before us with every running moment accounted for. If we went with friends to the Hamptons for the weekend or took his kids to Williamsburg, there were still two workouts a day to do. If I had a beer too many at a party, there would still be a morning run, headache or not. No more did I resent the workload; I knew that's what it took. Maybe there were other methods, but this was working for me. It wasn't pleasurable, but I was ambitious.

One telling difference was my attitude toward the dreaded speed work, where I never, ever did less that the assigned numbers of intervals. Before Boston 1974, I did them almost to prove Philip wrong—"See, I've done all you've asked and it doesn't work." Now I did them all in the firm belief that every single step and every single second counted toward reaching the goal. I even became superstitious—if I skipped one, it just might be the very one that would make the difference between 3:00 and 2:59.

It was an ungodly hot summer. I always ran in nylon bumhuggers, Vaseline, and a loose cotton T-shirt, carrying a second shirt with me on Tuesdays and Thursdays (speed nights) to change into midway through the workout when the first one became so wet that it weighed me down and dripped on the track. Sometimes I'd give it a wring and water splashed out as if I'd been swimming in it. I was stunned by my own body's vivid example of physiological adaptation to heat.

One hot summer Thursday evening, I was doing a speed workout of repeat miles. There were eight of them, so with the recovery laps, the warm-up, and the cooldown, it was a fifteen-mile workout, a long session. Early on during the workout, I saw Canadian Debbie Brill, the Commonwealth Games high jump gold medalist, arrive to do her workout. I hadn't known she was in town. Since I usually had the track entirely to myself, it was a bonus to have some company. For the first couple of miles, I'd see her at the end of the field doing some easy stretching and then arranging her gym bag. Then she went out on the back straight of the track and did a couple of easy strides, then back to the high-jump area, where she stretched some more. Every time I had a jogging interval, we'd exchange a pleasantry as I went by.

Finally, she adjusted the props and put a bar up and looked at it for a while, then went to her bag and changed her shoes. I ran another couple of miles, and then she made a couple of running approaches to the bar, stopped, and did a sort of rehearsal of an almost-jump. Then she sat down and looked at the bar some more and did some stretches. She looked up every time I whizzed by. Halfway through the workout, I changed my shirt, and when I jogged by again she waved. "C'mon, *jump*," I said to myself. I was desperate to see the real thing. Finally, two miles later, she did. It looked like a beautiful, slow-motion backward swan dive. "Oh goody," I thought, "just when my workout gets hard, I've got a little diversion." Then she went back to looking at the bar, stretched, and changed back into her other shoes and jogged a little on the back straight. "That's *it*? That's all there *is*?" On my next jog, she jogged over and said, "My God, you've been out here all night, I think you must be doing at least six repeats!" "I'm doing eight," I said, "and I'm wishing now I'd been a high jumper!!" To her credit, she laughed heartily.

Perhaps I fried my brain that summer, but I cannot remember a lot except the heat, the training to go under three hours, and all of us working to make the NYC Marathon a success again. Olympic Airways was back as an enthusiastic sponsor, and I assisted with the public relations again, Nancy Tuckerman kept giving me quiet reports that Aristotle Onassis was ill, and indeed it seemed every other day there was a photo of him or Jackie—never together—in one of the gossip papers. There was one picture of Onassis with tape holding his eyelids open; he had myasthenia gravis, a disease I had never heard of, which made it impossible for him to open his eyes voluntarily. I thought how sad it was that even with all the money in the world he still could not be made healthy. As naive as it sounds, it was probably the first time I realized that to have your health really is the most important gift in life.

The public relations for the New York City Marathon was good, cracking good. In addition to all the coverage from the daily papers and the wire services, *People* magazine was going to do a full feature on the race, and I had several long photo sessions with them in the park, resulting in some of my most treasured action pictures. *Parade* wanted a first-person piece from me for the Sunday papers. And maybe most interesting—and most promising in the longer term— was a one-hour special program being produced by ABC-TV for network broadcast called the ABC Women's Sports Special. Eleanor Riger, the only woman producing sports for ABC-TV, was making it and planned to cover my segment during the NYC Marathon. Donna de Varona was the interviewer and commentator for it. With all of the principals women, it was a historic first for women's sports and women's media. Donna was a network commentator who also worked as a sports anchor for the local New York station WABC-TV, and she came to the marathon with a camera crew to cover it for sports news, which was the first time the NYC Marathon was on TV in any form. Another era was beginning.

Most business meetings in those days were face-to-face, and I'd dash from place to place in New York on days I had AMF business as well, moving in a blur. Then I'd zoom back up to White Plains,

I'm deliriously happy as I run another personal best, this one in the December 1973 Maryland Marathon, held in Baltimore. My 3:10 was a six-minute improvement, validating the training schedule from my coach and boyfriend, Philip (far right). My mom, Virginia, is on the far left and my dad Homer is the tall guy behind me. Photo credit: Maryland Marathon.

In 1974, the New York City Marathon was four laps around Central Park. I was trying to break three hours for the first time on a freakishly hot day. Although I am on pace here, I am thinking how it will not be possible to run a personal best time after all.

We didn't have water stations in those days so my friend Zan Knudson, an author, crewed for me on the east side of the park.

I'm far in the lead in the 1974 NYC Marathon and while the men applaud, some women here are clearly not so enthusiastic. Women were often the hardest to win over in the battle for acceptance of women's sports. World-famous photographer Ruth Orkin documented much of the life of Central Park from her window but took this unusual race photo of me on the ground. My thanks to Ruth's daughter Mary Engel, a filmmaker and early runner, who has given me this photo. Photo credit: Ruth Orkin.

1974 New York City Marathon champion. Never in my life was I so glad to see the finish line! On my left is my friend Zan, and right behind me is a photographer from *People* magazine. Photo credit: Joan McCullough.

Afterward, I hung on my boyfriend Philip like a tent.

On the run to my personal best performance in the 1975 Boston Marathon. I felt like the road just came up to meet me. Photo credit: Jeff Johnson.

I was jubilant at the finish of the 1975 Boston Marathon! Although I was in second place, my 2:51:37 then ranked me sixth in the world, third in the USA, and first in New York City. Photo credit: Jeff Johnson.

A 1972 press conference at Tavern on the Green for the groundbreaking Crazylegs Mini-Marathon, Nina Kuscsik (left) and I (right) do a photo op with Joe Halper, who was then New York City Recreation Commissioner.

In 2002, a press conference commemorating thirty years' running of the New York Mini-Marathon was held again at Tavern on the Green. In attendance were (l-r) Allan Steinfeld, then President of the NY Road Runners; Nina Kuscsik; me; and Grete Waitz, former Mini champion and nine-time winner of the NYC Marathon. To demonstrate the positive benefits of running, I am wearing the same dress in 2002 that I wore in 1972!

In 1972 Fred Lebow was worried about getting publicity for the new Crazylegs Mini-Marathon so he enlisted some Playboy Bunnies to come for a photo op with Nina, Joe Halper, and me. Nina (bottom) and I (top) are not very amused.

June 3, 1972: The start of the first-ever women-only road race, and the beginning of a big history! Some IDs (l-r) include Nina Kuscsik, #1; me,#2 (with hair in bun); Jackie Dixon, with Bay to Breakers logo; and Pat Barrett (white shoes). Charlotte Lettis, far right, is #3.

This ethereal photo of two women running epitomized how many of us women felt when we ran. It became the ubiquitous image of the Avon International Running Circuit. Photo credit: Avon Running – John Kelly.

We are proud to announce the inclusion of New Zealand on the Avon Running Circuit.

INAUGURAL TWO RACE SERIES.

CHRISTCHURCH: 15 km
9 a.m., 18th September 1983.
$6.00 (reg.) $8.00 (non-reg.). **Free** T-shirt for all starters
• Pre-race clinic • spot prizes • age category prizes

Race Director: Rod Rutherford
Phone: 558-663 (Evenings)

AUCKLAND: 15 km
Mid 1984 (Date to be announced)
For entries and information write:
Sandra Main
Avon Cosmetics Ltd
P.O. Box 1828
Auckland.
Avon will send the first three Christchurch finishers to Auckland for the 1984 race.

The world's largest beauty company, Avon Cosmetics Ltd, invites all New Zealand women to participate in these two fabulous races.

Run the Avon in Christchurch this Spring!

Over a million women from twenty-seven countries participated in Avon Running events. Their numbers, international representation, and outstanding performances were pivotal in the official inclusion of the women's marathon in the Olympic Games, starting in 1984. Photo credit: Avon Running – Yellowdog Productions.

Lorraine Moller runs a 2:35 to win the 1980 Avon Marathon in London, while Elizabeth Phillips, my right-hand colleague and life-long friend, holds the naughty finish line tape. Photo credit: Avon Running – Yellowdog Productions.

We felt certain that the International Olympic Committee would make the women's marathon an official event after the triumph of the Avon Marathon in London. The winners' medals and eyes sparkled like the regalia on the Lord Mayor of London at the prospect. Left to right: David Mitchell, Chairman of Avon; Nancy Conz, 2nd place; Lorraine Moller, 1st; Sir Ronald Gardner-Thorpe, the Lord Mayor of London; Sir Horace Cutler, the Leader of the Greater London Council; and Linda Staudt, 3rd place. Photo credit: Avon Running – Yellowdog Productions.

get some stuff done in the office, do my hard afternoon workout, and drive back to the city. I never felt I was slipping under my boss's radar to do this, as PR contacts are PR contacts, no matter where they are made. Plus my running was giving AMF so much positive visibility that our VP came to me one day asking if AMF should get into the running-shoe business. My phone at home and at the office was ringing constantly, and often it would be ten thirty, after training, shower, and dinner, when I'd finally have a quiet moment to write press releases or edit a report for my boss.

None of this got me down except the domestic stuff, which I could never keep up with. In a life that was already full of hard repetition, the endlessness of laundry, grocery shopping, and cleaning the bathtub (bathtubs get filthy in two seconds in New York City, a phenomenon that has driven me to more tears than heartbreak) were the crushers. Philip criticized me for working too cheaply, saying I should charge Olympic Airways more, to which I'd say, "If the race is a success, that's all that matters." Almost everybody working the race was a volunteer anyway, and there was always the danger that the AAU would come up with some witch-hunt determination that I was getting paid for running and expel me.

Philip's manner was critical and impatient, but he was forty-two and I was twenty-seven, and he wanted me to avoid mistakes he'd made early in his career, not realizing that I had to live through some of my own. He was especially impatient for me to break three hours on September 29, 1974. Once again, he analyzed the route, prepared maps, and recruited friends to crew for me. For all our criticisms of the Boston Marathon, we know-it-alls in New York didn't have split timers or water stations, either, and the only toilets were the nice ones at Tavern on the Green or the dicey public ones in the park.

Things were looking good. The heat of the summer finally broke, and the last couple weeks of September were beautiful. Norb Sander and I were asked to go on the *Today* show two days before the race, and the field was looking strong; an unknown guy named Bill Rodgers, who finished fourteenth in the Boston Marathon, was coming, along with some other newcomers. On Wednesday, I got to sleep two hours later, since I had PR work in the city that morning and didn't have to drive up to White Plains until the afternoon. It was bliss to get some solid sleep with the race just five days away, and when I put on my sweats to go out running that morning, I felt marvelous.

I was in countdown for the race with no more hard work to do; oh, I loved the tapering week! It was one of those warm, sparkling, one-in-a-million September days. Heading south on the East River promenade, it was beautiful; sailboats were bouncing on the glittering river and everything looked clean. I let my mind drift as I watched a chunky black guy jogging toward me. I'd seen a few runners out here lately, and I liked the black guys with the towels around their necks; I knew they were local boxers doing their jogging and shadowboxing.

As he was nearly alongside and I began to say hi, he came close to me. I sidestepped to the left and was nearly on the river rail, saying, "Hey!" in an annoyed voice, when suddenly he was right there, turned and grabbed me around the neck with the crook of his elbow, and held a knife at my throat.

"I'm gonna cut you! I'm gonna cut you!" he kept snarling.

They say time stands still in such circumstances, and it really did. A million alternatives came to mind, but I remember thinking I should try to calm and defuse this guy, so I said quite reasonably,

"Gee, I don't think that's a very good idea." I kept looking at the knife. It was one of those cheap serrated steak knives they were giving away at the time when you bought ten gallons of gas or something. I thought of the incredible collections of knives my retired military father and my active-duty military brother had purchased or confiscated from all over the world, all of them kept oiled and razor sharp, a source of great masculine pride, and I thought, "Shit, I can't let myself be killed by a dopey gas station knife!" The problem was that this guy had the point of it right on my jugular, which had to be pumping pretty visibly. I kept arching my neck to get away from the tip and twisting to face the guy. He couldn't keep a grip with his elbow because by that time I was sweating so profusely.

"Give me your money, I'm going to cut you," he said again. I was a bit confused. Did he mean, give him my money *or* I'm going to cut you, or did he mean he was going to cut me anyway?

"I don't have any money, I'm just out here running," I said. I was amazed at how calm my voice sounded. I had on my expensive chronograph. He didn't notice it, so I assumed he was not a pro at this, which scared me more, since I'd rather bargain with a pro than a nutcase.

"You're gonna come with me, I'm gonna cut you,"

"Where are we going?"

"Over there, I'm gonna cut you." There was a grove of trees, I assumed he meant there. I kept squirming, and finally I'd turned so that we were facing each other but our heads were in a lock together with the knife still at my neck. Anybody casually going by us would think we were in some kind of weird embrace. He began pulling me toward the trees and I kept resisting, because, as he kept saying, he was gonna cut me and that sounded like an inevitability. I was still trying to figure out a way to maneuver out of it when he tried to karate-kick me in the stomach. That infuriated me, and in his moment of imbalance, I got an arm free and said to myself, "C'mon girl, you've got one shot at this." I slapped my hand to my waistband, grasped my dog repellent, and began spraying up in one movement toward his face. The gloppy mustard-orange goo stuck to his shirt and, I guess, his face, because he took off running in a sprint. He went uptown, which is where I would have liked to run home myself, so I sprinted downtown and ran howling up to a gardener in the park. He calmly suggested that I go into the park station and call the police, which I did. I also called Philip, who jumped in a cab and got to me before the police did. When the police arrived and took my statement, I couldn't convince them to hurry up and go out and look for a guy who would have to be trying to wash his burning face in a fountain someplace right now, but I did get a little lecture on what did I expect, being a woman out here running alone? I snapped back that I expected in a civilized country not to be attacked, that Manhattan was not a safari theme park where people have to stay inside and watch the animals roam about them. I was livid, and after I got home and took a shower, I got a little teary. After a cup of coffee, I felt grateful that I'd gotten out of it in one piece.

"He probably was going to rape you, or make you blow him," said Philip matter-of-factly. I winced at the graphic word. "So why did you fight him? Most women wouldn't have. You took a big chance." He didn't sound critical or admiring either. Just analytical.

"Well, he said he was gonna cut me; he didn't offer any alternatives. So I figured if I was gonna die anyway, I might as well fight. Plus, it was a dopey knife."

"It was still a weapon."

"It wasn't a gun."

"What if it was a gun?"

"If it was a gun, I'd probably have done anything he asked."

. . .

My first appointment that morning was with Ira Berkow, then the sports editor with Newspaper Enterprise Association (he later joined the *New York Times*), and when I arrived late, I was so rattled I blurted out the whole story of the morning. I thought a guy like Ira would be pretty jaded, but he was astonished, and upset, too, and he talked sensitively and at length to me. He understood quickly my long-term concern, which was not fear per se, but having to face hundreds of future training runs with the possibility of being mugged in the back of my mind. I was angry that the mugger stole a lot of my sense of freedom and gave people who thought runners were crazy anyway more reasons for not doing it. "I'm going do my Scarlett O'Hara and just not think about it right now," I said. "I'll run the New York City Marathon on Sunday and then I'll figure it out."

On Friday, Norb Sander and I were on the *Today* show, and, Gene Shalit made the flippant remark at the end of an otherwise perfectly delightful interview that at least we marathoners could outrun the muggers. Muggings were so common then that it had become a standing joke in New York City. I couldn't help but retort that I'd been mugged three days earlier but fought him off with dog repellent, so it wasn't very funny. It was a real "Outside of that, how did you like the play, Mrs. Lincoln?" ending to the show. Nobody was ever going to forget that show about the New York City Marathon!

The night before the race, with no warning, a huge warm front moved in over Manhattan. When we woke up slow and groggy on Sunday morning, the blissful Indian summer weather had turned to a freakish 95 degrees, bright sun, and insanely high humidity. It felt like a July day in the Louisiana bayou. Start time was ten A.M.—we thought that was early in those days—so the middle of the race was going to be during the worst part of the day. I was stunned by the heat and couldn't think clearly. All our friends with water buckets were showing up and checking in with Philip, and ABC-TV was fitting me with a card-deck-size transformer and wireless mike that I'd supposedly talk into as I raced. Reporters were milling around and Fred was running around frantically waving his arms as he always did before a race. The elegant general manager of Olympic Airways, in a white silk shirt and beautiful sport coat, was wiping the sweat off his bald head. Nancy Tuckerman was wringing her damp hands and directing the reporters who showed up late and demanding last-minute interviews. The *People* photographer was everywhere, shooting photos and sweating.

My plan to break three hours was fried—literally! I tried to get a grip on the new reality. What should I do? Nina wasn't running because the week before she had run Dr. van Aaken's international women's marathon in Waldniel, so there was little doubt that I would win. Should I jog now and save it for another marathon? But there really wasn't another one. I'd peaked for this one, and my body was in racing mode. I knew the answer before Philip even said it: "You're going to have to go for it."

When the gun went off, I felt as if I were racing into the mouth of hell. I went off at my sub-three-hour pace and I was going to hold it as long as I could. Ted Corbitt wrote to me later, saying I was just behind the pack of the lead men for a long time. I don't think that is quite correct, but I was happy hearing it from Ted, as he is a man I have always respected, and it would have been amazing to me to be anywhere near him in a race. The point of the story is that it was so hot that the men wisely went out conservatively, and thus I was not so far behind them. Gradually, the heat just broke everybody apart. I was better off than most of the people in the race because I was very heat-acclimated and I also had my own water crew, who were lifesavers. Nowadays, the race would have been rescheduled due to dangerous heat like that, but not having water or sponges on the course made it downright life-threatening.

People were ambling all over the park, bicyclists weaving lazily down the roadway, most of them getting in the way, totally oblivious that a race was going on. This was the most annoying thing about the NYC Marathon. It was a big-deal race, but the ordinary New Yorker did not understand it in a way that everybody in Boston knew about the marathon. Fred and I had talked dreamily about running the New York City Marathon through the main city streets but that was just a fantasy. We were such a small-potatoes club we couldn't even imagine having the resources to cordon off the inside lane of the park for a race.

My water crews were a very interesting assortment of people, and on the East Side included the poet May Swenson and her partner, the novelist Zan Knudson. Zan had attached herself admiringly to me a few years before by writing and calling and wanting to meet me for resource material for her young adult sports books. Zan was in awe of me, but a bit disappointed because I was "just too girly-girl." I had no idea what she was talking about. In her own words, Zan was an unabashed "jock sniffer," and where there were sports, you could usually find Zan. If it was women's sports, you could not keep her away. I was slightly homophobic then without even knowing what the word meant, but I was crazy about Zan because she was just so unafraid of being a bombastic butch lesbian at the top of her lungs and because she'd given up the nine-to-five pantyhose life to be a writer. She actually earned her living as a novelist, which is about as impossible as earning your living as a marathon runner. Zan was always telling me things that I should do to help the women's sports movement: "You should march up to those old fuddy-duddies at the AAU and the IOC and tell them to shove it up their ass. You're an important person! They'd listen to you!" How can you not love someone with this degree of naive chutzpah?

May was entirely different, a quiet, reclusive poet who wrote extremely beautiful verse. She was well published and highly regarded, but until she won a MacArthur "genius" award in 1987, I don't think she and Zan even had heat in their cottage on the Long Island shore. I was full of admiration for both of them, and here they were running along carrying cups of water for me in a marathon. Well, Zan did; she had the jock job and ran alongside shouting encouragement while May stood and quietly clapped, ever watchful and observant. The second time I came around, though, at about eleven miles, Zan handed me a cup of iced tea. "What's this?" I asked.

"It's iced tea, we had to run across the street and get it at a deli, one of the runners ran off with our jug of water! May bought it, she doesn't know, I told her you might get diarrhea if you drank this but that's all we have right now and May says she's so sorry!" I loved the story of how another runner ran off with the water jug and Zan, thinking she was such a hot-ticket jock herself, couldn't get it back.

I also had a sense of the desperation the guy must have felt to run off with a stranger's jug of water.

After two laps, and grunting only unprintable things into ABC's microphone, I took it off and tossed it to Ellie Riger as I flew by the camera position at the start line at Tavern on the Green. As small as it was, it was too heavy; after fourteen miles *everything* was too heavy.

"Can't do it," I shouted.

"Doesn't work, anyway," she shouted back.

There was a mob of people gathering in the roadway at Tavern on the Green. Like the finish at Boston, they'd filled the street and formed a chute for us to file through. Some had brought their own cups and buckets of water and all were cheering. As I came through, there always seemed an especially loud roar. "It's a girl!" I'd hear murmured all along the corridor of people. This was obviously pretty new to them. Then there would be "Oh, honey, look she's wearing a dress and hair ribbons!" Sometimes the applause would stop as women spectators looked surprised and somehow indignant, or didn't know what to do. Then a man would shout, "Hey, lady, looking goooooood!"

Philip ran along beside me as I entered lap three. "You've still got it, you can do it, " he said. He didn't sound confident. His shirt was soaked from the heat. Runners were stopping and walking dejectedly out of the park. I didn't blame them. The prospect of two more laps—twelve more miles—in this heat was just unbearable.

"This is the hard one," I answered. It's never the last lap that's hard, it's the interminable lap about halfway.

Then it was around the corner and up a slight hill and past the Carousel, which seemed to shimmer in the heat and the music seemed to be slow and warped, like a 45 rpm record played at 33. I'd had this warped-sound sense before, at the Puerto Rican Day Marathon in the summer of '72 and at the Munich Olympics after the death of the Israeli athletes, with the damned oompah-pah bands still playing. Both occasions were linked in my mind with desperation.

Then, there were Zan and May; they'd found water again, and Zan ran alongside with the cup chatting about how good I was looking, how I was making all the guys look like wimps. I loved Zan, but it was always a sexual contest with her, whereas it was never the intention of women runners to try to beat a guy. Then she said, "Ohhhh, Christ!"

"What?!" I said.

"You're wearing fingernail polish!!"

I could feel my mind drifting, and I was kind of worried somehow my old coach Arnie would find me out, running hard in the heat, after all his admonitions not to. "Heat is your only danger!" he'd intone. How many times had Arnie told me the story of Buddy Edelen? Plenty. And now I was replaying how Edelen won the 1964 U.S. Olympic Marathon Trials by an incredible—some would say foolish—twenty minutes on a scorching hot day. "He never ran well again," Arnie would say, mournfully.

Back at the twenty-mile mark at Tavern on the Green, Ellie's cameraman was filming away. I knew I'd fallen off the pace, but people were still screaming, "You can do it, only one lap to go!" I wanted to scream back, "I know I can do it, you idiot, I just can't go any better in this heat!" If anything, it had become even more humid and oppressive. It was even hard to breathe.

Philip was waiting at the bottom of the hill. He looked like he'd been swimming.

"Look, you don't need to tell me," I preempted him.

"You can get it back if you pick up the pace," he said. Was he pathological or what?

"I'm doing my best and it's not going to happen."

"Don't give up yet."

"I won't give up, I never give up, it's just out of my control now." And then I was gone.

On the East Side, near the Metropolitan Museum, Zan was saying, "May is so impressed, she thinks she'll write a poem. She thinks you look like you're dancing in your white dress and all."

"I feel like I'm on the Bataan death march," I answered.

"Yeah, it's awfully hot," Zan conceded glumly. That was gratifying, someone else realizing we were going through hell out here.

The air had become still. At times I felt like I was churning rather than running. As I headed toward the northern end of the park for the last time, it became overcast, and I saw flashes of light in the sky. At first I thought this was a sign of heat exhaustion, or a violent migraine, but then I realized it was lightning. The sky got black and the wind picked up. At the top of the 110th Street hill, the rain started pelting down in huge splats and people were running for cover as their Sunday newspapers blew all over the place. Fearsome bolts of lightning crashed all around us. We really shouldn't be out in this, I thought, up here on a hill, with trees nearby—CRASH!! Ka-BOOM!!! Yipes, that one nearly knocked me off my feet!

One of the weird things about running for a long time in difficult or dangerous conditions is how insensitive you become to the emotions of fear or fruitlessness. Your focus is just so narrow at that moment, and all the energy is expended on finishing. What was I going to do, stop and seek shelter? Actually, dying that moment by lightning strike sounded like a great way to end this. Rain pounded on the roadway in such blinding, gray curtains, it bounced back up. For a while, the road steamed, and then it began to fill. "Oh, come on, give me just a little break here," I thought, as I headed down the streaming inside lane past the Delacorte Theater and along the lake, where the route flattened out. I was ankle-deep in rainwater. I'd already lost my three hours, and now it was an insulting slog at the very end of a very hard race. Everyone around me was walking and I felt apologetic for passing them. I just wanted it to be over as quickly as possible.

At last, there was the finish at Columbus Circle. I crossed it strongly, but with my eyes closed. As I bent over with my hands on my knees, someone from ABC put a microphone in my face. My first utterance was "Shit." Several runners who had finished already and were waiting to cheer me in put their arms around me, a sweet gesture of support I didn't want or need, as I didn't want it to look like I needed propping up, at least until Philip got there, and then I hung on him like a tent. I looked like a drowned rat, but I didn't care—everyone looked like a drowned rat. I was alive, and that was all that mattered. Some of the runners were limping and crying as they came in, some retching, others congratulating each other for having made it. I don't recall joy or disappointment, only a sense of resignation, and one of gratitude. I was alive. I'd done my best. I'd won the New York City Marathon. Eventually, the rain piddled off into a cool drizzle, and then stopped. The air became crisp and fresh, perfect for marathon running.

My time was 3:07:29. Under the circumstances, even Philip had to admit it was a pretty good performance. It just sounded so slow, and yet I knew that for the effort I had expended, it was my best race ever. Even today I know that. Half the field didn't even finish. The next woman was twenty-seven minutes behind me, and in time, that bit of trivia became noted as the biggest margin of victory in the history of the New York City Marathon, but that was just indicative of how few women there were, not how good I was.

As we lay in the dark that night just before sleep, I said to Philip, "I almost died today." It wasn't meant to be self-congratulatory or melodramatic, it was exactly how I felt, that I'd gone to the edge and there wasn't another molecule left to give without falling over.

"What do you mean?" he answered.

"I feel the way you do when a car spins in front of you on the highway and you just miss it—lucky and grateful to have survived."

Chapter | 19

PR!

As tired as I was, I was happy to go to work the next day, because all my colleagues had heard in the news that I'd won (at last!) and it felt good to accept their congratulations. To tell the truth, after doing a tough job, it is nice to hear such reactions even if your time is not what you would have liked; they didn't know the difference between 3:07 and 2:07, anyway. My butt was dragging all day, though. Never had a race so taken it out of me. Fred called, sounding all hang-dog about the weather, saying he was thinking of moving the date into October, which I thought was a no-brainer. I desperately needed lots of no-running days and some sleep. I felt as if I'd dodged a bullet.

I was also still dodging that serrated knife. Philip declared that we'd have to move up to White Plains for me to train safely. I agreed with that. Why not? Running was the center of our lives now and saving commuting time would be a blessing. We found a small rental house and moved in. Then Ira Berkow came out with his syndicated piece about my getting mugged. It was a sensitive article that appeared all over the country, and, as it turned out later that year, won a national award for best sports writing. So all the letters and phone calls started again, and requests for more interviews, which

now involved issues of runner safety (and women's safety in particular) and psychological mind-set. Naturally, every relative in the
country called my parents, weighing in with admonitions not to run
or encouragement to continue. All this in the first few days after the
New York City Marathon; it was a full life, and I needed a vacation.

So we went to Greece. I had asked Olympic Airways to remu-
nerate me with air tickets for my PR work and managed to persuade
Philip to forget his fantasy of drinking expensive wines in someone
else's chateau in the south of France, and enjoy what he was convinced was "down-market" Greece. We had a brief disagreement
when he thought I should run the new Skylon Marathon in Buffalo
only a month after New York, to "take advantage of my sub-three
fitness." It was an insane suggestion. I was exhausted, and I was
beginning to wonder if Philip knew how hard this was. So for once I
said no. I had yearned for Greece through all those slogging miles and
sweating interval sessions that long hard summer. This was the reward
I'd promised myself.

We ate fish in Rhodes and drank ouzo in tavernas in Crete, and
everywhere we went, men would stop Philip and shake hands, twirl
their curled black moustaches, and wink. Philip would twirl his curled
black moustache and wink back, and then they'd all clap each other
on the back and buy rounds of drinks. Philip enjoyed being taken for
a native and began to admire Greece—and himself—immensely.
The only downside was that he spent every evening in the bars and
tavernas, the way he did in New York. Even after dinner, Philip would
go out again on his own to sit in tavernas and drink and smoke with
the locals. Since they couldn't talk to each other I suppose they just
twirled their moustaches. I was disappointed that our entertainment
had to revolve around alcohol.

It had only been two years before that I'd been to Greece on my own, having to look in my purse to see if I had five extra drachmas to pay for a shower with my ten-drachma room. Although Philip and I were on a tight budget, I bought myself a silver bracelet that I'd seen two years before and had longed for ever since, thinking I'd never be able to have it. One rainy night, when we stopped for dinner in a steamed-up taverna in Agios Nikolaos, there was a young woman sitting in the corner with a cup of coffee, writing in her journal. Philip saw me looking at her and said, "Reminds you of yourself, huh?" He was right. Had it just been a couple of years ago?

When we got back to New York, it was cold, the clocks changed, and after a couple of weeks of base work on the road, it was back to the track for intervals two nights a week. They seemed harder than ever. One night I took off my shoes, threw them into the fence, and burst into tears. It seemed so endless, the track so vast and dark and forbidding. I felt gypped by the 3:07 in New York; I knew I had a sub-three and doubtless even better in me, but it all seemed so hard, and Boston, the next shot at the goal, was five long months away.

While training it gradually dawned on me that Scarlett O'Hara had come back to bite me. You can put off thinking about something difficult or unpleasant for a while, but if you are running, it will eventually bubble up from the bottom of the kettle right alongside something nice, like a much-loved teddy bear from childhood that you think has been forgotten. So pretty soon the mugger who held me at knifepoint began surfacing. At first he was just a flash of face on a dark night at about twelve miles into a fifteen-mile run. And then I could count on him appearing at just the point where I got tired; he'd be a shadow that ran up behind me on a street (my own) or be leaning against the fence rail on the track watching me (the school custodian just making his rounds). He became a nightly fixture.

Finally, I had had enough of him. One night at mugger time I called out loud, "Okay, you creep, come on out and face me like a man! You two-bit predator, waiting until I get tired, come at me again and I'll kill you with my bare hands!" (Actually, I used more graphic words.) Night after night I invited him to appear, and night after night in an hundred different ways I fought him, maimed him, and killed him. I always won. I'm not sure I want to know what a psychiatrist would make of this grotesque fantasy, but we deal with our demons as best we can, and I think that in my case, I exorcised this one fairly thoroughly. At the same time, I was diligent about running with confidence, even with assertiveness, making note of my surroundings at all times, and yes, testing my pepper spray every now and then to make sure it worked.

Then the months blended, and for all practical purposes the passage of time was identical to the year before: the workload increased, the intervals got faster, and I could barely keep up with them. The difference was that I now had no doubt about my ability to run under three hours and in fact to be a contender—not among the very best of the women marathoners, but ever-improving in the second tier. It was a massive revelation to me: training works! I had been the worst judge of my own capacity, and for years I'd let it limit me. It was an amazing self-discovery—I, an ordinary person, could become an athlete! It felt awfully good.

A real indicator in my changed attitude was calculating my weekly mileage, which the year before had been around eighty-five to ninety-five miles a week. Now it was 100 to 110 and if the total was going to come out at, say, 105, I'd make sure to add an extra mile a day to keep it at 110. Doing 110 miles a week made me feel as confident that I had the old Secret Weapon as I did when I was sixteen and had started running three miles a day, certain that nobody in the world ran more than three miles a day. Roll on, Boston; I was getting ready.

I was still overextending myself with meetings, shooting a commercial for Colgate (for free, because of my amateur status), writing for magazines—including the important new *womenSports*—and putting together big press events for AMF. But one day, an invitation came to hear a reading by May Swenson at the 92nd Street Y in Manhattan. Forget about a track meet! To be invited to a poetry reading was to touch the stratosphere, as far as I was concerned. I rearranged my training so that I could go. Zan Knudson was greeting guests at the door. She said, "Oh, May will be so glad to know you are here!" May will be glad to know *I'm* here? Wow! A hopeful fantasy flitted through my mind that May might have written a poem about that hot New York City Marathon, but she hadn't. She read some love poems, which thrilled me. One in particular thrilled me again a dozen years later, in a different life, in a different country, when she read it as I married Roger Robinson, the great love of my life.

Since the Maryland Marathon in '73 and '74, I had kept up communication with Ron Hill. I didn't understand why one of the best runners in the world, an Olympian, a European and Boston Marathon champion, wasn't invited to every race there was. As we got closer to Boston and I was communicating with Jock and Will, I was disturbed that they weren't flying Ron over for the race; he was, after all, the course record holder. Will explained once again that Boston paid nobody's expenses, but he gave me permission to try to find a sponsor for him. How could this be the greatest race in the world I wondered? I called Ron, he said he couldn't afford to come, naturally; what runner could afford to fly from England? He had just left his job as a textile chemist to put all his savings into starting what seemed then a very risky business, making performance running clothes.

I called my friends at Colgate-Palmolive. I figured their English-sounding Wilkinson Sword Blades would benefit from sponsoring Ron and was pleased when they didn't hesitate at giving $1,000 to cover Ron's expenses. But I was stunned when the public relations director asked, "Can we sponsor you, too?"

I'd always organized sponsorship for everyone else. It honestly never occurred to me to look for sponsorship for myself.

"Gee, thanks, but you know, I'm okay. It's just a drive up to Boston and I'm staying with friends so I don't need any help. But thank you just the same."

"Well, okay then, good luck in the race, talk to you when you're back!"

Duh, duh, triple *duh!* I could have organized a nice sponsorship for myself right then and there, but I didn't even hear what she was proposing. What I heard was expenses to Boston, which I didn't need. Anything more than that put me on dangerous ice with the AAU. My ears didn't allow me to hear things like "appearance fee" or "endorsement," as losing amateur status was so onerous.

Will Cloney was so pleased that he told the *Boston Globe* what I had done to get Ron there, and I was happy to have helped Will with his race in a way that had nothing to do with me personally. When Will asked me if I thought Ron would win, I said no, Bill Rodgers would. Will had no idea who Bill Rodgers was, and when I explained that Rodgers just got third place and first American in the World Cross-Country Championships in Morocco, it was clear that Will didn't understand how cross-country could be a predictor of a good marathon performance. Most people don't know that World Cross is the most competitive race in the world, and if you do well there, you can do well anywhere. Plus, Rodgers was a home-town Boston boy; I was surprised Will didn't know him.

For once, I was totally looking forward to the Boston Marathon. The days had gotten longer and I loved training in sunlight in both the morning and afternoon. I felt expansive, powerful, and long-limbed. I was very lean and fit now and felt both light and super-strong. Nothing hurt anymore; I was recovering quickly from all my hard runs. I occasionally added an extra interval at the end of a workout just for luck, something I'd been too tired to do previously. My weight was well under 120 pounds, I was almost skinny for the first time in my adult life, and I was eating like a horse. At the office cafeteria, I needed the kind of hot meal the workmen had, things like stuffed pork chops smothered in gravy, to keep up my strength, and then I'd eat another dinner in the evening. The workouts were flying by—indeed, they were much faster—and the air was full of spring and sweet blossom smells. I had the radio on full blast every morning while I was in the shower, and if they played Maxine Nightingale's "Right Back Where We Started From," I knew I'd have a lucky day; the tune would stick in my head for the afternoon intervals and make me feel happy the whole time.

As always, the phone rang incessantly the two weeks before Boston for press interviews, and more so this year, as I suddenly was one of the favorites—by default! Nina was injured; Jacqueline Hansen, who had run a brilliant new world record 2:43 again in the Culver City Marathon in December, wasn't coming; and Miki

Gorman was pregnant, a dream come true, since she had wanted a child for so long. That left a whole sea of women runners I'd never heard of, plus all those from the year before who were improving as rapidly as I was. Fifty-two of them were starting the race, a huge number. So I had no idea what would happen. For all I knew, an unknown Daisy Mae, who had been training alone in Appalachia, could come out of the hills and win the race, too, and all joking aside, it had to be considered, since women's running was wide open at the time. My goal was to break three hours, and that was it. All of our old friends and our crew from the year before were waiting for us as we rolled into their house near Boston for the 1975 marathon.

The morning of the race, Philip woke me in with a huge smile, smelling of fresh outdoor air and imitating the Swedish runner's accent we heard when he was interviewed on TV the night before: "Veel I vin de race? Da vind, vich vay it blow?!" Sunlight filled the room already; how long had he been up and dressed? He was practically prancing. "Hey baby, baby! It's fifty degrees, bright sun, and a tailwind! You're wearing number seven, it's your seventh Boston, and the moon is in the seventh house! It's your day!!" I smelled coffee, I salivated for my pancakes, and I was ready to rock. In the car on the way to the start Maxine Nightingale was singing "Right Back Where We Started From." It was a good sign and I felt incredible.

I signed in with the dutiful Gloria Ratti and the other women at the church in Hopkinton and pinned on my number. When I stripped off my sweats, a lot of heads turned. Sara Mae Berman gasped, saying "My heavens, Kathy! Just look at you, you are *really* ready!" I was a whopping ten pounds lighter than just the year before, and I had been pretty lean then. Sara Mae hugged me and shook my arm. "I am *so* proud of you! You've worked so hard!" Sara Mae was, and still is, a woman who infallibly supports other women and their efforts, even if she is dueling head to head with them in a race. She knows her athletic stuff, though, and when she of all people gave me this appraising and knowing look, followed by that compliment, I felt absolutely wonderful.

The start area was utterly jammed. Will and Jock were frantic as usual, but this year 2,400 runners were there, so they were utterly overwhelmed. How could they not have known? Everyone had registered for the race; did Jock and Will think they wouldn't actually come at the last minute? It was another instance of an unworkable, pitiful budget, inadequate preparation, and pure naïveté. I'd done enough promotional work to see what was happening a mile away and I ached for Will and Jock, who were just trying to keep this race going, no matter how little budget they had.

It was both heartbreaking and hilarious. For instance, there were 2,400 runners and eleven Porta-Johns—I counted them. The runners gave up and shamelessly squatted everywhere, on people's pristine New England front lawns, in their tulip and rose beds, and of course, in the surrounding woods, which had no leaves yet on the trees. Modesty? There was no choice—everyone was in the same boat with a race to run. We women had a toilet in the church, but there were fifty-two of us, and like little puppies, we all had to go again and again as we warmed up, so we hit the bushes like everyone else. Perhaps nothing spoke as much to women's equality as our squatting not far from a man doing the same thing and both of us pretending the other was invisible.

I was given the first starting position but moved about ten rows back. It was still too close to the front, but I would run wide on the left and let the others pass on the inside as we made the right onto Main Street from Hayden Rowe. Philip was alongside, winding his watches. I was shaking out my hands and purposely quivering my legs like a track runner. I guess it was chilly—it was 51 degrees—but I felt perfect, I had on all I needed, which was my little tennis dress, my magic roadrunner pin, and my big gray cotton gardening gloves.

Philip handed me the card with the splits written on it. I looked at it, but as usual, I didn't focus on it, especially avoiding the final number, and put it in the pocket of my tennis dress. Handy, those pockets. I always kept a tampon in the other one just in case.

"How do you feel?" It was a question Philip had never asked before.

I looked him in the eyes, and then down the road ahead. "I am going to run the *hell* out of this race," I answered.

And I was, too. I wasn't even afraid of the distance, or the inevitable pain, or the competition, or anything at all. I just wanted to attack it. Every damn interval for the last two years had been aimed at going under three hours, every waking thought, every dream, every nightmare, every time I said no to a beer or got up to an alarm I hated, every run with my eyelashes and snot frozen on my face or heat so hot the tar had stuck to my shoes, had been for this. And what a gift! I was here at last and healthy and I was going to launch the final ship to see if it sailed over the edge of the earth. And there was a wind at my back!

"Have a good time," Philip said.

My first mile was 5:35, 10 seconds faster than the previous year, and like then the fastest mile I'd ever run, period. It was downhill of course, but reckless anyway, but I just didn't care. I'd settle down soon enough, usually at four miles when I felt awful for a while and regathered myself. But four miles came and whizzed past and I did not fall into a trough but into a smooth, steady stride. No other woman passed me, and this first four miles is where it would happen if she started behind me. I could see no women in front of me, but the crowd of runners was thick. Everyone on the planet had been training like mad; it was like a stampede!

My water bucket team was there at five miles. The water was ice cold and I wasn't thirsty, but I drank half a cup anyway and poured the rest on my head. The crowd groaned when they saw that, as it was a very brisk day for the spectators, but for me, with the wind at my back, it was perfect. I was comfortable—warm, even—but not sweating at all. The cold water on my head would cool me and help prevent fluid loss when I did start to sweat.

A crew that was filming George Sheehan, a popular author and our guru of running, and me in a movie being made for the President's Council on Physical Fitness and Sports was alongside the road at six miles; I saw them before they saw me, so I yelled, and they started to try to run with me. It was hilarious. I'd told them beforehand there was no way they'd be able to shoot from the side like that, but people just have no idea how fast even a mediocre runner like me is running. A guy carrying a twenty-pound camera cannot possibly run alongside. It was so funny—run, stumble, try to run, and then Zoom! I was gone and he was just shooting my back as it disappeared down the road. It gave me a good laugh for a few miles.

The crowds of spectators seemed thicker than usual; perhaps it was the sunshiny day, or the fact that the race was so much larger than it had been the year before. They were wildly responsive to me, leaning out with their cameras and shouting all kinds of encouragement, mostly "First woman, first woman!!" Occasionally, there were shouts of "Looking great, second woman! Second woman!" I was not particularly concerned. I was running as fast as I could run, and the crowd rarely knows anything with accuracy. They'd start telling me "Almost there!" just after the halfway point.

Philip was there at Mile 10 and ran alongside with water and the time, saying I was going just fine. Someone shouted "First woman" again and Philip said, "Don't listen to them. You are definitely in second and she is running very well, so don't even think about it. Run your own race."

I couldn't believe it was past ten miles already; it seemed the whole course was easy, going down, down, down. So far, it felt like the easiest run I'd ever had, but I didn't want to jinx it by thinking that. I concentrated on concentrating. Halfway, at Wellesley, it was impossible to concentrate, so I let my mind go for a while. The women just went insane. They screamed so loudly they were crying, and I felt my eyes well up, too. I pumped my fist a couple of times in the air in a power salute and they screamed again; I couldn't help it. I just wanted them to know that Yes, we are powerful women; I'm really doing this for all of us and we've come such a long way and thank you for your support.

Something previously vague was clarified and clinched as I came out of Wellesley that day. It was the sense that I was not just being cheered for being a woman, or a woman who ran, but a woman who was running powerfully. Maybe it was my imagination, or some kind of self-acknowledgment for my hard work, but it seemed that the crowd voice was different, just as the tone of the male runners around me was different than in years before. Before, I'd been cheered in a

Good for you! way for being a role model and a barrier breaker; now it seemed to have a tone of athletic admiration. I liked the sound a lot.

I went back to concentrating: monitoring, measuring, keeping it steady. I can't remember anything but the sense that the road was flowing toward me; I didn't have to reach out for it and pull it in. I had only to put my feet down and up again, as quickly as I could. I would keep it in control to Heartbreak; after that, I could cut loose. That was the deal with Philip. I would fly after Heartbreak. Down, up, right turn at the fire station, so many people, concentrate, and suddenly I was at the top of Heartbreak, and Philip was running alongside with water.

Someone screamed, "Second woman, you can catch her, you can catch her!!"

"Not a hope," said Philip. "You are running well, and the only way you will catch her is if a Mack truck flattens her at the next intersection. She's running a world record; just don't think about it and run your own race."

"Wow, good for her. Who is it?"

"Don't know, some German. Big. Tall."

Someone screamed "First woman, first woman!" again.

"They keep saying that," I said.

"That's because she is bigger than a lot of the guys so they are mistaking her."

"Never listen to the crowd!" I singsonged Arnie's old adage, which I'd quoted to Philip many times. Right on cue, someone shouted, "Just two more miles!"

"I'm breaking my promise," Philip said. "I don't want you running hard into the finish. You are right on target. Don't blow it, keep it steady."

"Oh, come on, I'm feeling so good!" I was really disappointed; I wanted to let it rip.

"Don't take any chances. You are doing great." And with that, Philip turned off into the crowd.

I went back to concentrating. It was hard. My body felt great but my brain was getting tired. I wanted desperately to disassociate, to look at the crowd, wave back, put my arms out like an airplane on the downhills, make it fun because it felt very good. I was tired of work. I began having a raging conversation with myself.

Just don't blow it.

Well, it won't hurt if I just let gravity help on the downhills. I'll just roll with it, let it help me with momentum to charge the uphills. Philip couldn't have a problem with that. Come on, concentrate. Steady.

Nothing bad will happen, just run like hell.

Just keep it steady, you jackass.

We were on Beacon Street now, and I was cutting through scores of—maybe even a couple of hundred—guys who had slowed or were walking. The crowd was very thick but they hadn't yet squeezed down to a single chute, so there was more room to maneuver. The more men I passed, the more I picked up the pace. I had absolutely no disappointment that I was second, nor did I harbor any secret fantasy that the woman in first would suddenly come into sight. And I was also secure that nobody would close on me. The only sensation I had was that glassy, fragile feeling in my legs and knees, as if my legs were stems of crystal wine goblets. Very strong until tapped in just the wrong location. The trolley tracks were just the place where they could be shattered, too. Just that funny angle. I had a mental image of my knees suddenly exploding into glass particles.

Put that out of your mind! Steady, concentrate. Careful over the tracks.

With about two miles to go, Nina Kuscsik appeared alongside on a bicycle.

"How are you?" she said.

"Okay, I guess," I grunted, not wanting to waste breath now. I was trying to put my feet down carefully.

"You've got your sub-three and nobody is coming. Just keep it up!"

"Thanks, Nina!"

For the life of me, then and now, I can't imagine how she could maneuver a bicycle alongside us in that crowd.

The Citgo sign, one mile to go. I didn't feel the hill. I was passing everybody; it was like I was in a different race. Someone I passed who was walking shouted, "Hey, Kathy," and began running alongside. It was one of the guys from my old Syracuse University cross-country team, someone I normally would have been pleased to see after all these years.

"If you can run with me now, why the hell were you walking with only a mile to go," I wondered angrily.

He tried to start a conversation, but I shot him a look that said, "Shut up!" and he said, "Oh," and dropped back.

Good, just leave me alone and stay out of my way.

Past the Eliot lounge, incredible screaming. *Someday I'll go have a drink there, right, sure, someday a century from now when I have a free evening, ha ha.*

Right turn onto Hereford so fast I'm leaning into it, and now here is my time. One last hill. I popped up it like a champagne cork, rounded the left corner onto Boylston, and heard the full effect of the crowd. Everything was working, the legs were fine, the knees weren't going to break, the whole finish area spread out before me in massive color, I was flying down the straight. I flung my arms wide in sheer joy. *I will remember this forever.*

It couldn't have been better, but then suddenly it was. Philip was on the finish line again, and I flung my arms around him before I even stopped running. I was laughing and we were both twirling around and I was saying, "Did I do it, did I do it?" which was silly. I'd known I'd done it, just not by how much. I figured maybe 2:56. Philip held up the watch shouting, "2:51! 2:51!" I must have looked stunned, because my first reaction was that I couldn't run that fast. Then the most beautiful image came into my mind, of a big electronic scoreboard going clackety-clack as it rolled over the new order of performance rankings. A whole bundle of names rolled down and mine rolled up and froze there. I was sixth in the world, third in the USA, and first in New York City. A huge weight was lifted from the top of my head; I felt light; very, very light and free.

We went quickly through the garage area under the Prudential Building, weaving our way past the rows of cots where many shuddering men were lying down or sitting on the sides wrapped in blankets. One guy vomited spectacularly as we passed. Another was having terribly bloody feet attended to by one of the podiatrists. I was laughing with a bunch of guys who were following us through the area and toward the elevators up to the cafeteria where we'd eat the infamous beef stew. Philip had never been through this zone before and he was shocked.

"Jesus God, it looks like a Civil War hospital tent!" he exclaimed.

"Oh, this is nothing! It's often a lot worse. They'll be *fine*," I said confidently.

"You have got to be kidding me," he said as we headed for the elevator and he looked back over his shoulder. He was pale. It was a shocking sight if you weren't expecting it, and Philip had never seen this side of the sport. Although he saw me plenty sweaty and with terribly beat-up feet, he never saw how truly brutal the marathon could be. His expression was a confused mixture of admiration, pride, and wondering how the hell he had gotten himself involved with such a bunch of lunatics.

In the crowded elevator, I had another wonderful moment when several guys said, "May I shake your hand please? You beat me, and you deserve to, you really did your homework." Another said, "I tried like hell to catch you, you are just terrific." The whole elevator was full of guys who were congratulatory. They, like I, knew this wasn't a woman-trying-to-beat-a-man thing; it was all of us running as hard as we could. If I'd beaten them, it only meant I'd trained a lot harder. I'd only ever wanted recognition from my peer group of runners, and these guys gave it to me.

Upstairs, Jock and Will presented me with my second-place trophy, this time in one piece. In the line for the stew, I met my 1971 boyfriend and introduced him to Philip, who for once was not jealous in the slightest. This old boyfriend was full of admiration, and was especially complimentary about my skinniness. I thought this had to be the only situation where a lover is happier to see less boobs than more.

And then in a wonderful surprise, Arnie appeared. He'd run about a 3:20, a hugely remarkable feat for a guy who was now almost sixty years old, and who had thought it was all over when he was fifty. It was also an hour faster than he'd run with me in 1967, a race which of course he sacrificed for me. He had never said that, naturally.

Arnie, always self-effacing, said instead that it was me who got him over his injuries and back to running. It was so good to see him, and it was the first time he and Philip had met.

What an occasion! It was marred only by the fact that Arnie went on and on, complaining about the backup at the finish line, about how it went all the way to the top of Boylston Street, and about how he'd never get his correct finishing time and that they were not allowed to run across the finish line. It took me some time to figure out what he was saying, but apparently after about 3:10, when the great deluge of runners descended on the finish line, the finish scorers could not write down their bib numbers and finishing times fast enough. It's hard today, with computerized chip timing, to imagine that such a thing could happen, but it was becoming an every weekend occurrence as the number of runners was growing faster than the technology. There were no display watches, digital clocks at the finish, or even a chronomix recording device in those days. So in 1975, the runners jammed back up the street; sad, weary pilgrims, unable to cross the magical line, leaning against each other with their faces on the back of the person in front of them, holding each other up as they inched forward.

No toilets at the start, no time at the finish, no expenses for your champions; and this was the Boston Marathon, the greatest marathon race in the world outside of the Olympic Games. Someday, I would organize a race—a Dream Race—that got it all right.

Still, it was a banner year for Boston and all of us knew it. The likelihood of having these kinds of conditions were one in a million, and they produced records in both the men's and women's races. If you ran that day, you knew you'd talk about it for the rest of your life because it was so rare and special.

Philip was right; the first-place woman set a new world record of 2:42.24. She was Liane Winter, from West Germany, another Dr. van Aaken athlete. Liane had run a 2:50 in his race in Waldniel the year before. She was awesome, and here in the press-and-beef-stew room, she was being crushed with interviews when I saw her for the first time. I only had a chance to shake her hand. She was the biggest woman marathoner I'd ever met, about five feet ten and 150 pounds, a fabulous powerhouse who completely dispelled my theory about the best being tiny and light, like Miki Gorman. I laughed right out loud; what a fabulous sport! It really *is* for anyone who wants to do it.

Liane improved her personal best by eight minutes; her nine-minute victory over my 2:51:37 is noted in the lore of Boston as the biggest margin of victory in the history of the race, something I find amusing after my similar statistic in New York. Boston's biggest story though, was my pick to win, Bill Rodgers, who improved his best by a whopping ten minutes to run a 2:09.55 for a new course and a new American record! The rest of the men's field let him go. They should have paid attention to his finish at World Cross. When Tom Fleming and I saw each other in the cafeteria, we hugged and shook our heads. Tom said, "Can you believe it? You and I ran PRs that we never thought we could do, and we both *still* got beat!" Like me, there was no malice, only amazement. Amazement and lightness.

PART IV | WARM-UP

The warm-up is designed to get you to the starting line mentally and physically ready to run. Stretching, striding, sweating, psyched.

CHAPTER | 20

LAST DANCE

This sense of feeling light was very real. People talk about walking on air and I understood now what that meant, but it was more than euphoria. For over ten years I'd been carrying the burden of having to prove myself. No matter how right I was in being a barrier breaker and pushing for women's equality, whether at Lynchburg College or Syracuse University or at the Boston and other marathons, there was still that element who said, well, she's not really a good athlete. Even I had said that! It shouldn't have made a speck of difference in the right of women to run, but it did, and it always has in the quest for women's rights. No matter how good Billie Jean was as a tennis player or how justified she was in her quest for equal prize money, world thinking changed most when she beat Bobby Riggs. Similarly, my marathon time now was good "even for a man" and a lot of people were compelled to admit that I was more than a sports agitator or media darling.

I felt light in another way, too, as if a flashbulb had gone off: If I, who had limited talent, could run this fast, thousands of women could run even faster. And millions who were just ordinary could achieve the unimaginable. All sizes, shapes, backgrounds; they've all got the ability. I was right, doggone it! All they needed was the opportunity to try. If they tried it, they'd feel it, they'd believe it, and they'd do it. God, I was happy!

And it was beginning to happen. The women's running movement was becoming stronger and stronger; we were rushing from discovery to discovery, and the media sensed both the excitement of it and our own urgency for wanting the marathon for women to be a lot more. My thinking focused more and more on the Olympic Games. Olympic inclusion for women's distance runners would mean two things: first, that the whole world would at last acknowledge women's physical capability, and second—but no less important— that women *themselves* would suddenly realize that they could be distance runners at the highest level. I felt it was as important as women having the right to vote, because talent, strength, and capability cannot be fully realized if there are no personal rights to allow them to be visible or be deemed significant in the first place. My own breakthrough was a spearhead for women everywhere. The Olympic marathon, the global mythic symbol of arduousness and courage, would be the best showcase of their capability.

I knew that people often believed only in what they could see; I knew there were many women training for shorter events in the Games because that's all there was and they didn't know anything else. Again, I felt strongly that it was going to come down to creating the opportunity to show them. It was not going to happen with protests and petitions and angry letters. It was going to happen by creating first-class events that showcased women and gave each a mind-expanding experience. It was like that line in the book *Shoeless Joe* (later made into the movie *Field of Dreams*): "Build it and they will come." But who was going to build it?

The media and various vocal groups of women wanted to rail against the stodgy old men of the International Olympic Committee, as that gave them a male patriarchy to hate. They dragged out the picture of Jock attacking me at Boston as if that were the situation for all women runners and that the mean old men needed to rectify it. Some started indignant letter-writing campaigns to the IAAF and IOC. I wanted to scream, *Oh, come on, they don't even know we exist and now you are antagonizing them!* Again and again in interviews and appearances, I tried to defuse that story and explain instead that we had a lot of homework to do to educate the powerful decision makers. Yes, it was true they were all male, but MOST men, particularly the runners, were strongly in support of us.

There were open meetings in New York of the AAU Women's Long Distance Running Committee to discuss the issues and tactics, and it is astonishing today to remember that some of the audiences for these meetings would fill whole auditoriums, with women packed against the walls. They were all passionate and vocal; it was clear that running had empowered them as women as had nothing before in their lives and was fundamentally changing the way they regarded themselves, their careers, their families, and their futures. Receiving Olympic recognition was important at a very basic level to them, no matter what their ability. They wanted to know how they could help make it happen and were willing to work on committees, write checks—whatever it took. They turned often to Nina and me for answers because we were the best runners in New York, and at times the pressure was overwhelming. Before, the pressure had been to run to prove women had the strength to run at all, then to prove we could be athletes. Now it seemed everyone was counting on us to create a miracle.

After an evening of trying to explain the intricacies of the athletics hierarchy, which was an arcane science at best, and showing the past dismal history of longer running events for women, I'd come home pretty discouraged. If a 3,000-meter were added in the next Olympiad (1980) and every Olympiad added another event, maybe we'd get the marathon in 1992. People didn't understand the laborious committee process. I'd worked long enough in corporations to realize that change took forever, so the prospect of implementing change in the old-line organizations AAU, IAAF, and IOC was daunting. I kept thinking there was another way to make this happen.

What kept me thinking positively was the steady increase in other women's sports sponsorships and the ballyhoo about women's sports opportunities in general. "You've Come a Long Way, Baby" was the slogan for both the Virginia Slims brand of cigarettes and the women's professional tennis circuit it sponsored, but it also became the ubiquitous tagline for anything having to do with women's sports and women's equality issues in general. The spirit of the slogan was recognized by just about everyone in America; maybe they didn't like the message, but they got it.

Ellie Riger finished her film for ABC, and Colgate had a big press conference to announce the Colgate Women's Sports Special. Inside the restaurant were giant photographs of many of us in the film; it felt great to be on the wall alongside Billie Jean and Carol Mann and Donna de Varona. My photo was the one of me running across Red Square; David Foster thought the onion domes in the background were fabulous and that I was a little daring and exotic for running there. I was amazed that David Foster even knew who I was. He was paying for the sponsorship of the film and paying to get it on network TV. I admired his fearless decisiveness.

Knowing what I know now, I might have gone to David Foster for mentoring advice. It never occurred to me then to ask for advice; I only dared to absorb it from afar. I think I felt I might look stupid and helpless if I asked for advice, and I was stubborn. I wanted to do things myself and think them out until I had a real plan to propose. I also had a theory that turned out to be right: When you are looking for sponsorship, don't go to the companies that are already sponsoring events. Carve out something unique for someone different so they create their own identity.

I'd become friends with Elizabeth Phillips, a stalwart volunteer officer at the New York Road Runners Club, and a back-of-the-pack runner who loved the way running had changed her life. Elizabeth worked for NFL films, and she knew a lot of big players in sports media. Thus, because of our jobs, we both had a different sports perspective than most of our runner friends. I'd often call Elizabeth when my head was spinning and ask her, "Am I crazy or what?" and she always gave me a good, no-nonsense answer. I came to value her opinion and our growing friendship.

I sometimes tried to interest my own company, AMF, in women's sports as a potential growth area. I was getting a lot of publicity as a visionary; you'd think they would have noticed, but I was met only with patronizing smiles. It's true: you're never a prophet in your own land—unless you are hired specifically to be the prophet. That's the trick, I thought. More grist for the brain mill over those long miles.

Then it was June, and time to start the four-month buildup to the 1975 New York City Marathon, which that year was designated as the second AAU National Women's Marathon Championship. From the outset, the marathon was lackluster, though, as Aristotle Onassis had died and Olympic Airways was in disarray. There was no sponsorship and we went back to a no-frills event. I concentrated on training. Although I had four hot months of summer ahead of me, the race had been moved to October, so there was no way it was going to be a steam bath again. My plan was to train hard all summer, finally get another sub-three hours and this time on the New York course, and win a national title. I was highly motivated, even though it was hard as always starting up the high mileage.

I bumped the mileage back up to 80 a week, planning to be doing 100 to 110 a week by mid-July. That would give me four very solid months of training for New York, including six weeks of over 100 miles a week. It felt so routine and I felt so confident of the workload that I hadn't given a thought of the risks of jumping from 50 easy miles to 80 harder miles in the initial week. In mid-June, coming down a long hill three miles from home, a pain went through my right knee like a bullet. In fact, my first thought was that someone in the nearby woods had shot me, accidentally or on purpose. My second reaction was how to stop and keep from falling, as I was going fast down a steep slope. Then I had to figure out how to get home. Limping was my only option; three miles took forever. So, this is what a real injury feels like; this is not blisters or a sore Achilles tendon or a crick in my back. I was totally screwed and I knew it. By the time I got home I was trying to figure out how to find the best surgeon and thinking of how many months it would take to build back the base I was going to lose.

On Billie Jean King's recommendation, I went to Dr. John Marshall, who said my kneecap was rubbing into the cartilage due to two things—first, an imbalance of my foot and the camber of the road, which can be corrected with orthotics; and second, my weak thighs. I needed stronger quadriceps muscles to hold the kneecap in place so

it would stay snugly in its "track." No surgery was n
mechanical things. This was a relief, but I was ins'
by the assumption that I had weak thighs. "These legs run .
a week," I said. I couldn't believe what he said was true. While we
chatted, Dr. Marshall invited me to "sit" opposite him, each of us
with our backs against the wall, without a chair. "This is what we
skiers do to strengthen our quads; you should do this exercise every
day as long as you can," he said. He wrote out directions for fitting
my orthotics and explained that running made the backs of my legs
very strong but didn't do much for my quadriceps. After seventy seconds, my legs were quivering and I had to stand up. He just smiled as
he continued to sit against the wall and write notes. As I left and we
shook hands, he said, "I love working with competitors."

Instead of smooth 100-mile weeks, the hot summer was a
rebuilding of base. I hated the orthotics, which gave me chronic blisters and forced me into a different stride, which caused stabbing side
stitches. There didn't seem to be any flow. To top it off, every night
after I ran, I had to face the prospect of sitting against the wall in my
invisible chair and working up from seventy seconds. It is a diabolical exercise, because your thighs sting after thirty seconds no matter
how much strength you build up. You can't even watch TV because
you keep looking at your watch in despair. After four months, I was
up to holding this position for seven minutes at a time. No skier was
going to beat me, and I was going to make sure I never had a knee
injury again if I could help it. The knee stopped hurting, and thirty-
two years later, if it hurts, I do this exercise and it goes away.

I was favored for the New York City Marathon, but I knew as the
day got closer it was going to take a miracle for me to win. The competition was just too fast to think I could stay with them after all the

training time I'd lost, and my stride was still off. If you're going to race people who are as good or better than you, the flow has to be flowing. Kim Merritt, a twenty-year-old track runner from Wisconsin, had posted fast times and was especially daunting. Miki Gorman was coming back after having had her baby, so was an unknown quantity, and others, like Joan Ullyot and Gayle Barron, whom I'd beaten at Boston, were coming on strong.

In the end, it was a triumph for the young Merritt, who set a phenomenal course record of 2:46; she even beat Miki Gorman by seven minutes. Five women broke three hours, and I was not one of them. I ran a 3:02; it was a tough run for me, punctuated by side stitches that could only be eased by walking. I remember waving Gayle and Joan past me during one walking stretch, feeling like I was in one of those nightmares you have when you can't lift your feet.

This race preceded the most difficult time of my running career, and as it turned out, my relationship with Philip, too, as I entered the long, dark winter season of training. I was lumbering. The Boston Marathon seemed a million years away and everything was suddenly wrong. At a certain level, I knew that some things in my life had been wrong for quite a while, but I either didn't recognize them or ignored them. It's the truth: When you are running well, the sense of self-esteem is very great, and it makes up for a lot else in life that is less than wonderful. I'd been in my job for three years and wanted to connect my career somehow with women's running. I'd been writing proposal after proposal, but each seemed small-scale. Doubleday publishers, at a memorable New York lunch, had asked me to write a how-to book of running. "I don't think anybody would read that book," I said. (Honestly, I said that. Two years later Jim Fixx's *Complete Book of Running* went on the bestseller lists for a year and sold over a million copies.) I promised to send Doubleday a proposal of something else relating to running, maybe a novel. But for months I'd done nothing. I was going nowhere. Professionally, I felt I was running in circles.

Worst of all, Philip's drinking had escalated into a nightly debacle. His business was a failure, so instead of drinking with friends after work to have fun, he drank to get over it and would come home angry and abusive, stumbling around the house and crashing into things. Sometimes he didn't come home at all. On one occasion when I met him the next morning at the train station he admittedly sheepishly that he'd spent the night in jail, having been picked up on a DUI and slugging the cop who arrested him.

I'd never experienced this kind of behavior, and my first instinct was to get the hell out of Dodge. But that seemed terribly unfair, after all, Philip had helped me achieve my dreams in running and now he needed a helping hand, even though he kept biting it. I began investigating alcoholism, and went to talk to a doctor who was an expert. Once I could accept that alcoholism is a disease, I was more convinced than ever to help Philip. I mean, you wouldn't leave someone because they had cancer, right?

Philip agreed to quit drinking and get professional help but refused joint counseling. Our lives were like walking on eggs, since without drinking Philip was wound up as tight as a clock. He lost his fun, his charm, his interest in life, and his interest in my running. Sex was nonexistent. The only thing he didn't lose was his sarcasm.

I felt I was living in two worlds. One was a rather gloomy private life nobody really knew about, not even my parents. The other was a public life in which I could persevere and overcome all odds. I didn't want to feel like a quitter on this relationship, or anything else. Sometimes uplifting things helped me through—like running, of course, which is always a balm, or other things, like Diana Nyad's amazing swim around Manhattan Island. This led to a great friendship when the two of us were featured together in a TV documentary made by the iconoclastic baseball player turned TV commentator Jim Bouton.

It was a brutal winter; it seemed that every day brought another snowstorm, but eventually I got used to the cold and ice, and the running righted itself. The stride eventually smoothed, all my workouts got faster than a year ago, even without Philip's supervision, and I was up to eleven minutes on the invisible chair. One night I was on a TV talk show with Billie Jean King, and who should be the third guest but Dr. John Marshall! He was so pleased that my knee was fine. After the show I said, "Hey, how many minutes should I be doing that thigh exercise? You said do it as long as I can and I'm up to eleven minutes and it's getting a bit time-consuming." Dr. Marshall's jaw dropped. "Gosh, I don't know anybody who can do that longer than four minutes!" I burst out laughing.

Philip announced in March that he was going to allow himself to drink again, but with extreme moderation, and he did. I was actually relieved; he was so depressed without drinking that he was like a zombie. In retrospect, I believe his doctor was giving him some kind of drugs, but Philip would never tell me anything.

Suddenly he wanted to see the training charts and was very pleased I was on schedule; it was like he'd been out of the office on sick leave. Then he called my parents and invited them to come up and watch me run the Boston Marathon, telling them that no matter how much I downplayed myself, I was a champion and they would be sorry if they missed seeing me run in my prime. I had always discouraged my parents from coming to marathons because they would be an extra organizational problem and I had enough on my mind as it was. You can't invite someone as important as your parents to a complicated event without accommodating them so they could actually see it. Now Philip was undertaking this for me. It was a wise and kind thing for him to do.

It had been cold and sleety for weeks, and the Thursday before Boston I went to work in a wool suit. When I came outside at five, it was suddenly 80 degrees! Everything I took to wear in Boston that weekend except for my skimpy running outfit was made of wool. The heat wave was so sudden that the public buildings couldn't possibly get air-conditioned and all the press conferences and meetings were sweltering. The heat kept rising alarmingly, 90 on Saturday, 95 on Sunday. George Sheehan, who was a physician as well as an author, gave a speech Sunday afternoon and focused the whole topic on the heat, intoning, "Someone is going to die tomorrow." There was a tremendous debate about the noon start. Temperature at race time was predicted to be over 100. Some said the marathon should be canceled. There was a rush on painter's hats, and a media plea to the public to hand out ice cubes for us to put in them.

It was like the heat in New York the year before. Philip, my parents, our friends, and I all moved in a kind of stupor that morning, trying to get organized, and left for the start twenty minutes later than usual. This normally would not have been a problem, but the Massachusetts Pike was backed up from 495, and 495 was backed up from the Hopkinton exit. We waited and inched along; thirty minutes passed, then forty, then an hour. A wave of panic hit all of us when we realized that all the cars in front of us were trying to squeeze into the tiny two-lane road into Hopkinton and get to the start. I found a piece of cardboard in the car, inked "7" on it, my race number, and pinned it on. At 11:45 I figured I could just make the start if I ran like hell, so kissed my folks and Philip, made a fast pee stop in the woods alongside the car with my hands covering my face pretending that hundreds of stranded motorists couldn't see who I was, and then beat it to the start. There was a roar of laughter and applause as I ran up the empty roadway right up to the front of the race where all the men were poised, just moments before the gun went off. Will Cloney was there and I gasped, "Will, it's me, we got stuck in traffic! I made my own number, please tell the officials even though I did not pick up my real one I started at the start of the race!" "Oh, Kathy," Will said, "please, please be careful, it is so hot, it is dangerously hot, please be careful!" I thought he was going to cry. I might have cried if I'd had time but the gun went off and the race was under way.

Despite all the talk about going out cautiously, the start was a mad rush. I had to go like hell just to keep from getting trampled. Kim Merritt flew by me, and then Miki Gorman. So much for *them* being careful! I was already soaked from my run to the start and by mile two I was dripping. I eased back and a couple of other women passed me, but less quickly. I'd give it to Framingham, I decided, just like I did in 1973, only 1973 was just a warm spring day compared to this. At Framingham, I knew that if I didn't pull back and make it a long training run it would be decided for me anyway. Save it for another day, I thought, it's never going to happen today. I was cooking hot and my feet were blistering already. Gayle Barron eased past with a pat, and then a slow parade of others began to go by. Philip and my parents were at Mile 10; seeing them was the best part of the race, I couldn't believe they'd even gotten there! I was only sorry I didn't have a better show for them, but they cheered me as if I were winning the damn thing. Boy, are they wonderful.

The entire roadway was lined with people with buckets of water, ice cubes, and garden hoses. When I saw one of my crew at Mile 15, I could tell he felt superfluous with a bucket of what was now warm water when we were all getting showered the whole way. It was as if we were swimming. My crew shouted that Philip had to go on to the finish; it was too crowded to try to meet me at Heartbreak. That was fine with me, as this was not a race but a survival contest, anyway. How he'd gotten himself and my parents through the crowd at Mile 10 was astonishing.

At Mile 16, Liane Winter passed me going up the hill. Here was the defending champion, having a terrible day, too, and looking like a big rag doll. As she came up on me she greeted me like a best friend found in a desert, shaking her head, saying, "Too *heiss*, too *heiss*, Katty!" and she stumbled on ahead, still shaking her head. I thought, well, she's come all the way from Germany in the hopes of a repeat victory and has had to bag it, too, so I'm in good company in the disappointment department.

Joan Ullyot came up to me at around 18 miles and chirped, "Well! We're the *smartest* people in this race! Those others ahead of us are going to pay for going out hard, and we'll be just fine." "Yeah, I've been thinking about Sheehan's speech all day," I answered. Joan was a physician, too, and smart as hell no matter what the circumstances, and I was glad she was agreeing with me. I began thinking about which marathon I'd do next to make up for this one.

Then the weirdest thing happened. When we went over Heartbreak Hill at Mile 21 and headed toward Boston and the coast, a sharp wind blew cold air in from the sea. This cold air had been trapped by the hills, so while it was ferociously hot and still west of Heartbreak, there was a 60-degree headwind on the east side of it.

Dripping wet and at the fatigue point in the marathon, we started the sharp downhills into what felt like a freezer. Even my strong thighs—my *very* strong thighs!—began to seize. Whenever the road flattened out, I tried to shake them loose, and whenever there was an uphill grade, I ran hard to warm them. I never thought I'd welcome uphills this late in the race.

I finished in 3:19. A woman sprinted past me near the finish and I heard her squealing to her friends afterward, "I beat Kathrine Switzer, I beat Kathrine Switzer!" I'm glad to give you this moment, I muttered to myself, and then silently thought, "Oh, just go shove it." Philip greeted me at the finish with, "If I knew you were going to tank the race like this, we wouldn't have bothered coming." I protested, and we argued into the finish area, where I said you could really harm yourself by pushing it on a day like today, and Philip said, "Oh yeah? It doesn't look like it hurt *her* any!" and he pointed to Kim Merritt, who sat slouched on the floor with the laurel wreath still on her head. "It was so damn dangerous that *she*"—he pointed again—"managed to run a 2:47!" It was an extremely impressive perform-ance; I didn't want to take anything away from her, but I said, "Okay, but we don't know what kind of price she's going to pay for this." In fact, Kim was later taken to the hospital and treated for hypothermia. Still, Philip had to snap back with the final word, "And you don't think winning the Boston Marathon is worth the price?"

I decided then and there that I would have to find another coach, perhaps work with a team. Philip would probably be delighted to abdicate the responsibility. Clearly, he'd lost interest, I was losing respect for him, and it was only now making an unhealthy relation-ship even worse. As it turned out, it didn't matter. Boston 1976 was my last marathon.

Chapter | 21

A New Race to Run

"My God," said Dr. Weisenfeld. "I don't know how you walked in here."

"Pretty disgusting, huh?" I answered. My feet looked like hamburger. The heat of the marathon, the chafing orthotics, the odd gait, had all contributed to the worst case of blisters I'd ever had. They were raw and bleeding, and my toenails were puffed up with huge black blood blisters underneath. Murray Weisenfeld, my podiatrist, usually joked with me about my bad feet and my shark's capacity for high pain tolerance, but this time he was serious. "There is absolutely no way you're going to be able to run for a month. Really, just forget about it and let the feet heal." I told him I'd had it with the orthotics and was going to start over in my old flat shoes; my knee was going to be fine.

But I had run my last marathon. That historic race and everything it had led to would remain vitally important in my life, but now, though I didn't know it, I was on the starting line of a different, equally challenging course. Its direction and contours would not be clear to me for another year.

Almost as soon as I limped out of Dr. Weisenfeld's office, new opportunities and problems began to appear. AMF put my speech-writing abilities to work for the company's president. I did my first race commentary for radio. I was invited to West Point to help the first cohort of female recruits through a very difficult time in their early training. I joined a group of significant women athletes, including Billie Jean King, Rosie Casals, Donna de Varona, Carol Mann, and Peggy Fleming, on an action committee convened by the visionary philanthropist Eva Auchincloss that was the pilot for the influential Women's Sports Foundation. I was even offered a job at *Runner's World.* That came during a wonderful weekend in California at *Runner's World*'s tenth anniversary, when I was named Female Runner of the Decade and Jim Ryun, the legendary miler, was named Male Runner of the Decade. The magazine also photographed me for the cover running in the grassy hills above San Francisco with the Golden Gate Bridge in the background. The job offer came to nothing because the publisher, Bob Anderson, would never commit to a contract, and I wouldn't move to California without one. So that was another possible course that I never ran.

Another major commitment came in a bombshell from Philip's ex-wife. She was breaking up with her second husband and asked us to take one of the two children. They were great kids and deserved the best, but this came at a time when I was very close to leaving Philip, who had slipped back into his destructive drinking habits. Some soul-searching brought me to the awareness that my job as an adult was to give any child a fair chance and sense of security. Another way of putting it might be that I am always willing to jump from the frying pan into the fire. But Eric was both sensible and sensitive, and thrived with me, despite finding it difficult to relate to his father. He was a good part of my life for the next four years.

Speech writer, journalist, military motivator, stepmother—I played many roles during the subsequent months, and each put off my decision to start training again. For the world around me, though, it was an astonishing time, a sort of "perfect storm" for sports: public relations, sponsorships, and event promotion had become the hot new thing. As advertising in general grew more expensive, sports sponsorship gave a lot more bang for the corporate buck. At the same time, running was simply booming, and women's sports and women's rights were bursting simultaneously into the public consciousness. Both were new, fresh, high-visibility, and incredibly inexpensive. Running was also participatory. For the first time a sponsor could get both sponsorship credit and directly touch thousands of devotees. To me, the biggest slam-dunk was going to be sponsorship of women's running. We never failed to get huge publicity. I kept going to meetings, kept stuffing the Idea Box. The phone rang and rang.

One important call came from Jess Bell, the president and owner of the family-owned cosmetics company Bonne Bell. A super sports enthusiast, he'd recently discovered running, and his new mission was to get everybody he knew doing it. Jess insisted that running had saved his marriage by putting order and discipline back into his life and giving both him and his wife, Julie, renewed self-esteem. This amazed me because they were wealthy, jet-setting, skiing people who didn't seem to be lacking in self-esteem, but it is astonishing what running can do. Jess and Julie were an attractive couple anyway, but Jess went on about how they lost weight, got toned up, and how all that was so cool because they were happy to make love with the lights on again. Well, people could be quite frank in the '70s!

Jess was staging a community race in Lakewood, Ohio, where the company was located and wanted Gayle Barron and me as celebrities. I also offered to help him with the PR, and in fact handled the press truck for him, which was more interesting to me than running his race. I was back to jogging, but not yet back to training. He was ebullient about this small race and told me how he wanted to get into sponsorship of women's running. I thought, this could be it—maybe there is an opportunity here for me. The original 1972 Crazylegs Mini had lost its sponsorship when Crazylegs Hirsch, a famous football player, sued Johnson's Wax over the appropriation of his nickname. Despite growing in numbers and prestige since then, the Mini was now surviving only through the generosity of Arno Neimand, a successful New York businessman and runner. When I told Jess that the 1977 New York Mini-Marathon would be a perfect race to sponsor and I could make it happen, he jumped at the offer.

This got me thinking. A job with Bonne Bell promoting races around the country would be a grand start to my dream of getting women's distance events into the Olympics, even better than working for *Runner's World*. I sent Jess a proposal on his series idea, stressing state-of-the-art race organization, AAU sanctions, and professional public relations. It was more than Jess wanted to spend—he just wanted a celebration of women. Still, he offered me a job. Unfortunately, it was for less than I was making at AMF. In the career quest, I've always thought one should take creative opportunities over salary, with one exception: The New York Rule. You can come to New York for less pay, but you must never leave New York for less pay. So as Jess and I chatted away all autumn about Bonne Bell promotions, I got paid as a consultant and we let the job discussion drift.

New York was more than ever the place to be, in running as in almost everything. Incredibly, the 1976 New York City Marathon was going to be run not the old obscure four laps around Central Park, but through the very streets of the city, linking the five boroughs in one ambitious 26.2 mile swoop. The fantasy was coming true! The idea was that of the political gadfly George Spitz, though Fred and lots of us had floated similar concepts for years, and the basic idea of a "city tour" marathon dates back to the 1900 Olympics in Paris. In New York, the logistics were horrendous, but when Manhattan Borough President Percy Sutton, real estate mogul Jack Rudin and his brother Lew, Manufacturers Hanover Trust Company's Charlie McCabe, and the publisher George Hirsch (a devoted and talented runner and founder of *New Times* magazine) all threw their weight behind it, and with the extra pretext of celebrating America's bicentennial, the city said yes. It was breathtaking, and Fred was close to apoplexy.

And oh, it was brilliant! The runners poured across the Verrazano-Narrows Bridge, in a tiny trickle at first and then seeming to fill three whole lanes, which I know sounds hilarious today when they fill six lanes on the top level and three on the bottom. Someone put a news helicopter overhead, and the resulting images were some of the most dramatic ever seen in sports. The runners screamed: "We own the bridge! We own the streets of New York!" If you weren't here, you missed the greatest thing in running!" Runners went streaming excitedly through streets where jaded New Yorkers, who had seen everything and could care less, responded with open-hearted cheers. They had a world-class field to cheer for, too. Bill Rodgers won in 2:10 and Frank Shorter, who had just added an Olympic silver medal to his 1972 gold, ran a 2:13. Miki Gorman stunned the world by running 2:39 at age forty-one, less than a minute off the world record and 18 months after having a baby. She and the runner Chris Stewart also led to the carpeting of the bridges, as their feet were lacerated by the sharp gratings, and Miki's tiny shoes kept getting caught in them.

My own blisters had healed, but I was still avoiding training, so I accepted a role as a radio commentator for the race. The event and the celebrations afterward made me realize how huge our little sport had become. Plus it seemed everyone I knew—people who were just *joggers,* for heaven's sake!—was writing a running book, and here I was writing nothing, with Doubleday calling regularly. I was just dancing around the edges as the perfect sports storm blew by.

Determined to get something done for Doubleday at last, I decided the only way was to hole up with no distractions. I booked Wednesday through Sunday at Gurney's Inn out in Montauk, at the end of Long Island, the last week in January, the cheapest possible part of the year. I was on the start line again. But yet another course was about to open up before me.

I was trying to get things done at work so I could take the days to write, when Eva Auchincloss called from the West Coast to invite me to a meeting called by the new Women's Sports Foundation in New York. Executives from Colgate, Clairol, Avon, Philip Morris, and *Sports Illustrated* would be there, discussing sponsorship and media opportunities. I'd never have this kind of opportunity again to meet such heavy hitters, and I wasn't going to miss it for the world. In hindsight, you'd think my employers at AMF would have sent a top executive to such a meeting, but women's sports were far from their consciousness.

I wore my best suit and was nervous at the palpable power in the room. But the joy and excitement overcame that quickly; Billie Jean knew everyone and set up an easy, casual, style while Eva kept us on track. Each of us attending athletes was asked to give a quick overview of sponsorship and media opportunities in our sport. Since I was one of the few actually working a corporate job in PR, my report was quite different from the others'. I presented not just what my sport needed, but what my sport offered. At the time, women's road running was incredibly small time—you'd have to be a cock-eyed optimist like me to envision what it has become today—but what I presented resonated. I could tell they got it. They were not shocked when I said women's running was going to become one of the biggest participatory sports in the world. Later, I realized that these were CEOs of some of the biggest consumer companies in the world, and what set them apart was their powerful sense of vision and creativity. That's why they were there. It was another Eureka! moment.

Lunch was brought in—sandwiches and coffee on a cart! I'd thought these kinds of top executives only dined in their thirty-sixth-floor corporate dining rooms, but instead they all descended on the cart, took a sandwich, and walked around chatting to everyone. In the *Wall Street Journal*, these people were referred to as titans, bull-dogs, tenacious, and uncompromising, so it was an eye-opener to see how human and friendly they all were. Mark Williams, the executive vice president of Avon, came right over to me, saying, "Hey, I just read about you in the *New York Times* the other day. And I was inter-ested in your remarks this morning. I'm wondering if you can help me out. We have just begun sponsorship of something called the Avon Futures Tennis Tour, which is the developmental satellite tour for the Virginia Slims. That's enough for us for the moment, but a few weeks ago we got a proposal from our general manager in Atlanta asking for consideration of sponsoring a women's marathon there. We take requests from general managers seriously, but I have no idea if this is doable. Would you be willing to look it over and give me your opinion?"

"Sure, I'd love to," I answered. "That's like asking me to open your Christmas presents!"

He took me to lunch at Orsini's the next Tuesday. An invitation to one of the most "in" restaurants in New York was a nice send-off for my writing "vacation," which was about to start. But first I skimmed the proposal. It was a two-page job and I smiled when I saw it was put together by old friends from the Atlanta Track Club. "I know these guys," I told Mark Williams. "They're good, they know what's going on, this is a good idea." Bill Neace, Richard Calmes, David Martin, and Jeff Galloway had been inspired by what Gayle Barron told them about the all-women's international marathon in Waldniel, so they approached the general manager of Atlanta's huge Avon facility.

I went right to the budget, which looked sufficient to pull off a nice local race but not make it international or give Avon the visibility I knew they would be hoping for. I was rattling off organizations and publications when Williams said, "I don't know any of these players or any of the structure here. Would you rewrite this to make it work? Could I have it back next week?" "Sure," I said. What the heck, it's an hour's work, something I love doing, would love to see happen, and maybe like Bonne Bell there is an opportunity for me. You never know.

Gurney's now is a very exclusive spa, but in those days it was a ramshackle old inn, remote and overlooking the sea. The plan was for me to work for three days and Philip would join me for the weekend. I loaded the car with the typewriter, my Greek fisherman's sweater, and a pile of books and files; at the last moment, I grabbed the Idea Box, since I thought I'd do a quick rewrite of the proposal for Avon when I needed a break from the book writing. Although I added to it regularly, it had been eight years since I'd looked in the Idea Box, but I thought I might need some inspiration to give this Atlanta proposal more zing.

Typical of my romantic naïveté, I figured you had to set yourself up like Ernest Hemingway to write a book, even a sample chapter, so I placed the typewriter in the window of my room facing a lashing sea, and put on my woolly turtleneck. Even though I don't smoke, I bought a pack of cigarettes for effect. I sure felt like Hemingway, but the prose came out like Snoopy atop his doghouse typing, "It was a dark and stormy night." The only real ideas that kept popping into my head were for the proposal I'd promised Avon. I kept a pad next to the typewriter, and every time I got a running idea, I'd jot it down and then go back to my "creative writing." By the end of the day, I had a whole list of scribbles for the proposal and a floor covered with balled-up paper from the fits and starts on the book. I took a run, had dinner, and went to bed determined to start again at dawn.

Dawn and black coffee, and more balled-up paper. Another run on the beach, watching a huge storm approach, then back to the room, where I shouted out loud, "Okay! Just do the damn Avon proposal! Do it fast, get it out of your head, so you can concentrate on the book." I started typing furiously. First the Atlanta rewrite, then my jottings, then important operational and budgetary items for that race. Technically, I was finished with what Williams wanted, but unavoidably, it had started an outpouring of ideas I'd had for many years. I could see a really solid program well beyond a single Atlanta marathon taking shape before my eyes. I'd wanted to write this program up for years, the brain was clicking and the keys were hot, and it probably wouldn't take too long to do. It was also a good time because I needed the practice of writing up a full program proposal directed at a specific company, and since Avon was interested anyway, it was a great model to start on. A good proposal should be tailored for the company you are pitching. If they say no, well, you rewrite it for another company. It's time-consuming but important, because every company needs to have uniqueness or they aren't going to get good visibility. Some companies have a natural fit, others need creative repositioning. Writing the first proposal lays the base for the others that follow. It would be great to get it knocked off.

The Avon fit was excellent, and it was unique because it was a beauty company sponsoring sports. I always felt beautiful when I ran; I guess everybody who is on an endorphin high does, so that meant other women did, too. I knew Avon pretty well, as I'd grown up on it, with neighbors selling it and my mom always being their best customer; she bought bags and bags of Somewhere crème sachet, Honeysuckle cologne, compacts, and lipsticks. Avon was the creator of the direct-selling business, and had helped the incomes and self-esteem of many women by giving them a sales opportunity. The more I wrote, the more I felt that the Avon sales concept was similar to running. The heart and soul of it was participatory, and success came from individual effort—the more you put into it, the more you got out of it. Avon was also a global company, and I wrote the proposal with an eye to its developing into an international program. I felt free to write the program the ideal way it should be because I was convinced it was a practice model.

I called room service so I could keep working, and during my coffee break, just for the hell of it, I opened the Idea Box. It was like finding some kind of marvelous treasure; all these notes frantically scribbled on old cocktail napkins, matchbook covers, whatever I could find fast to write on in those post-run moments before the idea fled my mind. Plenty of them still had sweat spots on them; a decade of nights, thousands of miles—and oh, the ideas were marvelous! In a million years, I would not have been able to recollect or reconstruct many of these ideas, and here they were for the unfolding of the papers. I'd gone this far, I thought, I might as well use the ideas, give it my all, write out the Dream Race, make it the proposal of a lifetime. Avon would never go for it, but at least I'd have written it, and some company would pick it up eventually. A gale pounded the inn, my window flexed dangerously, and I kept typing until the lights went out. The front desk called to ask if I was okay, and when I said yes, they encouraged me to come to the bar for some soup and where they had lantern light. I took my pages and reworked the copy there, while the locals gathered near the fire and told storm stories. It was more like Robert Louis Stevenson than Hemingway, and I reveled in it.

Friday morning was all cold sunshine and wind, but the electricity was back on. I finished inserting all the ideas, did a final edit, and began typing it cleanly for presentation. Maybe, just maybe, there was still time to do some kind of book outline before Philip arrived that evening. The Avon proposal was forty pages long, with some charts and budgets; clean typing in presentation format in those days took a lot of careful time. I am a fast typist but a lousy speller, so I lost time in looking up words, and more time waiting for the sticky correction fluid to dry when I made mistakes. By five P.M., it was done, perfect and beautiful. There was only time for a shower and some makeup before I picked Philip up at the train station. It was supposed to be a celebratory (and with any luck, romantic) weekend, but there was no book writing to celebrate. None at all. Despite getting the proposal done, it was not what I'd set out to do, and I felt deflated. Probably there would be an argument, at least some kind of sarcastic reprimand.

Couples perform strange dances that keep them together. A zillion times I'd been close to leaving Philip, only to have some outside occurrence—like the arrival of his son—compel us to remain together, or some brilliant flash of confirmation or insightfulness from him that would make my heart soar, rendering separation impossible. This evening was one of those moments. We went to the room before dinner and of course he asked, "So, how's the book? Let's look at what you've done." I took a deep breath and blurted out that I hadn't done anything creative. Nothing on the book! Only this proposal for that guy at Avon! I was feeling a little teary. Philip took the stack of papers and began reading, turning the pages slowly. He reached over for the pack of unopened cigarettes, opened them while he read, and lit one. We were late for dinner. Finally he turned the last page, looked at the pages a moment, then quietly tapped the sheets on the desk, restacking them neatly. He stood up, looked at me very seriously and said, "That, my dear, is the most creative thing you've *ever* done."

It was a wonderful dinner; it was like some of our first together as we fired ideas back and forth. Philip would listen, comment, and query as I elaborated on how my ideas came together and how the program would work. Essentially, it was this:

First: Women would run if they had the opportunity to participate in something appealing, accessible, and unintimidating. So I proposed a series of races all over the country, with a thought that they could expand to other countries. They would be my old Dream Races: women only, welcoming all levels of ability, and full of feminine touches, such as flowers everywhere, the T-shirt being a fashion item, clean toilets with tampons, real jewelry (instead of ugly trophies) as commemorative awards, and a festive atmosphere that would include lots of colorful banners, signs, tents, rocking music, and good event announcing (my goal was to have the name of everyone crossing the finish line announced, or as nearly as possible), and a swell party at the end with beautifully displayed great food (mounds of fruit, especially) and a place to actually sit down and enjoy it with friends while the awards ceremony took place.

The second thrust was to make each race a first-class athletic competition that the AAU, the IAAF, and even the IOC could find no fault with. They also had to demonstrate women's capability at different distances. Let's face it—if officials found flaws in women's events, they would use it as an excuse to say we weren't ready or sufficiently organized for international or Olympic consideration. That meant having official certification for accurately measured courses (both metric for international standards, and imperial—miles and yards—for American), official sanctions from the AAU, total safety and traffic control, flawless scoring and record keeping, and well-disseminated results. Concurrently, the program would be developmental and demonstrative: if we were to get the women's marathon into the Olympics, it was limiting to offer just 5K or 10K races to get them there. Bonne Bell could do the 5- and 10Ks; my program would stress 15-, 20-, 25-, and 30-kilometer events with the full marathon, a real international championship, as the culmination. All races would be open to every woman, and the marathon would also include the world's best. In effect, the marathon final would be the substitute Women's Olympic Marathon. The global component would start with every willing Avon country sending their best marathon runner to the International Championship.

It was important to have women-only events. Coming from me, the gender-barrier breaker, this might sound contradictory, but in fact I knew the IOC (like most people) assumed women couldn't do arduous things without male help and would say that women in mixed races were paced. It was also important to train women to take responsibility for pace and strategy; it's quite different when you commit to the lead of a race—often with cameras and press vehicles bearing down on you—than it is if there is a group of guys around you. And it's also great for a woman to be The Winner, not just the first woman.

The third part of the proposal was that every race would also be developmental at every level. Each would be preceded by a ten-week series of clinics featuring expert coaches, motivators, and team leaders. It was pointless to create a race for women who had not yet started to run or who had not progressed to a higher level without giving them encouragement and the tools to learn. At the same time, incentive had to be provided to the competitive runner. Since no prize money was allowed in those days, I devised a system whereby the top fifteen runners could earn points toward a championship, with the winner of every race automatically winning her way to the national or, in some cases, the international championship. Other point winners could go to other Avon races and accumulate enough points to win a trip. No paid stars would be brought in to take the points or discourage up-and-coming runners. The message was this: Not everyone can win a race outright, but many of us can work hard and win places. Sometimes you have to work at it several times to get the confidence to win or place. With this program, it was possible to run in Kansas City, drive to Chicago and win enough points to win a trip to Paris or London for an international championship. At last I'd devised a way around the old AAU stranglehold that limited athletes' opportunities!

That was only the first half. No proposal is complete without showing what the sponsoring company will get back, and it's a mistake almost all proposal writers make. They say something uninspiring, such as, you'll get your name on the T-shirt, you'll get ten signs on the course, and your company's name will be on the bibs. Big deal! A proposal needs to show how the publicity will happen, how companies get beyond the sports pages and into features, news, women's, and health issues; the roles their employees and sales force will play, how they can tie in their advertising, provide product samples, showcase their factories, bring in their communities, put their general managers on TV, and roll out the promotion from city to city, far beyond the race itself.

There was no doubt in my mind that my program could produce all this and maybe more. The concept was innovative for the whole sport, not just for women's running. It was scary, though, because if you proposed it, you had to deliver it. Philip and I discussed this in philosophical terms. We both knew Avon was not going to take this proposal, but we agreed that it was a very important exercise for me to get out there and make it happen somewhere, in some similar form. I had heard (erroneously, as it turned out) that Billie Jean King and Gladys Heldman had taken their proposal for women's professional tennis to twenty-four different companies before they secured Virginia Slims, and I took heart from this story as only a tenacious marathoner could.

A few days later, after adding photocopies of news clippings and some charts, I personally took the proposal to Mark Williams at the Avon office in New York. He was impressed that I got the proposal into his hands at the very time I said I would but looked a bit startled at its size. I chuckled. "Most of this isn't what you asked for. I decided that a program for women's running needed to be written up thoroughly. I had an awful lot of good ideas, and Avon provided a good excuse. Don't worry, I don't expect you to wade through it; there is an executive summary at the beginning along with your revised Atlanta proposal." He recovered and said, "I'm going to stay up tonight and read this." This time I laughed right out loud. "*Sure* you are, Mr. Williams! But thank you for saying that." As I sat on the train home, I had a deep satisfaction that come what may, at last I'd written up the Dream Race, the dream program, the dream proposal, and put it in someone's hands.

The next morning, for some unusual reason, I was in my office early, and the phone rang. It was Mark Williams. "I stayed up last night and read your proposal; I read the whole thing. You know, I have to be honest with you. We may never do anything with women's running, but if you can think like this, we sure could use your ideas at Avon." You could have knocked me over with a feather but I managed a thank-you. "What is your status at AMF? I don't want to be pirating employees, but would you consider working for us? We are looking for someone to handle that tennis project we've just started." I thought he was kind of flattering me, so I made a joke and said, "Sure, if the price is right!" "What range are we talking about?" he asked. I don't know what possessed me, possibly because I was not really interested in tennis and felt I had nothing to lose, but I doubled my present income of $15,000. "Thirty," I said with confidence. "We can handle that," he said. For a wild moment I wondered what he would have said if I said "Fifty," but then he was asking if I could come in and meet some people.

Tennis! Cripes, I knew nothing about tennis. Oh, I'd played, knew how to keep score, I knew Billie Jean!! But I had no insider's knowledge, no intuitive feel for it. Avon, of course, was looking at my PR skills and general sports background, which I always underestimated when I was in an unfamiliar milieu. I decided that if they made me an offer, I'd take it. Avon was a company that believed in women's sports and as far as I was concerned, that was enough of a foot in the door. Besides, it was a glamorous, highly successful Fortune 500 company, a coup to have on any résumé. When I came in for interviews, I was stunned—*stunned!*—to see so many attractive, well-dressed women in management positions. I came home to Philip and crowed, "Hey, you know all those women who were so smart in college and then disappeared? They are all working for Avon!"

It was an odd time, as I'd go into Avon for a round of enthusiastic interviews, then not hear anything. I'd get calls from all kinds of Avon consultants wanting to take me to lunch. Inevitably, these turned out to be sniffing-out sessions and exercises in the consultants' own self-aggrandizement. I hadn't even been offered the job, but all the consultants urged me to keep them on. They also gossiped unmercifully, especially about the director of PR, who would be my boss. I had an inherent distrust of anyone who bad-mouthed the boss to an incoming employee. I was capable of making up my own mind. I was making my mind up fast that if I got this job, I'd hold all these consultants at arm's length.

It was spring, and women's sports were just bursting onto the scene like the blossoms. I was so busy speaking at conferences that Boston was upon me, and I accepted a speech and a journalistic assignment there without even considering running. That was an amazing change, but I was so busy and full of forward-looking ideas that its significance didn't dawn on me. That took another year. The heat and disorganization in the 1977 race made me glad not to be running, anyway—it would have been another nightmare for me. Miki Gorman won in 2:48; if she'd had my cool tailwind of 1975, I believe she would have smashed the world record.

Then it was back into the perfect storm. There was a different conference every weekend—Smith College, suddenly proud of the fact that they had the first women's sports programs in America; Immaculata, with their great basketball tradition, Hobart, Columbia, University of Massachusetts, even West Point, just to name a few. Other athletes, especially Donna de Varona, and a few sponsors were always at these events, and the network grew. I was still interviewing at Avon and trying not to hope too much for the job.

Women's golf and tennis were givens as top-earning professional sports opportunities, with names like Judy Rankin, Donna Caponi-Young, and Mickey Wright in golf, and Chris Evert, Evonne Goolagong, and Billie Jean King in tennis. New faces added a broader dimension. The golfer Jan Stephenson, who was extremely attractive and sexy and was accused of getting undue press attention because of it, helped women's golf a lot by winning over old diehards; we were all were very happy when she won the LPGA Birmingham tournament.

Although Diane Crump was the first woman to ride in the Kentucky Derby in 1970, the jockeys Robyn Smith and Mary Bacon were also in the news. They rode a lot and won a lot of money, but they had to fight for every mount and were terribly discriminated against in that rough gambling-dominated sport. They were uncommonly attractive and skillful athletes who also had a knack for creating off-the-wall controversy. Robyn, in 1973 the first woman to win a major

American horse race, set us agog by marrying Fred Astaire, fifty-five years her senior. Mary Bacon, a tiny blonde, was irritatingly abrasive and later embarrassed women athletes when she made racist remarks and supported the Ku Klux Klan. We worried that bad news about a woman athlete reflected on all of us, and like faltering in the marathon, might set us back. Still, I cannot imagine how hard it was for these women.

If the jockeys had a hard time, Janet Guthrie had it worst of all, because her success in race car driving—particularly NASCAR—struck at the heart of all that was truly macho. She had the myths thrown at her that we all knew: women are too weak, too emotional, plus the jokes about women drivers, which of course spring from people's assumptions that women are naturally bad at anything mechanical. Janet is a driver and mechanic of genius. But still they said her very presence on the track would be dangerous. To overcome such visceral hatred and earn respect, money, support, and equipment to race at the Indianapolis 500 was an achievement of Herculean proportion. When Janet raced—and raced well—that Memorial Day in 1977, she broke one of sport's biggest barriers. My heart soared. (When she finished ninth overall in 1978, we popped the champagne!)

Women also were getting increasingly and more visibly involved in mainstream sports journalism. The magazine *womenSports* was our voice, but having women delivering general sports news, and getting women's coverage on the regular sports news, was the crossover we needed. Donna de Varona was our most visible commentator, doing men's and women's swimming and other sports for ABC-TV. It wasn't network football or baseball, but that would come, surely. Anita Verschoth was a regular and serious columnist for *Sports Illustrated*, and even the *New York Times* hired a woman sports columnist, Maggie Roach. Two years later, Le Anne Schreiber was named sports editor at the *Times*!

There were big issues to cover, including the controversy over Title IX, the Equality of Education Amendment passed in 1972. Many argued that sports should be exempt from the principle of equal opportunity and funding, since they believed that not enough women were interested. I had thought the same until I ran the Boston Marathon in 1967. But that was ten years earlier and reflected the inexperience of a naive nineteen-year-old. Anybody who had their eyes open could see that there was now a rising tidal wave of women's sports participation. Already, the provision for women's college sports and the eligibility for sports scholarships was beginning the transformation; when this was made into law in 1978 it was wonderful! It would—and did—change the face of women's sports. At the same time, there was a lot of contentiousness brewing. The controversy continues as I write this thirty years later.

The New York Mini, in 1977 known as the Bonne Bell Mini Marathon, was a great success. Allan Steinfeld, Fred's second-in-command, was assigned to be race codirector with me. Low-key, thoughtful, detail-oriented, and incredibly intelligent, Allan was an electrical engineer and radio astronomer, and how he got hooked into working for peanuts for the New York Road Runners was beyond me, but as I say, running does funny things to people. Allan and I worked well together, put together a strong invited field, and had great operations and signage. With the combined firepower of the NYRR, Jess Bell's PR firm, and the sheer numbers and enthusiasm of the women, we had tremendous publicity. Jess was happy, and I was convinced more than ever about my direction with women's running, but I knew my future wasn't with Bonne Bell. I kept thinking about organizing a marathon for Avon, and I wanted that job!

Avon had been interviewing me for four months. I took a deep breath and called Mark Williams. Was he going to hire me or not? That is the kind of call that can sink your ship fast, but I didn't care. The women's sports race was streaming by and I felt like I was in the ladies' room of the gas station on the route of the Boston Marathon trying to cut the legs off my tights so I could get back in the race in time. Williams was stunned that I hadn't yet received an offer. It came the next day, and I started with Avon the next month. The gun had gone off, and I was racing the course to my future.

Chapter | 22

The First Avon International Marathon

The Avon job started with a hallelujah moment: they were indeed going with the sponsorship of the women's marathon in Atlanta, on March 19, 1978, just this one race and just this once. It was a major career breakthrough and a wonderful bonus on top of my main work, the eight-city Avon Futures tennis tour, beginning the first week in January. I was only thirty, already a manager (and one of the youngest in the company), making $30,000, and I had my own office on the thirty-first floor with a floor-to-ceiling glass window overlooking Central Park. It was, as they said then, good *even for a man* to do that!

Before I could call my parents with the news, Fred Lebow phoned. How Fred found out an hour after I accepted was one of life's mysteries and one of Fred's magical gifts. He was concerned that I would be spending most of my time and talent on tennis and was not convinced when I told him that I had to do the tennis in order to do the marathon. Another call came just as quickly from Jess Bell. Although he was disappointed to lose me, he was also encouraging, and we vowed our programs would never compete. We supported each other in various ways for almost thirty years, until he passed away in 2005.

It was already August. Every night after work for my first few days I was at the U.S. Open, staged then in Forest Hills, trying to meet many of the people my boss said were important officials, and to absorb as much tennis as I could. Philip proved an asset at this time, with his maturity, urbanity, and knowledge of tennis. I loved the concept of Avon Futures Tennis, because it was about opportunity, like my running proposal. The Futures was a developmental circuit that gave players the chance to experience a national tour, get "match tough," and play for the reward of an immediate "wild-card" entry into the Virginia Slims if they won a Futures tournament. Some amazing talent came through the Avon Futures. "There are a lot of Tracy Austins out there" became one of our taglines after the then-unknown youngster went right to the top.

At the office, I was scrambling. I had to get logos and ads prepared for the January magazine issues, and I was learning that in a corporation such things take time to get approval. My appointment had been left late, I had problems with a secretary reluctant to work for a middle-management "girl," and I was struggling to get on good terms with my boss, Joe. He had come to head up the PR department after being Avon's director of security, a career path that suggested little natural empathy for women's sports or my role in advancing them. Only a month into the job I presented him with a problem when I was invited to lead off a torch relay on the first leg out of Seneca Falls, birthplace of the first women's rights convention. The relay would go on to Houston, for that year's National Women's Conference. It had the endorsement of President Ford's 1975 National Commission on the Observance of International Women's Year, but some fiery activists were associated with the relay, and Avon, and especially its cautious former head of security, was leery of anything that could be construed as political. Eventually, approval was given, since the invitation was to me as a running pioneer, not as an Avon employee, and I ran quietly through the dawn mists of Seneca Falls and missed all the media hype for the "feminist icons" who later carried the torch on its final leg into Houston. Everyone was happy except my mother, who didn't understand why I wasn't in Houston with her idol, Billie Jean King.

My main feeling was that it was incredible that more than 125 years after the first women's rights convention, some people were still opposed to the Equal Rights Amendment, with the most vocal opponents being—you've got it—women themselves, the people who had the most to gain. They reminded me of the women who used to try to run me off the road when I was training. In time, I thought, it will come—a lot of those women drivers have already taken up running! They're getting their own Secret Weapon! In ever-increasing numbers, they also were transforming events like the New York City Marathon.

The 1977 NYCM came soon after my Seneca Falls run. The 1976 big-city, five-borough experiment had become a phenomenon. This year the marathon was an even bigger citywide and worldwide success, with more than five thousand starters making it the biggest marathon and one of the biggest sports events of any kind in history. Miki Gorman and Bill Rodgers repeated as champions, but I was so busy with my own Avon Atlanta marathon organization that I was only marginally involved.

With some luck, the pieces came together. A powerful logo is one of the most important things for the success of a program; it creates an image and establishes an instant identity. We found a terrific graphic artist named Al Corcia, who got our typefaces and printed materials together quickly. We hired vendors who had been kind to running and women's sports, companies like United Emblem, who had been reliable supporters of the New York Road Runners when we didn't have a dime. It was great to turn down the many new charlatans and carpetbaggers of running who came calling with phony theories, accessories, apparel, you name it.

Then I found a brilliant running photographer, John Kelly, whose portfolio included a shot that jumped out at me: two lean, fit women running across a sun-dappled meadow, working hard but looking beautiful and lost in a long run. It was positively ethereal. With that picture, and the tagline it inspired—"the beauty of women in motion" —we had an image. Soon we also had a name for the Atlanta race, the Avon International Marathon. We had red and white as our color theme, for both tennis and the marathon ("Red is for brave women," someone said), and we had red French-cut T-shirts with white printing on them, because I knew that red would photograph in newspapers as black and that the white printing with a big AVON would jump out in every image, especially important when journalists didn't mention us as sponsors. I ordered French-cut shirts since I knew the women would wear them again and again to run in and with their jeans. I wore at least a dozen different sample shirts in training myself before I found one that really breathed, looked great, and held up after washing. Naturally, it was more expensive, which occasioned my first real argument with boss Joe. He didn't understand the significance of pure cotton and soft shape, or understand how much visibility women wearing the shirt can bring. Eventually I won on the shirts by compromising on nipples.

Yes, you read that right. We had adopted the legendary woman runner of ancient Greece, Atalanta, as a sort of patron saint, and her seminude image appeared on our race awards and finishers' medals. At Joe's insistence, for the first time in three thousand years, Atalanta was represented in full running stride with her nipples sanded off.

Meanwhile, the Atlanta Track Club and I had worked out a huge operations checklist, far beyond the scope of any previous running event in America or anywhere else, as far as I know, with the probable exception of the New York City Marathon. Everything was started from scratch, and I was extremely anxious to avoid any screwup that could doom women's chances and make Avon look bad. Plus, I knew Avon would not be impressed with some rinky-dink draw-a-line-on-the-road event, and since we were willing to pay, we pushed the limits. We were, for instance, the first to give medals to all finishers. The Atlanta people were hard at work with the course, starting and finishing on the grounds of the beautiful Avon distribution facility (great restrooms, changing areas, pressroom, and cafeteria). Additionally, the event was on public roads, which created new traffic, crowd, medical and legal considerations, so we had to work with the police and municipalities to provide medical support, placate the churches who didn't want their congregations held up in traffic, and handle grandstands, scaffolding, toilets, and all the myriad aspects of a professionally organized marathon—many things that had not been done at Boston.

I wound up spending weeks in Atlanta working out details and I'm sure I was often a royal pain. But despite my relentless pushing and increasingly frenetic behavior, I made great friends with the Atlanta group. One in particular was Dr. David Martin, a runner and professor of exercise physiology at Georgia State University, who was also an expert on the marathon, as a physiologist, coach, statistician, and historian. His many talents have made him a Fellow of the

American College of Sports Medicine and have been the source of an enormous contribution that still continues (the two American medals in the 2004 Olympic marathon owed much to him, for instance). Dave and I concurred in an ambitious plan to invite the top twenty-five women in the world, identified through his precise stats. It was a big PR expense for Avon, outside the original budget, but it was a gesture that would strike a very loud blow for how serious women's running had become. Besides, you couldn't have the best without giving them a way to get there, as I had long lamented. Dave and I were giddy at the thought of it.

A few months before, I'd also quite serendipitously met Mike Harrigan, a lawyer who was an expert on amateur sports and the Olympics. He told me that for an event to qualify for Olympic inclusion it must be practiced in at least twenty-five countries and on three continents. This piece of information was a bonanza and became a critical part of my plan to get the women's marathon into the Olympic Games. To assist this effort, I again pushed the idea of having the best woman runner from each country where Avon does business also sent to the marathon. This would give our countries a sense of ownership in a global promotion as well. In exchange, they'd get buildup, send-off, and "results" stories from a specially developed national PR kit I developed. Germany was especially important, with several runners in the top twenty-five, and of course Dr. van Aaken was a big story himself and our guest of honor. The invitations, in an era before e-mail or even fax, proved to be a big logistical project!

The final marathon press release, with names, numbers, and bios, was accompanied by a beautiful glossy poster of our two women runners. We secured fourteen of the world's top twenty-five women, an amazing show of solidarity. In all, there were 152 women from 26 states and 8 countries—the USA, Japan, Germany, Brazil, India, Hungary, Canada, and New Zealand. When they descended on Atlanta, so did the press corps. Already, the buzz on the marathon was delivering more news than the tennis.

I had no idea we'd pull this kind of firepower, especially in a suburb of Atlanta. The atmosphere projected both strength and celebration. And the media totally got it—women wanted a marathon in the Olympic Games and here was a marathon to prove they deserved it.

All my predictions came to pass—a young unknown named Martha (Marty) Cooksey from California won the race, defeating the world's best, a perfect example of the wealth of unknown talent in women's running. She won a tactical and competitive race, overtaking the Olympic track runner Julie Brown at Mile 21. Yet another dimension was added by the runner-up, Sarolta Monspart of Hungary. She had to jump through hoops of communist bureaucracy to accept our ticket to Atlanta and deeply touched the crowd with her courageous plea for national, as well as women's running liberation. Manuela Preuss Angenvoorth of Germany, third, made the podium truly international. Gayle Barron, by now also a TV commentator in Atlanta and one of the reasons the race took place there, held up well under the pressure and finished fifth.

After all the speeches, flowers, awards, and congratulations that night, I called Philip. "I monitored the evening news," he said excitedly. "You were on all three networks. That's Sunday night, baby!" And the coverage rolled on and on: the *New York Times, Sports Illustrated,* an ABC Wide World of Sports feature, numerous radio stories, and saturation in the Atlanta media. I recalled all those nice post-marathon mornings in Boston, reading the papers over coffee at the muffin house; this was a million times better because it was all about us women, and an event that launched us. It captured the public imagination, stirred the spirit, and won massive support.

The publicity flowed over to boost the Avon tennis, also in Atlanta, which occupied me all the following week. I was exhausted. But for one last jolt of endorphins, on the way home, I stopped on my way to the airport at Six Flags Over Georgia to ride the roller coaster, my favorite way to scream at the top of my lungs. The kids giggled at me in my business suit and high heels, but after outrunning them for the first car and riding eight times, shouting *"No hands!"* I won their respect. "I wish *my* mom would ride roller coasters," a youngster told me as I headed to my car.

It was safe to say Avon had never received publicity like this. From the doorstep of the Avon facility in Atlanta, it made our local people look good; when it went national, and then international, I finally had proved myself to my cautious boss. He praised me, circulated the clippings, complimented me to others, and then said, "Get out your original running proposal. If you put a presentation together, I'll get you on the chairman's calendar."

What a break! Everyone loved the program and the chairman approved it on the spot. I proposed a pilot series of six races in the USA, each at an Avon regional headquarters location, culminating in 1979 in an Avon International Marathon in Waldniel, West Germany, as a tribute to Dr. van Aaken, and a plan for global expansion by taking the marathon to a different country the following year. There was handshaking all around. I thanked Joe for the opportunity. He laughed. "Usually the employee rides the boss's coattails to success. But maybe I'll ride your coattails!" It was a compliment reminiscent of Jock Semple's makeup kiss on the starting line at Boston in 1973.

Joe and I were at loggerheads plenty of times in our years of working together, but he also brought out the best in me and gave me a huge opportunity to create the Avon International Running Circuit. Women runners everywhere and I owe him a big debt of gratitude.

Philip was pleased for me, feeling proprietorial in affirming my creativity, and enjoying a role in a career so much more interesting than his own. Philip's son Eric joined in the celebration. It was one of our happiest times, and the following month, in one of those manic triumphs of hope over much more relevant experience, Philip and I got married quietly in the little stone church in Chappaqua, with only my parents, his kids, and two friends attending.

There was one big loss at this positive time. At that year's Boston Marathon, working again as a journalist and speaker, and watching the glamorous Gayle Barron lead home an astonishing twenty-nine women under three hours, I was suddenly overcome with sadness. I ached to be a runner again. I came home weeping. A month later, after the successful corporate presentation, Philip forced me to face what I could not admit. "If you do this program, you know your competitive running days are over. You will never have the time or energy to do both. Be happy in the decision, and use the energy to go forward." With that I broke down again into really mournful sobbing, as if I'd lost an old friend, and kept it up without shame until I got it off my chest. Wow, two crying jags in two months, a record; I hadn't had two crying jags in two *years!* Then I thought about all those times I looked forward to not having the pressure of training and realized I hadn't lost a friend at all. My friend had just become a jogger. I never looked back on the decision. Running became more fun than it had ever been. Thirty years later, it still is.

Chapter | 23

Going Global

I sent the reworked plan over to my friend Elizabeth Phillips for her advice. With her usual directness, Elizabeth mailed it straight back with a scribble at the top: "If you do this alone you will either have a heart attack or get a divorce and probably both."

My only help was my secretary, but I had to start, so I dived in. The excitement of the Avon Marathon in Atlanta and the announcement of the new circuit reverberated at Avon offices all over the world. Avon Japan, Belgium, and the UK were calling and asking to sponsor races in their countries, and I was duly dispatched to give advice.

Whenever I conduct business in another country, I pride myself on doing my homework about the culture and protocol. It's important to be patient and remember that I'm a guest. In those days, this was a zillion times more important if you were a woman, and in my case, because a lot of previous publicity had given me the reputation as a firebrand, I had to win people over with an especially cooperative attitude, even if it meant privately chewing nails from time to time.

When I arrived in Tokyo in 1978, I was amazed to see how traditionally women were regarded in an otherwise stunningly modern and technologically advanced nation. Many were well educated and had responsible jobs, but they still deferred totally to their male colleagues, and quite sophisticated women walked three feet behind their husbands on the street and through hotel lobbies. When I gave women-only running clinics to the jogging clubs, the women were embarrassed to take off their long track pants because they thought they had unattractive legs. There had been one Japanese entrant in the Avon Marathon in Atlanta, supported by our Avon division in Japan, but she was quite the exception. Although there was a growing over-forty jogging movement there, races were for elite runners only. The Japan Amateur Athletic Federation (JAAF) controlled athletics and the athletes with an even tighter iron fist than we'd had in the United States in the '50s. To a great extent, they still do.

Avon was a new American company in Japan and was willing to spend a chunk to make a good impression. Japan does not make it easy for foreign businesses, so Avon decided to create a big publicity and advertising program there that stressed how it gives women an opportunity to succeed: in business, in the arts, and, *ta dum,* in running. A Tokyo women's road race was part of that plan.

It was obvious that JAAF wasn't excited about a race that included beginners and joggers. And *women!* That's something that hadn't even occurred to them. They didn't think Japanese women would take part. They thought women's distance running was possibly dangerous. (*That* again!) They were suspicious of an American company and a new idea, and they weren't wild about having to talk to an American female as the expert. Whenever I spoke, they answered only to my male colleagues. (That sound is me chewing nails.) It didn't help that, in my high heels, I was enormously taller than all of the officials. Finally, it was decided that JAAF would sanction the event but it could be no longer than 5K and no woman under sixteen could run it (because of the "danger"). I am sure there was a substantial sponsoring fee, but I didn't want to know, as it would have rankled me. Avon and the ad agency were going to do almost all of the operations and publicity.

I sat down for three solid days and evenings with my colleagues from Avon and the agency and worked out a complete operations list, including road closings, race applications, timing, toilets, working out a sample budget, and drawing pictures to show them how a race was done. I've never seen anybody work more assiduously and enthusiastically, and absorb ideas more quickly, than these Japanese friends did. These were people who had never seen a running shoe or a stopwatch up close, and they took every idea and made it better. Eventually they got so good that we started using some of their ideas in our own program. I had no time to be a tourist; if it hadn't been for a few early-morning runs through the city, I'd have seen nothing of Tokyo. So much for the glamour of travel.

Belgium was easier because of the longtime race director Jacques Serruys, whose successes included some of the best road races in Europe, notably his pioneering international 20K for masters in Brugge. Jacques also wanted to organize a women's race and had contacted the local Avon office in in Brussels. The essential ingredient in making something like this happen is the vision of the organizer, and Jacques Serruys was a leader ahead of his time. He was like the guys in Atlanta, the New York Road Runners, even my old pals in Syracuse—all of them were willing to give their all to help the sport, whether it was for women or men. None of them even thought about getting paid; just having a sponsor in those days was reward enough. It felt pretty wonderful when I considered how hard it was for women jockeys or race car drivers.

I went on to Germany to start the wheels turning for the Avon International Marathon in Waldniel. I especially wanted Dr. van Aaken to be happy. This was his home, and the race was a tribute to his vision. I had no worries about working with the Germans; heavens, they invented organization, and of course Dr. van Aaken and his Olympic Sports Club Waldniel had organized women's marathons three times already. Even at the massive and glamorous Avon Germany headquarters near Munich, I was stunned by the corporate enthusiasm. Before I even asked them, they had set up official meetings with the Deutscher Leichtathletik-Verband (DLV), the German athletic federation, and already some media.

My global groundbreaking tour ended in London where I felt the most important meetings of all would take place: those with John Holt, executive director of the IAAF, and Marea Hartman, chair of the women's committee of the IAAF and the longtime secretary of the Women's Amateur Athletic Association in England. It was the IAAF's voice that went right to the IOC. I wanted and needed them desperately to be in favor of women in the marathon. Meeting John worried me the most, because I knew he was on the receiving end of many of the abusive letters the IAAF and IOC were receiving about their unfair treatment of women runners. He sounded nice enough on the phone but there was a chance he'd think I was coming to harangue him in person.

Instead, we began by talking about our running. John had been outstanding in the 800 meters at Oxford and ran internationally for the British team in the early 1960s, and he had a sense of vision and good deeds for the sport. He was also the best kind of gentleman—kind, without the slightest self-importance. So I just told him how my own running had led to where I was today, what my hopes and dreams were with the Avon program, and about the international races that seemed to be springing out of Avon countries already. I now understood the IOC requirement that a new Olympic sport needed first to be contested in three continents and twenty-five countries. I told John I thought we could meet that, and I asked him whether I was doing it the correct way. The last thing we wanted to do was to alienate people. We wanted to make it happen. John gave me advice, telling me who I needed to get to know in which countries and how a recommendation is put forward. We agreed to run together the next time I was in town. When I left his office I was thrilled beyond measure.

Then I was off to have lunch with Marea Hartman. Chairing the women's committee of the IAAF actually made her more important for me than Holt, but I really needed both of them on the same page. A lifetime official, Marea had been in charge of UK women's athletics for so long that many thought of her as conservative and inflexible. I was considerably younger and didn't want her to think of me as a young American whippersnapper. As we looked at the lunch menu, I broke my usual lunchtime rule and said impulsively, "Shall we have a little drink to start?" Her eyes lit up. We ordered Bloody Marys. I had maybe two and Marea maybe three (maybe more). It was a wonderful laughing lunch, and Marea rattled on with some of the funniest sports stories I'd ever heard, the best being when the then-premier of the Soviet Union Nikita Khrushchev felt up her leg under the table at some international sports reception. Talk about a missile crisis! The lunch broke the ice.

High jinks aside, Marea was an astute, longtime player in international sports politics. She understood quickly the importance of the women's marathon. She was impressed with how much work I was doing organizing the global events to get the countries we needed. As time went on, my eyewitness reports of how our races were transforming women's lives, especially those in poor and nontraditional athletic places particularly resonated. She could see this was about more than another sports event, and she could also see that this was more than a job to me, that it was a passion. Marea became a strong supporter of our women's marathon movement, a wonderful adviser, and a very good friend.

I came back from this trip buoyed by my contacts and experiences, but my desk was two feet deep in important work. My boss Joe finally relented and told me I could hire a temporary freelancer. Elizabeth Phillips was my preference; she was a runner, pulled no punches, and best of all knew budgeting, which was my weakest suit. But the uncertainty of working freelance made it impossible for her to leave her job. Then I thought of Valerie Andrews, a good friend and a skilled writer. She could help with the writing while I did operations and stumbled through the budget. Valerie had left New York to go to Greece for the summer, so I sent a telegram to Poste Restante, Mykonos, saying, "Want a running writing job call me." Our press conference was only six weeks away. When Valerie arrived at Avon for her first day, she was wearing a flowery, insanely low-cut dress, and proceeded to tell Joe how the telegram arrived when she was sitting bored on the topless beach at Mykonos. Joe nearly swooned, and Valerie was a breath of fresh air among us buttoned-up Burberry girls, writing fast copy and calling everyone on the press list. By that time, I had all the race directors, organizing clubs, and dates set up for Chicago, Los Angeles, Kansas City, Cincinnati, Atlanta, and Newark, Delaware—all cities where we had major Avon facilities.

The only thing I found difficult was getting public relations consultants to help with the races. Nobody had done running PR before. Valerie and I spent too much time teaching professional agencies all about women's running. It was more effective to take a club runner and teach them PR. There were those who worked for a radio station, or were involved in the Junior League or some community group, and they had great contacts. (I'm proud to say that many of those women later started their own PR agencies.)

The press conference had a packed house: notable runners like Amby Burfoot and Nina Kuscsik, organizers like Fred Lebow, the sports and women's press, and the Avon brass. I emceed, Chairman Dave Mitchell made the announcement of the program, and then we heard from special guests, starting with our Avon Marathon champion, Marty Cooksey. As circuit spokesperson, Marty exemplified the theme of opportunity. "There are a lot of Marty Cookseys out there" became our catchphrase, as with Tracy Austin in tennis.

We also introduced Miki Gorman as the spokesperson for our race in Japan. Nobody had been forewarned about how extensive the program was, and the room was bubbling with excitement. And I had another surprise behind the curtain. I introduced "the man who, in spite of himself, has probably done more for women's marathon running then anyone else in the world—Jock Semple!!" It brought the house down, and old Jock was beaming from ear to ear.

Once you promise it, you've got to deliver it. On top of the running circuit, I still had an eight-city tennis tour to direct. Soon Valerie was chugging away full time, the new secretary was ostentatiously displaying a bottle of Maalox on her desk, and Joe was jumping in, because I was on the road doing operations and PR in fourteen American cities as well as Tokyo, Brussels, Munich, London, and

Waldniel. Every city needed to be woven into the design to make the whole piece of cloth strong and support the push for the Olympics. Memos and telexes would arrive from other Avon countries asking me to visit and talk to them about setting up a running program, and I would just look at Joe and say, "We're drowning here! We have to hire Elizabeth Phillips." But Joe would always say it needed to go through Avon human resources to do a proper search.

Then, on October 28, 1978, a big chunk of marathon history was made that had nothing to do with Avon but which helped enormously in the Olympic campaign. Everybody was gaga over the New York City Marathon, as Bill Rodgers was going for a third victory and Christa Vahlensieck, the women's world record holder, was also running. (Christa had to forgo the Avon Marathon in Atlanta because she was running in the World Cross-Country Championships.) She was the main subject of my radio broadcast with Ed Ingles for CBS on race morning. I saw nothing of the women's race. We were with the lead men and our coverage of the women was to be constructed from spotters. For a while, the leading women's number they phoned through was Vahlensieck's, but then the number given was "1173." Impossible, I said to Ed. All the competitive women have low numbers. We asked for more information. Number 1173 had blond pigtails and was wearing red shorts and a white top. No help.

Traffic was ridiculous, and we were diverted to the finish, not far ahead of Bill Rodgers making a beautiful run in 2:12. We waited for the mystery woman. She hit the finish line in 2:32:20, a world record by over two minutes! Like every other reporter, I rushed down the finish chute with a microphone and tape recorder. She didn't want to talk to anyone. She was extremely irritable, and when a man walked beside her she tore into him in a Scandinavian language. Some things don't need translation, especially when she took off her shoes and threw them at him.

Eventually we all circled her. She spoke excellent English but was exasperated. Finally, her name: Grete Waitz. Of course, the Norwegian winner of the World Cross-Country Championships, and 3,000-meter world record holder! At last, a thoroughbred had tried the marathon, and the landscape was changed. Her last-minute entry was genius on Fred's part; pity he didn't think of telling the media, and I felt like shaking him. It's now a legendary story how Grete's husband, Jack, thinking she was probably in the waning years of her track running career, thought the invitation would make a neat way for the two of them to have a free New York holiday. Grete had never run more than 20K (about 13 miles) and wasn't even too sure how long a marathon was, but Jack said just go out with Christa Vahlensieck as long as you can. Grete found the pace slow, passed Christa midway, and kept going, despite the inevitable suffering from a fast marathon, because she never knew where she was in the strange city and on a course marked only in miles, not kilometers. The distance seemed endless, she was furious with Jack, and she snapped at the media, "I'm not a marathon runner, I'm a track runner." It made for an anticlimactic radio interview. But the world took notice.

Early one December morning, Joe passed my office with a cheery good morning and did a double take. "You look awful," he said. And then he noticed that I was wearing the same clothes as the day before. "Don't tell me you've been here all night." "Yep. And I'm not even close to being caught up with my work." Joe agreed to start the search process and to meet Elizabeth Phillips. But that was not for two more months. I have no idea how I got through that Christmas. I figured, no matter what, a few days at Christmas with my parents, grandmother, brother, and his pregnant wife might be more important in the long term than anything else. Despite eight people in the house and all the cooking and fuss, I was right. Philip was as well behaved as I'd ever seen him and it was the last nice family time we had.

Then it was an Avon float in the Rose Parade in Pasadena on New Year's Day (trust me, this was not my idea) titled Avon's Salute to Women in Sports, and I got to ride up there in the roses with ice skater Linda Frattiane, golfer Donna Caponi Young, and some other athletes. It was fun, in a surrealistic way. Right after that, our tennis program began, and that occasionally proved surrealistic, too, mostly because U.S. law courts had decreed that Renée Richards (née Richard Raskin), the transsexual player, had a right to play in Women's Tennis Association events if she could qualify. That included the Avon Futures Tour. I absolutely agreed with the law and Renée's right to play, but it was a strange sight to see a much older, six-foot two-inch, and still quite masculine-looking figure battling it out on the tennis court against teenage girls in pigtails.

At the opposite extreme, Avon Japan was telling me that the Japanese women were excited about the 5K but timid about training in public and bothered by the old loss-of-femininity myth. I had the idea of sending Miki Gorman to do a media tour, taking along her three-year-old daughter. They were a PR hit and fueled the popular success of the race. A then-incredible eight hundred women showed up to run, all proud to be part of the first-ever women's road race in Japan. They made history and opened the doors to a new era for Asian women. The oldest runner was seventy, born in 1908, when many Japanese were still binding the feet of their baby girls. Tiny feet meant helplessness, and, thus, perversely, femininity. A woman born into that era, and who had since known wars, famine, and nuclear holocaust, could now run freely through the streets of Tokyo. The thought still brings tears to my eyes.

In Tokyo, the French-cut T-shirts, this time in orange, were also a sensation, a must-have fashion item. Avon's advertising agency decided to pre-pin all the bib numbers on them so that all the women wore the orange shirts. The ensuing river of orange through the Tokyo streets and around the emperor's palace was spectacular, the media coverage extensive, and Avon visibility—on the chests of eight hundred women—exceptional. Far from being the flop the JAAF had predicted, the event was a bigger success than anyone had dared to dream.

Once Avon's human resources had gone through all the endless stages for a job search, Elizabeth Phillips was finally allowed to apply. Joe came by my office to say she was terrific, which of course was what I'd been telling him for a year. He still tried to shortchange her by a thousand dollars on salary, so I got out my own checkbook. "You bitch," she said thrusting it back at me. "Take your stupid check! When do I start?" It was the beginning of a thirty-year working relationship and a lifelong friendship.

In the Boston Marathon 1979, the world met an amazing runner named Joan Benoit. It was also the start of yet another career for me, or one more aspect of my single-minded career commitment to women's running. For the first time, a marathon other than the Olympics was televised nationally. Producer Greg Harney, a legend at WGBH-TV, lined up the witty and astute Bud Collins to emcee, Larry Rawson to do commentary for the men's race, and me to do the women's. I'd been on TV a lot, but this was my first time as a commentator. When Bud asked me to do a stand-up at the start, I looked like a deer in the headlights. A *what?* I was fine, however, on my pre-race interview with Roberta Gibb, near the forsythia bush she'd hidden behind in 1966 before she first ran the race. I talked explicitly about her being the first woman to run Boston, and hoped this national interview would lay to rest a lot of that confusion.

The show was on same-day tape delay. The race began at noon and we were on the air at six P.M. It was a breathtaking undertaking for WGBH. It was difficult for Larry and me, making solo commentaries on videotape while riding on underpowered electric golf carts that dropped behind the runners on the uphills. Every few miles, at designated points, we would pull aside and throw a big 3/4-inch cassette tape over the crowd to a waiting courier on a motorbike who would zoom it back to WGBH for editing, and then we'd hustle back into the race.

The day was cold and drizzly, and being on an open moving vehicle I was soaked through and seriously chilled. But it was still amazing to see 520 women runners and watch close up a great race between Patti Lyons and Joan Benoit. Benoit hammered the last five miles for a 2:35:15 course and American record. Another speedster had arrived, to hold up alongside Waitz for IOC scrutiny.

I was feverish that night, and the next day, Elizabeth's first at the office, I was so sick with the flu that I could not move, my first illness since I was ten. Not for the last time, Elizabeth saved me. When I was out of the office, she had taken all the out-of-control projects off my desk and created functioning systems. Soon we were off together to London and Waldniel to get her connected with the players there, as Joe was sending me to Thailand, the Philippines, and back to Japan.

We called on John Holt at the IAAF office near Hyde Park wearing our running clothes, since he wanted to run at noon and we could conduct part of our meeting at the same time. John was surprisingly fit, started quickly, and Elizabeth immediately said a cheery "Too fast for me!" I hung on, pretending the pace was fine, although my lungs, guts, and quads were burning. I used my old technique of asking probing questions that required detailed answers so I had time to breathe. As I said, people tell you secrets when they are out running; there is something about the endorphin rush that frees them. John gave me more key names and ways to contact them. Then he said, "You've got to get to your own guys in L.A. They have a lot of leverage." He gave me two—Peter Ueberroth, president of the LAOOC, whom everyone had heard of, and Dick Sargent. "Who's he?" I panted. "He's Ueberroth's right-hand man, his first executive on staff." Afraid that in my oxygen-depleted state I would forget, I kept saying the name over and over until we finished.

Back in John's office, two astonishing things happened. First John said to his staff, "I can't wait to tell Adriaan Paulen I had a run with *Kathrine Switzer!*" Paulen was president of the IAAF, a rather forbidding character who intimidated the hell out of me. I was greatly flattered. The second was a call from the head of JAAF in Tokyo, asking John whether it was within IAAF rules for athletes to wear sponsor identification on their T-shirts. In particular, they were questioning the legality of putting "Avon" on the Avon Running shirts. And there I was, sitting right in the office! John put them on hold and I pulled out the photos and held up the shirt. "Wow, that's a really nice shirt!" he said. "Do you give that to everyone?" and I said, "Yes, and the women love it; look here is a photo of eight hundred of them wearing it." "I don't see any problem with a nice gift, and it's the name of the race anyway," John said, and told the JAAF person that the shirts were fine. One run with John Holt had saved months of work and anguish in Japan and on the Olympic front. It also put another big idea in my head.

First, though, I thought it was underhanded of JAAF supposedly to be in partnership with Avon and yet try to deny us the visibility we needed. With friends like this, who needs enemies? I quickly called Avon's general manager in Japan to alert him to what had happened. "Forewarned is forearmed," he said cheerily. We were now preparing the groundwork for a whole series of Avon Women's 5K and 10K races, in Fukuoka, Osaka, Sapporo, and Tokyo. It was breathless how fast Avon Japan was moving and I didn't want any underhanded stuff going on with our program.

Over dinner, I told Elizabeth all my news; it was wonderful to talk to someone who really understood the sport. Then I gave her the new idea that had grown out of the run with John and the phone call from Japan. "All the real power in running right now is here in London. This is where we have to have the 1980 Avon Marathon. It's got to be a big deal, a *really* big deal, because 1980 is when the decision is made for new events for the 1984 Games."

"Oh my God," said Elizabeth, "I think you are serious."

"I am totally serious. Little Waldniel is nice, but it isn't going to cut it with the IAAF and the IOC."

"How about Chicago? Now there's a bigger town. How about *New York*! Fred and the New York Road Runners would love it," said Elizabeth.

"No. That makes it just another splashy American idea for foreigners to hate. We need to put this race right in the front yard of the IAAF. London."

"Oh, God," Elizabeth moaned, and then started laughing. "Oh, God, it's going to be fabulous! Oh, God, we're *both* gonna die!"

Chapter | 24

Coalescence

There's a wonderful moment about thirty-six hours before a major marathon when all the material and people suddenly coalesce. For the organizer or race director, it's the moment when all the plans and hopes become visible, if not yet quite enacted. Ordinary streets fill with the colors of posters, welcome signs, and fluttering banners and flags. The grandstands are up, slowing traffic. People stop and look, and there's a general bustle in the shops. Lithe runners, babbling in a variety of languages, dart about in multicolored warm-up suits adorned with their national insignias. You greet each of them, cross their names off the Arrivals list with a relieved smile, and suddenly feel grateful for the miracle of safe travel. Many have never before left their hometowns, much less traveled the thousands of miles across national boundaries to arrive here. And the scene is never quite the same from race to race. All marathons have their own distinct characters, and they take on their own lives. We organizers are merely facilitators.

Before that life begins, and after all the mounting preliminary hubbub has finally ended, there is a moment of stillness just before the gun goes off, and in that short interval all the work of weeks and months and years hangs suspended before you. For the athlete or the organizer, it is the same great sensation.

I experienced it all over again at Waldniel on September 22, 1979. The second Avon International Marathon was another triumph. It brought in runners from places as new to the marathon as Bolivia and the Ivory Coast (which sent a 200-meter sprinter with no shoes to run in). It gave worldwide recognition and corporate endorsement to the visionary research and coaching of Dr. Ernst van Aaken, who for so many years was a lone voice for women's long-distance running. And it brought another star runner and remarkable woman to the forefront, through the commanding victory of England's Joyce Smith. At age forty-two, in only her second marathon, she ran a 2:36:27, the fifth fastest ever, and demolished centuries of prejudice about age as well as gender. She joined a minor British tradition that began with Violet Piercy, a mystery figure who supposedly ran a world-best 3:40 marathon in 1926, and was followed by Scotland's Dale Greig, who definitely did in 1964 with a 3:27, and the dedicated Leslie Watson, who was running every race available. From Joyce Smith to Paula Radcliffe, the tradition would grow.

For me, and for the long campaign to have the women's marathon added to the Olympic Games, Waldniel was a stopover, not a final destination. Like the preparations for a race, that campaign swirled confusingly for a very long time and demanded huge work, until finally, thankfully, it all coalesced. The key events happened all around the world—Los Angeles, Tokyo, Rio de Janeiro, Paris, Boston, Moscow, and London. All contributed, through strategy, personality, or by sheer accident.

Los Angeles

My travels and the campaign began where I hoped they would end in success five years later, Los Angeles. On John Holt's advice, I went straight to Peter Ueberroth and Dick Sargent at the Los Angeles Olympic Organizing Committee (LAOOC), the key players in the preparations for the 1984 Olympics. They were informative and encouraging. I learned a lot about the commercial and international politics of the Olympics, how Kodak lost their sponsorship spot to Fuji Film, how the Soviets were pushing for inclusion of rhythmic gymnastics, the financial implications of adding any event (new venue, new tickets, more athletes to house). I learned that it wasn't as simple as saying women "deserved" the marathon; there were all kinds of trade-offs. When I provided statistics on women's marathon participation and research on the medical implications, Ueberroth was very interested and asked for the information in the form of a report. Most encouraging, Dick Sargent accepted my invitations to an Avon media dinner and to the Rose Bowl Stadium in Pasadena to present the awards at the Avon Half-Marathon we were holding there. I was blown away when he ended his short speech to the crowd with, "I hope you get your marathon in the Olympics."

Tokyo

Tokyo seemed like a slap in the face. On the way to Japan, I launched our new races in the Philippines, Malaysia, and Thailand, that's how international the Avon Circuit had become already. We also had series in development in France, Holland, Belgium, and Spain. My life on the road of hotels and meetings was more congenial at this time than life at home. With his drinking, lack of career, and resentful attitude toward his son Eric, Philip had become almost entirely negative and critical. I stayed only because I thought I could be a buffer between him and Eric, who was very pleasant company. (Twenty-five years later, after his father's death, Eric thanked me and told me how important this support was.) So it was not home-sickness that made my Tokyo visit an unpleasant one, but the response from the men on the board of the JAAF when, after our hugely successful 5K Tokyo race, we suggested that the Avon International Marathon come there. They howled in protest. "No, no, *no!* No woman's marathon here, *ever!*" "Well, gee," was about all we could say.

I said a lot more two months later when the news arrived at my office in New York that the JAAF had announced it was putting on an all-women's marathon in Tokyo sponsored by the cosmetics company Shiseido. Suddenly the undermining phone call to John Holt at the IAAF became clear. I lost my temper for the first time since I put my boot through Tom's television screen. In one swipe I threw everything off my desk and kicked the trash can clear out of the door. Elizabeth looked out from her cubicle and said, "I've been telling you for weeks to clean off your desk."

Then I laughed. The JAAF had just confirmed that the women's marathon was worth scheming for and the stakes were high. And the real winners were the women runners, because the Japanese vote on the IOC was a lot more sure now than if an American had been pressuring them for it. So when Japanese event organizers in identical blue blazers suddenly popped up at the Avon Marathon in Waldniel, bowing and handing out gifts and taking notes on everything in sight, I was nice, but I made sure they were firmly excluded from the media room. Our media arrangements were unique and I was going to protect our secrets. I even got my boss Joe to reprise his head of security role as pressroom doorman.

Rio de Janeiro

Avon's races in Brazil happened when I met Eleanora Mendonça, their top woman distance runner, a part-time resident of Boston. She began running Avon races in the United States and came with us to Waldniel. Talented and multilingual, she was a natural as a race director in Brazil, and Avon Brazil loved the idea. So I got to witness the total body-culture of Rio's beaches, where a G-string (called a tanga) and two postage stamps are formal attire and beach volleyball the national pastime. The race, we decided, would have to reflect this sense of fun in the sun, and be wholly unintimidating, so we made beautiful posters utilizing our theme of two women runners with a tropical background, and we chose a course right along the main drag alongside Ipanema beach. But there was another aspect of Brazilian life I wanted to touch on, too, and that was the myriad of women living in extreme poverty. Running requires no fashionable equipment. We would provide all amenities, including the light tricot singlet. It was a new setting for my old theme: opportunity.

The head of the Brazilian federation was not hostile, merely bored, when I called on him. "The women of Brazil are very feminine," he drawled (his passion was polo and his blazer had buttons made of real gold). "They would never run on the roads." I said that I'd noticed an awful lot of women on the beach playing sports and they sure didn't look masculine, and I invited him to attend. He sighed and agreed, but stipulated that his wife would not, nor would he permit (permit!) his daughter to attend.

Three thousand women showed up for the first race. By the third, it was ten thousand. You cannot ignore ten thousand women running along the main street of Rio de Janeiro in shorts. Some saw the race as another celebration of the body, and were in full tanga regalia with their postage-stamp tops. Many others saw it as an opportunity to leave poverty behind for a while, or perhaps they even ran it for a free shirt, a medal, and a lipstick, all things they had never had before. These were women without shoes. And I don't mean Adidas or Nike. I mean they owned no shoes, and ran in their Avon shirts and bare feet. The race gave them a sense of recognition and significance that was as unfamiliar as a medal. With a new sense of self-esteem and confidence born of this program, many—*many*—of these women went on to a better life. A public relations program for Avon had turned into a social revolution. And gave me some of the proudest moments of my life. Sometimes when I got discouraged, or so exhausted from my work and travel that I could barely stand, I thought of all the women—especially these poor women—and knew the effort was all worthwhile.

When I see twenty-first century "charity" runs or walks that are restricted to women who can donate or raise thousands of dollars, I regret the loss of the much greater charity that the old Avon circuit served: opportunity for *every* woman.

Senhor O Presidente was impressed. "Oh, senhor," I gushed, as he proudly handed out the awards, "we couldn't have done it without you." He was on O Globo TV every night for a week, looking important, looking like an innovator. He was happy. I had another safe IOC vote, and from a new continent. I was happy.

Paris

The report that Peter Ueberroth had asked for still wasn't written. I didn't even have time to turn in my expense reports to Joe, who grumbled that I was screwing up his books, as well as carrying a major out-of-pocket expense myself. There was simply no time. It seemed that I was in daily communication with every country in the world, often actually visiting them. There was always another race to plan, and, in the other extreme, I was trying to think about a divorce. Then I hit upon it—I'd con Valerie Andrews, my writing lieutenant, into a weekend at Gurney's in Montauk! She loved the story about how I wrote the Avon proposal there, and now the old inn had become a deluxe spa. Seducing her with promises of salt scrubs and massage between bouts of writing, I found a rare free weekend and we absolutely whaled into the writing. With no distractions, we finished the report and had our bodies overhauled at the same time.

So "The Avon Report on the Status of Women's Distance Running" came into existence, birthed among herbal wraps and lingering facials. A five-minute film on the Waldniel race was designed to accompany it. Soon after, I called on John Holt in London. It was John who made the brilliant suggestion that I hand out the report and make a short presentation when the full IAAF delegation met in Paris in March 1980 for the World Cross-Country Championships. I wasn't permitted to attend formal IAAF meetings, but John suggested that Avon host a cocktail reception at the delegates' hotel after a day of meetings and before an official dinner. Our Avon colleagues in Paris set up the reception in a jiffy.

Also in on the plot was Marea Hartman, who skillfully steered all the delegates into our salon as they exited their meeting. Many were already friends with whom I'd organized events, so the atmosphere was positive. As the report was distributed, I sincerely asked for their help in the next few months as we pressed for a decision at the IOC meeting in Moscow, saying that all the information they needed was in the report. The reception was under the official radar, but as John Holt had predicted, very effective. At last the facts were in their hands. Two weeks later, Holt himself used the report in his recommendation to the IOC in Lausanne that the marathon for women be included in the 1984 Games, as well as the women's 400-meter hurdles and the 3,000-meter track race. The IOC discussed it again in June.

I found myself meeting more influential people that weekend at IAAF dinners and receptions, the most astonishing being a champagne dinner show at the Moulin Rouge, where Adidas, sponsors of the weekend, hosted the IAAF and all the nations' team leaders. It was eye-opening in every way, because of all the beautiful naked (well, there were a few feathers) dancing ladies (when I mentioned the live dolphins in the decorative fish tanks, one delegate distractedly said, "What dolphins?") and because I calculated the cost of this one dinner at about $50,000, my entire budget for the Avon Marathon in Atlanta! Now I saw why Adidas shoes were on the feet of almost all the athletes in major world competitions. I also began to see how expensive it could be to be a major player in the sports sponsorship world. By comparison, our Avon budgets were chicken feed. We made it look big time because we did it all ourselves, in house.

The next day at the World Cross-Country Championships, I sat in the stands at the Longchamps race course with Dave Martin, whose research material had figured so prominently in the report. It wasn't just the convincing stats about the international growth of women's running but the vitally important medical evidence that showed women's unique ability for endurance running that would be imperative in decision making. Dave's research, along with that of Dr. van Aaken, Paul Milvey, and others scientifically refuted the age-old myth of women's weakness and fragility. We were jubilant. Then, around the racecourse, the American runner Craig Virgin stormed home to victory, beating the best athletes in the world. "Gold Medal 10,000! Gold Medal 10,000!" we chanted, as Virgin looked to be a hot contender for the 10,000-meter race in the 1980 Moscow Olympics. It seemed like a very good omen.

Boston

Our same team from PBS-TV (WGBH Boston) was back doing that year's Marathon broadcast. It was a warm and bright day and I was again on the golf cart leading the women's race.

Patti Lyons was the favorite, though I also knew Jacqueline Gareau, a nurse from Quebec, who was a sub-2:40 marathoner and had run in the Avon program was strong. Jacqueline took the lead at eight miles and held it, frustrating Lyons, who could see her but simply not catch her. From time to time on my golf cart I would drift back, and I could see that Lyons was just not going to be able to close the gap unless Gareau disastrously faltered, which looked most unlikely.

We had to get the cart off the course at Mile 23 since we were not sure the battery would last, so at about 22 miles I went up to the back of the second men's group, who were running about 2:25 or so, to double-check that my old nemesis, the unknown "Daisy Mae out of Appalachia," hadn't sneaked ahead, as Liane Winter did in my best year, 1975. I came back to Gareau and confidently gave her the Number 1 sign. But when I arrived at the finish area and strolled over to our TV truck, the producer said "Yah yah yah, Kathrine, we got the woman winner, here, take a look." He rolled the tape and I saw someone coming down the finish line I'd never seen before.

"Who is *that?*" I screamed.

"Number fifty. Some gal named Rosie Ruiz. From New York."

"I am going to kill Fred Lebow with my bare hands!" I said, assuming Fred had once again brought in a dark horse without telling anybody. "Roll the tape back again please."

Down the finish stretch she came again, all jiggling cellulite and flailing arms. It was weird. Here she was, running a 2:31, a new course and new American record, and she wasn't even thin. I knew every runner in New York City who could run under three hours, but maybe she's not really from New York. Where was she on the course?! I was there the whole time. How on earth had I missed her? All this was flying through my mind. I was scared. I had called the whole race wrong! Oh God, I had wrecked the broadcast of the women's race! I had to do something fast to repair the damage.

I ran back to my golf cart. The cameraman, a Japanese, was just leaving. I took his arm and said he had to come with me, pulling him to the finish area. He spoke hardly any English but kept gesturing that he was out of tape. I said "Please, *some* tape?" He held up his fingers to indicate a few inches. "Okay, let's go," I said, and we pushed our way through the crowd and into the underground garage to a makeshift press area. It was pandemonium. In the middle of it—who else!?—Jock Semple and Fred Lebow were shouting at each other. I barged in and grabbed Fred by the coat, accusingly demanding, "Okay, Fred, who is she?" He said, "She's a cheater! She didn't win the race!" I was stunned. That had not occurred to me. Who would ever cheat in a marathon? The ultimate victory is over yourself, so there's no point.

Where was Ruiz? Fred gestured across the room. Indeed, there was the very woman, making her way to leave. I ran over to her, cameraman in tow, asking to do an interview. The cameraman moved fast but warned me: "Little tape," he said.

At the first question Ruiz began to sneeze. We couldn't stop and do it over, as we didn't have enough tape. She kept trying to move away from me and the camera, so I held her tightly by the arm. I was trying madly to read her face and body, which was disorienting me, because she was so at odds with any post-marathon look: there were no salt stains on her clothes, no creases in her face, no sign of that almost beatific expression around the eyes that speaks for accomplishment and resignation. I've only otherwise seen that look in women after they've given birth. Finally, she didn't smell right. Post-race elite marathoners are drenched in a sharp adrenaline scent. It's a distinctive warrior smell, definitely not regular old body odor. Ruiz didn't have it. She didn't have anything I could recognize.

We proceeded. It was bizarre, like a comedy spoof of an interview. Only not funny.

"You just ran a 2:31! How many miles a week do you do in training?"

"I run fifty miles a week!"

I expected to hear a hundred, so I said "Wow, you must be doing incredible intervals." (That's the only way anyone could possibly do a 2:31 on fifty miles a week.)

"What are intervals?" she answered.

Now, twenty-seven years and hundreds of interviews later, I'd have asked her harder questions, but she sufficiently incriminated herself. It was my first-ever TV finish-line interview and I was intimidated and felt I had to give her the benefit of a doubt. What if, somehow, she really had won, and on TV I asked her if she cheated? I made my way morosely back to the studio to close the show. I wanted to crawl in a hole.

The studio was in pandemonium, as the ticker tape was firing in reports of a possible cheating scandal. I told my producer Greg Harney that I'd done an interview with her but that it probably wasn't any good. He racked the tape and everyone rushed from their editing desks to watch it. Greg came over to me and put his hand on my shoulder. "That was great, kid, just great."

By six o'clock, the whole country knew there had been a cheater at Boston. And we had the only finish-line interview with Ruiz.

On Boston Marathon day every year, a bar one mile from the finish hangs a sign, "Rosie Ruiz starts here." Jokes abound, like "Rosie Ruiz Pantyhose: Guaranteed Not to Run." She has become a comic iconic figure, almost a proverb: "Doing a Rosie," runners say. But many of us think it's disgraceful, and here I am annoyed all over again. The full story developed piece by piece. In the 1979 New York City Marathon, she left the course in Brooklyn, took the subway to the finish, and was mistakenly scored as a top ten finisher. Seeing her name in the paper the next day, her employer encouraged her to run Boston, and she submitted her fraudulent New York time. Whether for fame, or to appease her employer, or out of some delusional fantasy, we will never know, but she jumped into the race somewhere very near the end (no sweat under her armpits, even) and made the mistake of doing it ahead of the front of the women's field. Many people credit my interview as the thing that unmasked her, but any runner would doubt her floppy style and daisy freshness as evidence of a 2:31 marathon. She tearfully denies to this day that she cheated and has refused to give back the winner's medallion.

So how can I claim this petty cheat's scandal as a positive thing for women's running? Because, as the author (and my husband) Roger Robinson said in a recent *Running Times* article, Ruiz showed "how glamorous success as a runner must have appeared to someone with no such image of aspiration and attainment in her life." Because Jacqueline Gareau probably got even more kudos (which she fully deserved) when she was given her victor's laurels and medal in a nationally covered ceremony later in the week. Because Boston finally had to clean up its act, institute crowd control, identify the lead women, and time and score them properly. Because it made the Avon Marathons look good; it could never happen in our races! And finally because millions of people who had never heard of women running marathons finally did and had to admit that if a cheating incident was newsworthy, then the sport itself was worth taking seriously and that women now were real runners, trained and competitive, not patsy novices. Those millions would include, I hoped, some members of the IOC.

Moscow

The second shocker actually occurred a week before the Boston Marathon, on April 12, 1980, when President Jimmy Carter declared that the United States would boycott the Moscow Olympics in protest against the Soviet invasion of Afghanistan. Throughout history, Olympic boycotts have been useless. Nobody remembers who boycotted, they only remember who won. A magazine asked me for a quote about my thoughts, and I said, "My country, right or wrong, my country," by which I meant that I thought it was sad but was resigned to it because the United States was not going to change its mind. I was not in favor of Carter's action. It was a tragedy for many athletes—like the aforementioned Craig Virgin—who had dedicated their lives to an Olympic dream and would never have this prime time again. Another sentiment emerged from all this, however. Now people knew how women distance runners felt, being denied even the opportunity of an event in the Olympics.

In practical terms, the boycott helped Avon and the women's Olympic marathon cause. NBC-TV was not going to Moscow and so had a very big hole to fill. I began working on them to broadcast the Avon Marathon in London on August 3. I nudged every contact I knew, and NBC decided they would cover our London race with a national show. The UK did not join the boycott, but the BBC could not be outdone by an American TV company, so it decided to cover the Avon Marathon also. Then Eurovision jumped on board, along with O Globo from Brazil. Avon did not pay a cent for this coverage, and Elizabeth thought I was a genius. Best of all, the women's marathon and our Olympic quest were going to have worldwide television coverage. Nothing in the modern world had more influence, and millions of people—including important officials—were going to see it.

Moscow delivered yet another disappointment in July. While they had voted in the women's 3,000 meters, the IOC had found the women's marathon issue too controversial and postponed the decision to their board meeting in February 1981. "One member said there was not enough supporting medical evidence," Dick Sargent told me. "But our L.A. medical guy held up your report and said, 'Yes, there is! We've got it right here!'" We had dodged a bullet and had another chance. And before then would come the Avon Marathon in London. I told Dick that by February the IOC members would not have any doubt in their minds about the women's marathon.

London

Was it possible to run a marathon through the heart of London? It was a preposterous thought. The streets of downtown London had never been closed for any sports event. Even the 1908 and 1948 Olympic marathons used courses away from the central city. One argument in our favor was the recent spectacular success of New York's downtown marathon experiment. Another was the team who discovered us as much as we found them, notably Bryan Smith, husband of Joyce, a brilliant event organizer and coach. He and his club-mates Paul Lovell, Dave Billington, and Vera Duerdin had already thought of such a race and even had a course mapped out. Influential friends Marea Hartman and *Athletics Weekly* journalist Cliff Temple also jumped in without reservation. There were plenty of snags and problems, and for a while things were desperate, but in the end it was Sir Horace Cutler, the leader of the Greater London Council, who made it happen. Intrigued by New York's success, and attracted by the visibility to be gained for the mayor and the city, he embraced it and turned the administrative and police taps on for us. Bingo! It was a go! We'd put the women's marathon cause in the front yard of the most influential decision makers in the world.

At a champagne reception that he hosted before the race itself on the Parliament Terrace, Sir Horace rose to his feet against the background of the Thames and Big Ben and reminded us of the historic significance of the streets of London being closed for the first time for a sports event. "We have only done this before for the Queen. Congratulations, ladies," he said.

Because such history tends to get rewritten, or appropriated, another episode has to be reported. One day in London in the early stages of organization, I got a strange phone call from Chris Brasher, asking to meet me for a drink. Chris Brasher was a legend, an Olympic gold medalist, and equally famous for being one of the teammates who helped Roger Bannister to break the four-minute mile barrier in

1954. Brasher was an excellent sports journalist and an entrepreneur who started Britain's first chain of running stores. He was known as dynamic and successful, yet he seemed quite agitated about something. He wanted to know about "my marathon" and let me know that he didn't think having it in London was a good idea.

I remember I had just started a glass of white wine, and he'd already knocked back a martini, and I thought, whoa, I need all my faculties here because I'm not sure what is going on. Over another martini, and another, Chris began listing the many other courses in the UK that would be better suited for our race. I am usually talkative, and interject a lot, but I just nodded to encourage him to go on.

"Edinburgh!" he said.

"Edinburgh?"

"That's it! Edinburgh is the perfect place to hold your race.'

"Good heavens! Why would we want to go to Edinburgh?"

"It's colorful! It's historic!"

"I thought London was colorful and historic," I said.

"Yes, but Edinburgh is more manageable."

"I've never been there; I wouldn't know."

"Trust me, that's the place for you!"

"I hear it rains all the time in Edinburgh."

"It rains in London!" he answered.

"Yes, but when it rains in London, at least you are still in London!" And I laughed; I thought this was pretty funny. He was very pissed off by this time because the conversation was going nowhere, and I still wasn't sure what was going on. Plus I wanted my wine badly but dared not drink it. Finally, Chris left and I went to meet Elizabeth for dinner.

"How did your drink with that Brasher guy go?" asked Elizabeth over dinner.

"He wants us to hold the Avon Marathon in Edinburgh."

"Good heavens! Why would we want to go to Edinburgh?"

"It beats the hell out of me, Elizabeth."

A year later, Chris Brasher founded the hugely successful and high-profile London Marathon, whose official histories always explain how he got the idea from Fred Lebow, and so created the first marathon through the streets of London. Later we became friends, but Chris never admitted that the "official" story is less than the whole truth, or that we beat him to the punch.

Another strange conversation at about this time occurred when I had the opportunity to go back home for a while and take a break from London and its labors. I was exhausted. Philip took one look at me and burst out with resentment and jealousy over totally imagined affairs; he was a real Othello. Perhaps the most revealing moment in a time of sheer misery was when I asked him to stop telling me how to do my job. "Let's just be married," I said. "That's not what I want, I want to be in charge," he shouted. It was hard for him, with all my long absences, my celebrity and success, and his own career a failure, but the stress was catching up with me, and this fight was one too many. I had lost appetite and weight, I was cold all the time, and I tried to keep alert with eight cups of coffee a day. I passed out on one long flight, and was too weak to pick up my suitcase. The body never lies, even if the heart does. I was a classic thyroid case. The prescription was no coffee, no beer, regular food and sleep, thyroid medication, and a marriage counselor. The last did nothing. When Eric left for college, I sadly began separation and divorce proceedings and flew back to London.

Part V | The Race

The race is the moment it all comes together: you commit, and put it all on the line.

Chapter | 25

London: the Deal-Maker

I always flew with heavy baggage. Every time Elizabeth or I went to London, much to the horror of the Avon UK receiving office, we'd carry two giant suitcases full of banners, T-shirts, press kits, and even the solid-gold and silver necklaces that would be given to place-getters. We never got stopped by Customs and we saved a bundle on shipping. Getting this kind of stuff held up in Customs is a nightmare.

The winners from all of our international races had won their trips, and the point winners and champions from the domestic circuit were ready to go. The point system proved an amazing incentive. Women drove all over the country, and whole teams would travel by van to Avon races for points that would get them to London. In some cases, it would have been cheaper just to fly to London, but they wanted to win their way. It was a badge of honor. Indeed, we treated them well, not just to a trip, but to goodies and special recognition at the press conferences. As usual, we also invited the world's best, including Joan Benoit and New Zealander Lorraine Moller, who had just run one of the fastest debut marathons, a 2:37 at the Grandma's Marathon in Duluth. On a last-minute whim, I invited Moller. In the ensuing years, she became a close friend and confidante.

The travel arrangements were delegated to Hal Higdon, the famous running writer and former Olympian, who with his wife, Rose, had formed a travel agency specifically for runners. In London Hal would even take groups for training runs every day, and soon the Higdons were part of our Avon Running traveling family, along with photographers Jane Sobel and Arthur Klonsky, who documented every move in every race we had in the States and many abroad. We called ourselves a running Chautauqua.

Valerie Andrews, practically a sister by this time, also came early to London. A friend offered a sublet apartment in Knightsbridge, and we showed the ever-watchful Joe that it was cheaper than a hotel. That apartment became Marathon Central, and Valerie and I worked furiously there at PR, media, and operations. It proved a convenient place to meet journalists with coffee or tea, and nearby Hyde Park was perfect when they wanted to take action pictures. The park, in fact, was a godsend, and Valerie and I managed to get in a couple of runs a week. In the early evening, Elizabeth, still in New York, and I would have our daily trans-Atlantic update, and at about eight P.M. in London, we'd knock off and have dinner, usually at a funky place around the corner called Borscht and Tears, where the menu said you could dance on the tables if you wanted to.

The London police and Scotland Yard surprised me with their positive approach to this all-day job of closing streets. Their sense of humor was something I had never encountered in American law enforcement. Then there were meetings with St. John's ambulance, the mayor's office, volunteer groups, the race hotel, caterers, our Avon HQ in Northampton, and most of all the calm and tireless Bryan Smith, the race director. For Joyce, as the star British runner, the pressure was considerable, but she was patient and helpful as always. With two young daughters at home, and both Joyce and Bryan working full time, the Smith household was more than busy.

An unexpected problem was that the pound sterling was very strong in the summer of 1980 against a weak U.S. dollar, so doing business in London was costing a fortune. One evening at Bryan and Joyce's, we recalculated the budget. We were short by $30,000, an astronomical sum in those days. I called Elizabeth in a dark mood. She said she'd figure it out and she did. It was my turn to think Elizabeth was a genius.

As race day approached, Elizabeth arrived and we all moved into the Kensington Gardens Hotel, the official race hotel. I chose it because it was on the same side of the street as the gardens that led into Hyde Park, so the runners did not need to cross the busy road to reach an ideal training location. Something that bothered me more than it should was the number of wealthy Arab sheiks living in the hotel, lounging around the beautiful lobby all day in their headgear and long white robes, smoking, having coffee, and ogling our runners. Really, it must have been astonishing for them to see these young women who were so liberated that they could be athletes and wear short-shorts and tiny tops in a public place. Many of the runners, oblivious to how they looked, would gather in the lobby and languorously do their stretching together. I became overanxious, and even called an emergency meeting and lectured the runners on propriety, saying they had to do their stretching in their rooms, and when they were in their running gear, they had to enter and exit the hotel quickly. Elizabeth sat giggling at me, later telling me that I'd become an old mother hen. I told her that as far as I knew, there was still an undercover but active female slave market in the world and all we needed was for one of our runners to be kidnapped! She howled with delight. I got my comeuppance when I saw Gail Volk, an invited runner who happened to be tall and utterly gorgeous, with long, naturally platinum blond hair, walk into the elevator followed by a bellboy with an expensive armload of long-stemmed red roses. I ran after them and slammed myself into the elevator doors, forcing them open and snapped at her, "Gail!! I demand to know who those roses are from!" "Gee, Kathrine, they're from my boyfriend in Spokane. It's my twenty-first birthday!"

The Arab women showed how extraordinary our women were in the context of human culture and history. Covered from head to toe in a great black tent of cloth, with masks over their faces, they would cluster in the lobby and flutter in and out of the hotel like flocks of blackbirds to go shopping. One time, wearing a bare-shouldered sundress, I found myself in an elevator full of black-robed Arab women, whose leader kept hissing at me from behind her gold face mask until I jumped out quickly at the next floor. All these years later, I wonder if those women have been changed at all, as so many other Muslim women have, by the women's sports movement, and the breakthroughs that their few courageous sisters have made.

Nothing terrible happened at the Avon International Marathon in London, only good and wonderful things. It was so good, it was like a dream evolving. Crucial to the campaign for Olympic inclusion was the fact that twenty-seven countries and five continents were represented, exceeding the IOC's formal requirement for considering new events. Women's marathon running was an established global sport. London was the proof. They *can't* refuse us now, I thought, and we have six months to remind them.

I went out very early with some helpers to the start area in Battersea Park to erect Avon banners and other signage. The BBC was very strict about "commercial exposure." By the time they showed up, it would be too late for anything except begging forgiveness for all the on-camera visibility Avon would get.

I spoke about the moment of coalescence in my description of the Waldniel race. There is another that is quite magical, and that is race morning at dawn, when, minute by minute, a deserted park begins to awake and gets adorned for the start of a marathon. Tents pop up, tables open, scaffolding is draped, banners are unfurled, cables are taped, and microphones tested. Someone brings coffee at last. People arrive with all the paraphernalia for their specific duties, dressing the part whether they are helmeted and leathered motorcycle drivers, orange-vested photographers, or TV commentators in their spiffy blazers. Things you have discussed for months are unfolding like a ballet. On this day, a fleet of big red double-decker buses parades in, carrying Elizabeth and the athletes, officials, and invited VIPs. At the final moment, the runners burst onto the roadway, striding back and forth like the nervous thoroughbreds they are, until they are cor-ralled behind the start line while a helicopter beats low overhead.

Then in a whoop of cheering and streak of color, they are gone.

I always went in the lead press vehicle with the journalists, and Elizabeth hustled the officials and VIPs to the finish. I could brief the media and be on the spot for any on-course problem, not the least of which was to make sure that the route was followed correctly. (Don't laugh; disasters have happened even in the Olympic Games.) Elizabeth made sure everything was in place for the finish, at the magnificent old Guildhall in the heart of the City. She had to check timing, scoring, announcing, flowers, awards, camera positions, press control, and much more, and she had only a little over an hour to do it, after getting her big bus across London. I never worried about the finish if Elizabeth was there, and she never worried about the course.

But in London we didn't worry much at all, because Bryan Smith and his team had it all so well covered. As the race progressed, I could see that Bryan had remembered every detail discussed in meetings. There was the first water station! By golly, every single volunteer was wearing their red Avon Marathon shirt! There was a tricky cobblestoned corner; Bryan had a course marshal steering the runners outside the curve.

There were moments of bliss. Perhaps the greatest for me was standing in the front of the big red bus and leading the runners across Westminster Bridge. Hundreds of years, millions of people, and we were the first race in history to cross the Thames by the iconic bridge. I felt like Hannibal crossing the Alps.

The bliss moment for Lorraine Moller came at Mile 21, in the rather dreary Isle of Dogs area of the course, through a disused section of the Docklands preparing for its present-day gentrification (and incorporation in the London Marathon course). It was deserted on this Sunday morning except for the race leader, Nancy Conz, and our bus. Conz, from Massachusetts, had won a ticket to London as a prize from a non-Avon race. I knew her to be a big threat and had picked her as the dark horse. It was a great story—another unknown bursting onto the world marathon scene. The other favorites, including Joyce Smith and Joan Benoit, were not in sight, but we soon saw Lorraine Moller moving up. She and Conz were both running strongly, but Moller was in a higher gear. With no word or look exchanged between them, Moller just slipped by Conz, who did not attempt to go with her. It looked easy, but the reality was that both women were giving it all they had.

As good as the Nancy story was, the British were delighted with Lorraine, who was at least running under one of the former empire's flags. That helped make up for their dashed hopes over the hometown girl, Joyce Smith, who, bless her heart, ran the race despite having just had a case of chicken pox picked up from her young daughter. Lorraine then was a Commonwealth Games 800-meter finalist, but she was so new to the marathon that she didn't even own racing shoes, and ran in a pair borrowed from Gary Bjorklund, who had recently won the Grandma's Marathon in Duluth, Minnesota.

With just over a mile to go, we gunned the red bus to Guildhall and everyone dashed to grab spots in the finish area. On cue, the giant bells of nearby St. Andrew's began to peal a joyous, reverberating welcome. In response, our pipe band struck up a stirring march. It gave us all goose bumps. Elizabeth and I shared a quick teary glance, a private, microsecond salute to each other. Then the multitalented David Martin announced Lorraine down the cheering homestretch. The pushy Fleet Street journalists surged forward against our homemade fence of English rugby players. When Lorraine was fifty yards away, Elizabeth and I pulled the Avon finishing tape from our pockets and stretched it across the road. There wasn't time for the BBC or NBC to object; it was our final wicked act but we had to do it. Lorraine broke the tape in 2:35:11, another Avon record, another startling world-class performance, and another contender to strengthen the Olympic case. Nancy Conz kept it together and finished second in 2:36:02. In one of the most heartwarming moments of the day, tiny Linda Staudt, who won her way from Canada, took the bronze medal in 2:37:39 by battling past Joan Benoit in the homestretch, and fell weeping into Elizabeth's arms.

All three medalists defeated better-known champions, and went on to championship marathon careers. As the Lord Mayor of

London, with his own splendid regalia glinting in the sun, awarded the medals and necklaces, you could see the prospect of their futures lighting up their eyes.

Valerie had major media to handle that day (at the last minute, even *People* magazine had flown a reporter from New York!), but I laughed myself silly when I saw that she had still managed to put terry-cloth bathrobes with the Avon monogram on the winners as they were taken to the interview area. After it was all over, the head BBC producer came over to Valerie and me, smiling and complimenting us on the event, but adding, "You are very naughty girls!"

• • •

As the remaining marathoners continued to finish, a lovely luncheon reception for all our guests and officials was taking place in the magnificent gallery of Guildhall, but those of us working the race didn't have a moment to attend. Finally, I knew I really should at least say hello and thank you. When I came into the hall and down the old stone steps, the room burst into applause. I looked behind me to see who they were applauding and realized it was me. It was another blissful moment, not just for me but for the whole team that shared the vision, worked tirelessly to make it happen, and changed the future together. There was a lot of lobbying yet to do to make the women's Olympic marathon a reality, and that mission would dominate my life for the next six months, but the hardest work had been finished. This race was the deal maker.

That night, Elizabeth, Valerie, and I danced on the tables at Borscht and Tears. Much later, in the wee hours, when all of London was quiet, I went out and ran across a deserted Westminster Bridge.

PART VI | THE BREAKTHROUGH

Training works. Sometimes it takes years and sometimes it happens quickly, but there will be improvement. Suddenly, one day you'll be running and you're a lot better than before.

CHAPTER | 26

LOS ANGELES, 1984: THE BIGGEST
RACE OF ALL

SIX P.M., February 23, 1981: My hands were cold and sweaty as I waited for Madame Monique Berlioux, executive director of the International Olympic Committee, to rise and make the announcement. "This was not an easy victory for the women, but it is a very important one," she said. The Board of Directors of the IOC had voted in favor of including the women's marathon in the 1984 Olympic Games!

Madame was right: it was not easy. "Nobody will really understand how important this is until the first woman comes through the tunnel and into the Olympic stadium in three years," I told the reporter from the *Los Angeles Times*. "Then the world will be changed."

The announcement, though, sounded like angels' harps after all the years of work and the final six-month push. I thought the vote from the attending eight members of the board was going to be close, since each had their own agenda. Months before, I had enlisted advice from Donna de Varona, a personal friend of Mme. Berlioux's, to find where allegiances lay. Report in hand, I flew to L.A. in advance of the meeting to lobby the undecided and to ask those in favor to influence the others. In a generous and unprecedented statement, Peter Ueberroth told members that the LAOOC had only one request at this meeting and that was to ask them to approve the women's Olympic marathon.

The only dissenting vote on the IOC was from the Soviet Union delegate, even after some LAOOC people had tried to warm him up with a fun visit to Disneyland. The meeting adjourned to the lobby cocktail lounge with handshakes and hugs. As Valerie and I sat with our journalist friend Anita Verschoth of *Sports Illustrated*, who had followed and supported the women's marathon cause for years, a bottle of champagne arrived from Peter Ueberroth. I looked over with a happy wave of thanks, and he smiled and saluted.

The three years following this vote confirmed the wonder and honor of the decision. As the word spread that the marathon was official, many existing athletes refocused on the longer event, while many beginners hit the roads. Being official eliminated a lot of fear and hesitation. The Avon program exploded into twenty-seven countries, often with complete national circuits, many of them becoming national championships, some even IAAF championships. Eventually, over a million women runners in Avon races ran in every climate imaginable around the world, wearing shorts, pantaloons, burkas, T-shirts, tunics, tanga, and headscarves, with shoes or without. They now had a destination, not just a dream. Opportunity had made it happen, and opportunity would get them to the starting line in L.A.

Opportunity can make other things happen, too. I took another of several monthlong trips to Avon races in Malaysia, the Philippines, Thailand, and Japan. Not surprisingly, our five-city Avon Running tour lived quite companionably alongside the world-class Tokyo Ladies Marathon. Later, I shared a pre-race speaking platform in Australia with Roger Robinson of New Zealand, the world's top master runner at the time, and an author and university professor. I'd sworn off romance but fell in love at first voice. Roger did, too. Despite our very different careers, and often living ten thousand miles apart, we got married and have been deliriously happy for twenty years.

The other opportunity was an additional new career in television. That medium suddenly needed a knowledgeable woman to cover the female division in various city marathons, and especially the upcoming first-ever Women's Olympic Marathon in Los Angeles.

So on that important day, August 5, 1984, I was in the ABC-TV studio in Los Angeles, in my spiffy blue blazer, ready to broadcast the race of my life with colleagues Al Michaels and Marty Liquori. I was a lot more nervous than if I'd been running, and here is how it went, on air, and in my own thoughts:

The room is too small, filled with too many cameras, too many statisticians, and it seems, too many technicians. Al Michaels's IFB, the earpiece that links the commentators you see on your screen to the director and producer behind the scenes, is wired into another Olympic event; he's shouting to have it fixed. Our studio monitors are too small to read numbers, a sinking feeling, as you realize that two billion people will see a picture better than you, the "expert." Calm down, I tell myself, you know every woman in the race. *Every* woman; you don't need their numbers. The cables on the floor look like great snakes, and the technicians scramble, tripping over them in their haste, pale with worry.

In my earpiece: "We don't have time for a rehearsal! We're going *live* in four . . . three . . . two . . . one."

So began the day I'd dreamed of, many had dreamed of; talked and wrote about; worked, plotted, organized, and ran for. It was the marathon, the *Woman's Olympic Marathon* and it was the *first*. After today, everything would seem like history. But I didn't have time to philosophize. Tomorrow, perhaps. Later, anyway.

Camera pan, starting line: American Julie Brown looks a bit too cavalier this morning, especially for someone so shy. Gosh, she was pale and gaunt when I interviewed her last week. Grete Waitz was smiling. She has a kind of "What could ever surprise me?" look. Lorraine Moller appears Madonna like, a religious pilgrim setting out on terrible journey, while her countrywoman Anne Audain looks annoyed at the prospect. Ingrid Kristiansen is positively jocular, happy, relaxed, out for a Sunday run. I instantly peg her as the one to beat. (Well, not instantly; I had interviewed her two days before, as she bounced her eleven-month-old son on her lap. She had set the world 5,000-meter record only a few weeks ago, and I was impressed with this quality of sharpening and how happy-go-lucky she seemed about everything.) The camera pan confirms my intuition.

Now, there is Benoit, and she looks . . . how? Like nothing. Totally vacuous. With her jaw slack, mouth slightly open, and eyes glazed, she looks—well—almost retarded, certainly not of this world. Even her uniform, a blah gray, hangs limply.

Earpiece: "What are they thinking, guys, what are they *thinking*?"

What they are thinking is that they don't want to think just now. I refrain from saying that and concentrate on sorting out my information. Just educate the viewer . . .

Most of the faces easily engendered comments. But Joan's defied analysis. She was probably vacating her thoughts, push-brooming out everything to simply let the energy flow and her superb racing instincts take over when the right moment came.

She was definitely trying not to think about her knee, of the seventeen days before the May 12, 1984, Olympic trials, where she went through a living nightmare of going from the best shape of her life to a sudden knee injury, surgery, and rehabilitation, and almost didn't get to run in the Olympic trials at all. If she's thinking about her knee, she's telling herself that if it held up in May, it will hold up in August.

Joan had become the American poster child for the quest for the women's marathon, especially when she set a world record, 2:22:43, in Boston in '83. She had run two Avon Marathons, supporting their primary purpose to provide an Olympic-like opportunity and message. She also knits and picks blueberries at home in Maine. Mostly alone. And she runs her thirteen-mile loop there, reputedly in a consistent 1:08 this hot summer. Her opponents today have trained at altitude in Boulder, in the summer heat of San Diego, or the humidity of Florida. Few have been home. Advantage, Benoit.

Earpiece: "Okay, up front with a graphic on the weather, talk about the weather." The worst smog in L.A.'s history miraculously disappeared only days before the Opening Ceremonies and the good air was holding. (There *is* a God.) After talking about the L.A. heat factor for four years, race morning is gray and a cool 68 degrees. As long as this can hold, we're grateful. The women have left nothing to chance. They have all dumped water on their heads already.

I looked at Benoit's face again. Part of the difference was that she had cut her hair. So had Brown, Isphording, Kristiansen, Mota, Mendonça—all, supposedly, for coolness and convenience. But to me they were all unwitting Catherines in Hemingway's *A Farewell to Arms.* A commitment from which there is no turning back.

Benoit pulls on a painter's hat.

Earpiece: "Give me the laps at the start." At the gun, forty-nine runners from twenty-eight nations move in a pack around the fairly empty Santa Monica City College track, which seems a bit silly, since there are hundreds of thousands lining the streets outside. It's a gloved applause here for the overture.

Japan's Akemi Masuda bolts out ahead like a petulant—or panicked?—school child who has never run a road race. For a scary moment, I thought of Kokochi Tsuburaya, the male Japanese Olympic marathoner who committed suicide because he felt he had let his country down, and I hoped that after Masuda's DNF today (as I surely knew at that moment she would be a Did Not Finish) her tiny body and strong heart would have the courage to try again. Such things are important to the Japanese. But to the television audience, I talk only about Masuda's training and her great race in Osaka earlier this year, as I slip my handwritten stat card about her to the bottom of my stack.

Earpiece: "Okay, out on the road, give me the direction." There are a lot of runners in the front pack. The opening pace is brisk, but I count nearly a dozen runners there who are already running faster paces then they ever have before. For them it is a matter of how soon they will break and who will hold on the best. Maybe one is ready to pop a big one, although in the Olympics, it's unlikely.

We expected a group of three or four to establish the pace, but no one breaks. Benoit eases ahead at about two miles. I am not sure she is serious. Suddenly, at the 5K mark, the big pack swerves right and one little gray runner runs left. Our camera wobbles indecisively and then tracks on the solitary woman.

Earpiece: "Go with Benoit, go with Benoit."

She bypasses the first water station completely, one dancer out of step with the colorful conga line that swooshes past the rows of cups and bottles. Her coach, Bob Sevene, told me earlier in the week that the first water station would be very important. It's cooler than we guessed, then. Either that or it's a helluva psychological ploy. Benoit's got 25 meters on them.

"Nobody is going to take this race out hard," said Grete Waitz's coach, Johann Kagestaad, when I talked to him, too, earlier in the week. "The race is going to be won on details. We are concentrating on all these details, especially the water stations." At first, Benoit's move looks like just a little surge, an extra jolt of unexpected adrenalin. Then it must have felt good and she keeps the quicker pace. Suddenly, she puts a 50-meter gap on the pack. In a flash, it's a 100.

She looks back now over her shoulder at them, and shakes her head in a gesture of bewilderment and disdain. This is the only time Joan Benoit would ever look back in the race.

Earpiece: "Okay, turning on San Vicente." This is the best part of the course, running a smooth and shady downhill to the ocean. The asphalt is even, the grass trimmed, and the houses expensive. It is a good place to get a lot of intelligent reinforcement, and at ten miles, it's early enough to feel great, and it's a cinch to break open the race early if it just happens to be your day.

I watched Julie Brown fly down San Vicente last year when she won the Avon Marathon on this same course. It was the U.S. women's championship, and for almost all of the 1,800 women who were there and who would not be in the Olympic Games or the Olympic trials, it was their Olympic moment. Julie won that Avon in 2:26 with her front-running style, making her as good a bet for Olympic gold as anyone else. Today she's with the pack, biding her time, trying to be sensible.

Her teammate and another of our Avon champions, Julie Isphording, is falling back; it's awful to see her struggling with the plantar fasciitis that has crippled her all summer. Isphording is not running so much as praying. The pain in the foot is excruciating even with painkillers.

The New Zealanders are all in white with "New Zealand" on their shirts in black. They finally convinced their federation to switch from the traditional all-black uniforms with white lettering to accommodate the heat. Lorraine Moller is with the pack, but I know from her three Avon Marathon victories that she doesn't like a crowd and won't stay here long, either moving ahead or dropping back. Moving ahead is risky, since Grete Waitz is competent and controlling this pace and everyone is deferring to her, especially her teammate Ingrid Kristiansen, who I think is actually faster. That's interesting. Dropping back is not a good idea. I would not presume to read Lorraine's mind, on air or otherwise, although I know her very well.

I expect Joan to fly down San Vicente and she does. Soon the pack behind is out of sight. Joan's face now has expression: sheer concentration, fearless but not arrogant. Knowing, but not know-it-all. Concentrating on the work at hand, but not overwhelmed by it.

Benoit flattens out on Ocean Avenue at about thirteen miles, and starts serious running as if her surge down San Vicente was a tease. I knew the breeze off the ocean here; it should be slightly behind, on her right side. "Creates a perfect vacuum in front of you," old Arnie used to say to me, "better than a tailwind." I never understood that, so I resisted the temptation to say it on the air.

Joan is putting together miles of 5:16, 5:15, 5:16. She has opened up 200 meters.

Earpiece: "Coming into Venice. Look for the weirdos." This course is typically L.A. Some ritzy suburbs, some golf courses, some ocean, some ticky-tacky houses, and some freeway. And some Venice. I always speculated that the strange folk from the East Coast kept migrating west, and when they got to Venice, they could go no farther, thus the preponderance of exotic people: pink hair, roller skates, plenty of tattoos, various costumes or states of undress. Running through this mob, Benoit laughs at something. We speculate for a while on what and after the race learn it was a banner from her alma mater, Bowdoin College, that friends occasionally surprise her with during races. Her smile fades; she resumes her unchanging expression of concentration.

Earpiece: "Eighteen miles, coming into the Marina." There is a U-turn at Marina Del Rey. Joan will be able to count the seconds between herself and the rest of the field. She may decide that she has gone out too fast. Or, the rest of the field will have to make some important decisions. Waitz in particular.

"Joan knows that Ingrid and Grete are faster," said Kagestaad. "If they are together at 30K, well. . . ." He smiled. "Anyway, the race will be decided at 30K. If Joan goes out at the pace everyone predicts, well, God bless her." We are at 30K, and Joan is 110 seconds ahead.

Waitz is pretty stubborn; one would expect that she would stick to her race plan, but at this point even she has to wonder. I speculate about all this talk about strategy, anyway. A marathon is exactly like living; you try to plan but are forced in the end to deal with it as it comes. The runners move onto the Marina Freeway.

Earpiece: "Go to the helicopter." The distance Joan has opened up—500 meters—looks incredible from here, a perspective that makes the difference insurmountable. The vista from above, as well as at ground level—of the isolated runner on an enormous and empty L.A. freeway—is as surrealistic as any in sports.

I feel that if she can maintain pace on the glaring and unresilient concrete, the race is hers. I begin to look for a weakness in her right knee, any catch, any lack of spring, any imbalance. It would go here, on the harder surface. I feel superstitious and guilty in my journalistic scrutiny, and relieved when she shoots down the exit ramp at last and back into city streets: soft asphalt, people cheering, shower hoses. The sun makes a first hazy appearance, and Joan turns the visor down on her hat.

Camera close-up, Benoit's face: She may have begun to think of alternative endings. She may even have composed a speech, different ones for different endings, just to be safe. In any case, she doesn't dare think of actually winning. No marathon runners ever do that, despite bravado, until they safely cross the line.

Suddenly she is outside the Coliseum, running past a giant mural of herself winning the 1983 Boston Marathon in Nike shoes, running faster than all the men's gold medal performances up to 1952. Although that's not a fair comparison, I can't resist doing it because it's so dramatic. She's going down a long chute leading to the entrance tunnel.

Earpiece: "When she gets on the track, let the crowd take it." Ninety thousand people scream and cheer and weep. Joan circles, the same expression of concentration on her face. Her form is unchanged. At 200 meters from the finish line, then and only then does she seem to feel absolutely sure that she can acknowledge this victory. She takes off her hat and waves it briefly at the crowd, a modest flourish that is received by a roar that explodes from the stadium. And from our hearts.

She crosses in 2:24:52. It is the third-fastest marathon ever run by a woman.

Now Benoit is running around the track in a victory lap. Someone has jumped out of the stands to give her a giant American flag and she runs her lap so fast it looks like she is still in the race. There is a lot more in the tank. Over a minute later, Grete Waitz enters the stadium, the crowd roars again, and she finishes with dignity and resolution in 2:26:18. Waitz made up a lot of distance on Benoit in the last few miles, but later said, "It was too late. The train had left the station."

Portugal's smiling Rosa Mota, who in 1982 was the first European Games champion in the new women's marathon, took bronze in 2:26:57. Ingrid Kristiansen was fourth, in 2:27:34, and Lorraine Moller fifth, in 2:28:34. Thirty-nine-year-old Priscilla Welch set an age-group record with her sixth-place 2:28:54, and forty-six-year-old Joyce Smith ran 2:32:48 for eleventh place.

Earpiece: "Throw it to the finish-line interview."

Benoit looks back then, at last, to describe the race, but more, to thank the women pioneers who made the event happen. She is grateful for the honor of being the first—unstated, but it was clear.

We are about to wrap the show when emerging from the tunnel on our fuzzy monitors comes the unmistakable and always frightening sight of a runner staggering with heat exhaustion. The crowd gasps and grows hushed.

Camera closeup, face of Gabrielle Andersen-Schiess.

Earpiece: (Shouting) "Stay with her! Stay with her!"

Oh God, not this, not now, please not after the triumph of all these world-class performances.

Here it is at last. The nemesis of the women's marathon we had tried our best to avoid, the graphic display of near-collapse. The media will shred us. They will say we're not capable of the marathon. Horrified officials might pull the marathon from the program just like they pulled the women's 800 in 1928.

I know Gabrielle. Her Swiss federation had imposed a ridiculously strict time qualifier on her to be able to run in L.A. She spent the last year chasing it and is tired and dehydrated. At thirty-nine, there will not be another Olympics for her. I try to defuse it. We disagree on-air.

The director wants to play it for all its melodrama. For six long minutes every camera is trained on Gabrielle as she drags her contorted body around the track, medical personnel alongside, careful not to disqualify her by touching her.

I desperately want her to finish. That's what the marathon is, above all else, a quest to reach a destination. When she falls across the finish in the arms of the medics, the crowd roars its acclaim. Far from shredding Gabrielle, women, or the marathon, the media make her a new heroine.

Earpiece: "Up music, roll credits."

I always knew that nobody would understand how important this is until the first woman comes through the tunnel and into the Olympic stadium. That's when ninety thousand people will get it. But it's more. That's when 2.2 *billion* people watching TV will get it. In tradition-bound households from America to Afghanistan, where women have faces covered and are not allowed an education, every culture knows that 26.2 miles (42.2 kilometers) is a long race. Both men and women have walked or bicycled or even ridden a donkey over the distance and they know it is far. And here are women *running* it, with strength, courage, speed and grace. In one dramatic race, they showed the world the limitlessness of women's heroic capability.

Earpiece: "Okay! Reroll Benoit finish, here she is again, wrap it, wrap it, from entering the tunnel."

She is a perfect symbol now for much of women's history, as once more we see her enter the darkness, obscured for a few seconds, then stride out of the darkness to run powerfully and beautifully into a shimmering stadium, to a welcome that reverberates to the ocean.

Twenty-five years later, January 2009

Already there are now more women runners in the United States than men. The women's Olympic Marathon, contested seven times, has become a "glamour" event, as has women's participation in the Big City marathons. These women ignite public acclaim and have created a new class: the professional woman runner.

Prize money has changed more than the sport; it has changed women's social and financial status globally. In Africa, their winnings build schools, sanitize water, and earn respect and justice previously denied them for centuries.

Japan has had no global heroines in their whole history until Olympic marathoners Yuko Arimori and Naoko Takahashi. Now an elite woman runner in Japan is a rock star.

England's Paula Radcliffe rewrote world notions of women's capability when she ran a world best 2:15:25 marathon and then went on to be a mother, barely breaking stride and smashing several old barriers at once.

Joan Benoit Samuelson, now fifty, still runs and sets age group records. Lots of ordinary women start running at sixty, seventy, and even eighty, proving age is no limit to success.

This story is only beginning, because it is not just about running; it's about changing women's lives. Men's too, for that matter. I will continue to try to tell it, just as I will continue to run, because running has give me—given many of us—everything. Especially ourselves.

Chapter | 26.2

Appendices

It's been forty-two years since the famous Boston Marathon "incident," an event that changed my life, and thus the lives of millions of other women—and men, too.

The following are reflections on that amazing day, April 19, 1967, from five friends who were a part of it.

Frank Litsky of the *New York Times* was an eyewitness to the incident; Joe Henderson, the most prolific of all running writers, was running his first marathon; John Leonard is the only other surviving member of our Syracuse team who was in Boston; Harry Trask is the Pulitzer Prize–winning photographer who best captured this event for history; and John Linscott, a longtime New England–area runner, wrote this funny poem on the occasion of a testimonial celebration for Jock Semple in 1978.

• • •

Frank Litsky of the New York Times *is the distinguished elder statesman of running journalism. He was alongside the famous Shoving Incident and sometimes brags, "I was there for the birth."*

I was there when it happened, the moment the world met Kathrine Switzer.

The morning was miserable—40 degrees, raw and drizzly—and the runners were bundled up. K. V. Switzer was wearing baggy sweatpants and two sweatshirts; from the back, she looked like another guy.

An old yellow school bus served as the press bus, and it weaved through the field of runners. Sportswriters, portable typewriters on their laps, would write a mile by mile account of the race, and photographers would snap rolls of pictures. Every few miles, the bus would stop at appointed pickup points, and messengers would grab the stories and photo rolls and rush them to the newspaper offices.

The bus also carried marathon officials. One was Will Cloney, a scholarly former sports writer who had become the race director. Another was Scottish-born Jock Semple, a crusty man devoid of humor. Four miles into the marathon, humor was far from his mind. As the press bus twisted its way through the running traffic, a reporter spotted No. 261. The drizzle had stopped, the hooded sweatshirt was gone, and there was no mistaking it: No. 261 was a woman.

This was a big story. And for the Boston reporters, who loved to needle Semple, it was a double dream.

"Jock," one reporter said loudly, with his best Scottish brogue, "Therrr'zzzzz a woman in yourrrr rrrrrrace." Semple screamed for the driver to stop. He and Cloney rushed out and headed for K. V. Switzer. They were convinced she had committed fraud to get the official race number.

As it turned out, all the paperwork was in order. But Semple didn't know that, and if he had he wouldn't have cared. He just wanted that number back. Cloney wanted that woman out of his race.

Neither succeeded. Switzer was running between Arnie Briggs, her coach, and Tom Miller, her boyfriend. Cloney tried to block her. She ran around him. Semple yelled, "Get the hell out of my race," and he reached for her number. Briggs pushed him away. When Semple tried again, Miller, a 235-pound hammer thrower, bumped him away.

Next day, the *New York Times* carried my main marathon story and a Switzer sidebar accompanied by two Switzer vs. Semple photos. I wrote that Switzer was not an official finisher because the timers and clerks folded their tents after four hours and she had not appeared.

Two days later, No. 261, whom I had never met, telephoned me. "There are some things about me you don't know," she said. "First of all, I finished in four hours twenty minutes. I was tired, and this was my first marathon and I wanted mostly to finish."

Cloney was upset for weeks. "Women can't run in the marathon," he told me, "because the rules forbid it. Unless we have rules, society will be in chaos. If that girl were my daughter, I'd spank her."

Cloney never spanked that girl. They became good friends. When Switzer ran Boston an hour faster, Semple realized she was a serious runner, and he became a friend, too. The AAU sort of spanked her, suspending her for six months. To this day, Kathrine Switzer insists she did not know the Boston Marathon was for men only. I'm not sure I believe her, but that is beside the point. The point is that women are allowed to run marathons and everything else now, and for that they can thank No. 261, K. V. Switzer.

• • •

Joe Henderson is the most published of all running writers, with more than twenty-five books and innumerable articles to his credit. He ran his first marathon at Boston in 1967.

The running world took little note that my first marathon came on the same day and course as Kathrine Switzer's. Not that anything I did that day was memorable to anyone but me. But by early afternoon of that April 19 we already had something in common: a run-in with a certain Scotsman.

That morning I'd heard Jock Semple before seeing him. He had stood near the Prudential Center, haranguing runners as we boarded buses to Hopkinton.

About seven hundred of us had registered for that race. We all tried to escape the near-freezing outdoors by crowding into the Hopkinton High School gym, there to take the pre-race physicals then required. A doctor listened to my racing heartbeat only long enough to pronounce me living.

Then I wandered the halls, looking for a bathroom without a long line, and came upon the boys' locker room. Greeting me there was the same loud, angry, Scottish-accented voice I'd heard earlier.

Jock Semple shouted words to the effect: "This is the dressing room of the stars. Bums like you don't belong here. Get out!"

I retreated. After the race I again met Jock, this time being introduced to him as a new hire at *Track & Field News*. He remembered the incident and apologized.

Not until the next morning did I hear what Jock Semple had done to Kathrine. Actually, it was the greatest favor of her life. All of running, not just women's running, would be better for what had happened that April 19.

• • •

John Leonard was the fourth member of the Syracuse Harriers team that traveled with coach Arnie Briggs to the 1967 Boston Marathon. He is now the executive director of the American Swimming Coaches Association.

"Kathy Switzer is tough as nails." That was my first thought as we finally came to the top of the Heartbreak Hills. I'd focused my eyes on her calves as we plodded up the slopes. The only thing that kept me moving was the need to not wimp out with Kathy and Arnie ahead of me. The only one talking, or encouraging anyone, as we worked our way up those hills was Kathy. She was the only one remotely able to talk. She got us . . . hell, she got *me*, to the top of that damn hill.

I'd met Kathy one early fall day with Arnie Briggs. Arnie said something like "This is Kathy Switzer and she is training for the Boston Marathon." My first thought was *Uh-huh, and I'm training to be Miss America.*

Over the next eight months, I trained with Arnie and Kathy most weekdays. On weekends, the two of them ran long training sessions in marathon preparation, and I skipped too many of those, due to my God-given right as a college student to party every Friday and Saturday night. Arnie would get mad, but I lacked both perspective and enough respect for what we were doing, to listen.

Kathy and Arnie and I ran in the cold. We ran in the snow. We did serious, long, nasty runs in the snow in January and February. Lots of snow. A whole big mother lode of snow. We'd come in from a two-hour run in the gathering darkness of a February Saturday evening, and I'd look at the other two with their frost and the refrozen ice on their eyelashes, their faces, frozen sweat covering their cotton sweats, and say to myself, *My god, these people look ridiculous!* Then I'd see the mirror. It was during that winter that I first realized that Kathrine V. Switzer was to be taken seriously.

Running shoes are from another planet now, compared to what we had in the '60s. Blisters came every day, then. Looking at a runners feet you could see how seriously they trained. Kathy's feet looked like a war refugee's who'd been walking barefoot for weeks.

The Jock Semple incident was considered by the runners around us as absolutely ridiculous and uncalled for, to put it politely. The runners welcomed her. It drained us for a while, but eventually we made it up and down the hills and got to the finish line, which was almost an anticlimax. But I survived my first marathon. I'd go on to run forty-nine more, through 1990.

The next morning I was in bed in my dorm. The pay phone down the hall rang and one of my hallmates called out, "Hey, Leonard, your dad is on the phone." My dad had gotten on his commuter train and gotten his cup of coffee. As he sat down, he opened his copy of the *New York Times*. Immediately, the Harry Trask photo leaped out at him. He spilled coffee all over his suit as he saw his son, supposedly at class in Syracuse, involved in what looked like a brawl in Boston. And on the front page of the *Times*. The phone call was not one of the highlights of my life.

I tell myself that I'd like to begin training for "just one more" marathon and what I need is a tough lady like Kathy to train with and get my butt out of bed in the morning. But those women are hard to find.

• • •

The most famous of the many photos of Jock Semple attacking me are those in the three-part series by Harry Trask of the now-defunct Boston Trav-*eler. Harry had a great eye for news and moved unflinchingly fast to cap-ture it. The Boston series was included in Time-Life's* 100 Photos That

Changed the World. *His photos of the actual sinking of the Andrea Doria in 1956 won him a Pulitzer Prize. The* Boston Traveler'*s photo archives were acquired by Associated Press and Harry moved on to teach journalism, then retired to run a bait and tackle shop in Cohasset, Massachusetts. He passed away in 2003. Many years ago he gave me the following interview.*

April 19, 1967: When I came into the *Traveler* photo office that morning, all of the good cameras were gone. We had to check out and return cameras in those days, and the guys covering the baseball game at Fenway Park got all the long lenses and motor drives. I just had a regular crank camera, 35mm. I was annoyed by that and also because it was a bitter sleeting-raining kind of day and I had to sit on the back of the Boston Marathon's open photo truck for two and a half hours, not a great assignment.

After the start of the marathon, the photo truck moved from the back of the runners through to the front, with the press and officials' bus behind us. Midway through the field, in Ashland, we came upon number 261 who was clearly a girl and we began shooting. It was the first time a girl wore numbers as far as any of us could remember! Anyway, the next thing I saw was the bus had stopped and Will Cloney, the race director, got out to stop the girl but she ran on right by him. Then Jock Semple came running off the bus after her.

Since I didn't have a long lens, I jumped off the back of the truck to get in closer. I knew the photo truck could have gone on and left me, but I knew Jock! Wherever Jock was, there was going to be action. It was worth the risk. I cranked off three shots as fast as I could.

You never know for sure until the prints are developed, but when I saw the sequence I was pleased. In fact, I don't think they could have been better even with the fancy equipment.

'TWAS THE NIGHT BEFORE BOSTON
By John Linscott

'Twas the night before Boston and all through the Pru,
The rumors were thick in the land of beef stew.
At noon on the morrow one would break the hex,
A runner would run—of the opposite sex.

A girl in the race? The thought troubled Jock's slumber.
To add insult to injury—she would wear a number.
Jock has sworn by his name—just as firm as a rock,
"Nobody runs—'less they're wearing a jock."

Jock scanned all the entries, and medical checks,
Which attested to fitness, but not as to sex.
"Now what's in a name? I'll find one that fits her."
He checked every name, but he missed one—K. Switzer.

A "K" could be a Karl, a Kurt, or a Kim.
This "K" stood for Kathrine, who's a her, not a him.
So the plot has been hatched, now 'til noon we must wait
For the big confrontation—our sports Watergate.

On the 19th of April at Hopkinton High
The runners were dressing with one watchful eye.
They'd heard 'bout the girl, and read all the reports,
One had to be careful when changing his shorts.

But as the time passed, and the noon hour was nigh,
No runner appeared with a mascara'd eye,

Nor with legs that weren't hairy, were slender, not bowed,
Yes, a female was rumored—but nobody showed.

Well, the gun it was fired, after all of the fuss,
Jock sighed with relief and mounted the bus.
"Thank God there's no women to mess up my race,
Imagine a runner in shorts hemmed with lace."

But there in the pack with a shape and a curl,
Jock spied Miss K. Switzer and he cried, "It's a girl!
They're all right to dance with the Charleston or rumba,
But girls can't run Boston while wearing a number."

So he sprang from the bus to collar the phony,
As he leaped to the pavement from the grasp of Will Cloney,
He weaved through the pack like a hound on the hunt,
Now he grasps for her number—no, Jock!—not from the front!

Now advancing toward Jock and before he could pull back,
Came a friend of fair Kathy, who was built like a fullback.
They met there at noon on the Marathon course,
The gritty old Scot—the Immovable Force.

The damsel was saved, and she sped on her way
The story's been told and retold to this day.
And I heard Jock exclaim as she ran out of sight,
"I think I was hit—by a woman's right."

WOMEN'S WORLD MARATHON RECORD
PROGRESSION
(As of October 2008)

Time	Name (Country)	Date	Location Run
2:15:25	Paula Radcliffe (UK)	April 13, 2003	London
2:17:18	Radcliffe (2)	October 13, 2002	Chicago
2:18:47	Catherine Ndereba (KEN)	October 7, 2001	Chicago
2:19:46	Naoko Takahashi (JPN)	September 30, 2001	Berlin
2:20:43	Tegla Loroupe (KEN)	September 26, 1999	Berlin
2:20:47	Loroupe (2)	April 19, 1998	Rotterdam
2:21:06	Ingrid Kristiansen (NOR)	April 21, 1985	London
2:22:43a	Joan Benoit (USA)	April 18, 1983	Boston
2:25:29	Grete Waitz (NOR)	April 17, 1983	London
2:25:29a	Allison Roe (NZ)	October 25, 1981	New York
2:25:42	Grete Waitz (2)	October 26, 1980	New York
2:27:33	Waitz (3)	October 21, 1979	New York
2:32:30	Waitz (4)	October 22, 1978	New York
2:34:48	Christa Vahlensieck (GER)	September 10, 1977	Berlin
2:35:16	Chantal Langlace (FRA)	May 1, 1977	Oyarzun, Spain
2:38:19	Jacqueline Hansen (USA)	October 12, 1975	Eugene, OR

2:40:16	Vahlensieck (2)	May 3, 1975	Dülmen, West Germany
2:42:24a	Liane Winter (GER)	April 21, 1975	Boston
2:43:55	Hansen (2)	December 1, 1974	Culver City, CA
2:46:24	Langlace (2)	October 27, 1974	Neuf-Brisach, France
2:46:30	Adrienne Beames (AUS)	August 31, 1971	Werribee, Australia
3:00:35a	Sara Mae Berman (USA)	May 30, 1971	Brockton, MA
3:01:42	Beth Bonner (USA)	May 9, 1971	Philadelphia
3:02:53	Caroline Walker (USA)	February 28, 1970	Seaside, OR
3:07:27	Anni Pede-Erdkamp (GER)	September 16, 1967	Waldniel, West Germany
3:15:22a	Maureen Wilton (CAN)	May 6, 1967	Toronto
3:19:33	Mildred Sampson (NZ)	July 21, 1964	Auckland
3:27:45	Dale Greig (SCO)	May 23, 1964	Ryde, Isle of Wight, UK
3:40:22na	Violet Piercy (ENG)	May 29, 1926	Chiswick, England

a: aided. In New York, 1981, the course was found to be slightly short, and Boston has a net elevation drop

na: not authenticated, despite research

OLYMPIC WOMEN'S MARATHON CHAMPIONS

Year	Place	Athlete	Time
1984	Los Angeles	Joan Benoit (USA)	2:24:52
1988	Seoul	Rosa Mota (Portugal)	2:25:40
1992	Barcelona	Valentina Yegorova (Russia)	2:32:41
1996	Atlanta	Fatuma Roba (Ethiopia)	2:26:05
2000	Sydney	Naoko Takahashi (Japan)	2:23:14
2004	Athens	Mizuki Noguchi (Japan)	2:26:20
2008	Beijing	Constantina Dita (Romania)	2:26:44

AVON INTERNATIONAL MARATHON CHAMPIONS

Year	Place	Athlete	Time
1978	Atlanta, GA	Martha Cooksey (USA)	2:46:16
1979	Waldniel, Germany	Joyce Smith (UK)	2:36:27
1980	London, England	Lorraine Moller (NZ)	2:35:11
1981	Ottawa, Canada	Nancy Conz (USA)	2:36:45
1982	San Francisco, CA	Lorraine Moller (NZ)	2:36:13
1983	Los Angeles, CA	Julie Brown (USA)	2:26:26
1984	Paris, France	Lorraine Moller (NZ)	2:32:44

PERMISSIONS

Page ii: © Jeff Johnson.

I. Base: Page xiii: Kathrine's family, 1960. Photo courtesy of the author.

II. Build-Up: Page 61: Kathrine's bib number from the 1967 Boston Marathon. Photo courtesy of the author.

III. Sharpening: Page 151: Kathrine with her third-place trophy just after the 1972 Boston Marathon. Photo courtesy of the author.

IV. Warm-Up: Page 291: Kathrine running in Madrid while organizing the Avon Running Circuit there. Photo courtesy of the author.

V. The Race: Page 369: Avon Running—Yellowdog Productions.

VI. The Breakthrough: Page 379: Avon Running—Yellowdog Productions.

Appendices: Writing selections from Frank Litsky, Joe Henderson, John Leonard, and John Linscott are all published with kind permission from them.

Statistical Tables: Thanks to various sources, especially including: David Martin, PhD; Avon Running; *The Marathon Footrace* and *The Olympic Marathon*, by David Martin and Roger Gynn; *Running Encyclopedia* by Richard Benyo and Joe Henderson; and the *ING New York City Marathon Media Guide*, among others.

INDEX